International

RELATIONS

Using
MicroCase ExplorIt®

James C. Roberts
Towson University

Alan J. Rosenblatt
Stateside Associates

WADSWORTH

THOMSON LEARNING™

Australia • Canada • Mexico • Singapore • Spain • United Kingdom • United States

For more information about our products, contact us at:
Thomson Learning Academic Resource Center
1-800-423-0563

For permission to use material from this text, contact us by:
Phone: **1-800-730-2214**
Fax: **1-800-731-2215**
Web: **www.thomsonrights.com**

Asia
Thomson Learning
60 Albert Complex, #15-01
Albert Complex
Singapore 189969

Australia
Nelson Thomson Learning
102 Dodds Street
South Street
South Melbourne, Victoria 3205
Australia

Canada
Nelson Thomson Learning
1120 Birchmount Road
Toronto, Ontario M1K 5G4
Canada

Europe/Middle East/South Africa
Thomson Learning
Berkshire House
168-173 High Holborn
London WC1 V7AA
United Kingdom

Latin America
Thomson Learning
Seneca, 53
Colonia Polanco
11560 Mexico D.F.
Mexico

Spain
Paraninfo Thomson Learning
Calle/Magallanes, 25
28015 Madrid, Spain

CONTENTS

ABOUT THE AUTHORS

James C. Roberts is Associate Professor of Political Science at Towson University, where he is also the chairperson of the political science department and director of the international studies program. He teaches courses in political research methods, simulation and games, international relations, and political economy. He taught in the Department of Computer and Information Science at American University and was the Associate Director of American University's Quantitative Teaching and Research Laboratory. Roberts received his Ph.D. in International Relations from the School of International Service at the American University. He received his B.A. in Political Science from the Ohio State University and his M.A. in International Development Studies from the American University. Prior to his career in academia he worked for the United States Government evaluating the effects of international and domestic development programs. He has worked in Central and South America and in the Middle East. Roberts has published articles and chapters in the areas of research methodology and theoretical political economy. He has also authored numerous U.S. Government sponsored research reports. This is his first book.

Alan J. Rosenblatt is currently Vice President for Online Advocacy Services at Stateside Associates, a state and local policy issue management firm in Arlington, Virginia. Prior to his current position, he was Associate Director of the Delaney Policy Group and Assistant Professor of Government and Politics at George Mason University, where he taught courses in the politics of cyberspace, research methods, public opinion, political persuasion, and propaganda. Rosenblatt received his Ph.D. in Political Science from the School of Public Affairs at the American University where he also served as Associate Director of the Social Science Research Laboratory. He received his B.A. in Political Science and Philosophy from Tufts University and his M.A. in Political Science from Boston College. He has published in the fields of the politics of cyberspace, political persuasion, and international political economy. His most recent publication is "Online Polling: Methodological Limitations and Implications for Electronic Democracy" in the Spring 1999 issue of the *Harvard International Journal of Press/Politics*. This is his first book.

PREFACE

International relations may be the most important subject one can study. That may seem like a pretentious way to begin a text on the subject, but where else do students learn about making decisions that affect the lives of so many people? Decisions to go to war, decisions to provide foreign aid, decisions to open or close trade relations are all the subjects of international relations. These decisions affect the life and death, health and welfare, and employment of large populations. Yet, there is no one guide or one approach to this important subject that provides the answers. Indeed, in some areas there is little agreement about the very nature of the subject matter. This subject, however, is not something external to and remote from our own lives and experience. Unlike the molecule studied by the chemistry students or the cell studied by the biologists, the social and political institutions and events studied by students of international relations are created by our own actions and are therefore constantly changing.

Thus, we are faced with a dilemma. What may be the most important subject we can study is both an enigma of definition and in constant flux. We need tools that can examine this subject from various points of view and lead us to an understanding that may benefit the human condition. While our view of the subject may be pretentious, this book presents what we hope is a modest attempt to discover those tools.

This book will introduce you to the theory and practice of international relations by exploring data about events, people, nation-states, international organizations, economic relations, and other phenomena. You will see how to use simple statistical and graphical methods to test hypotheses and describe data. The tools we will use include an easy-to-use software package called MicroCase Student ExplorIt and data about nation-states, events, and time periods. The book merges theoretical discussions with analysis of data. The theoretical discussions are drawn from many different disciplines such as political science, economics, and psychology, because international relations is an interdisciplinary subject.

The book begins with a general introduction to the subject. Exercise 2 introduces the organizing concepts of international relations. Exercise 3 discusses the various actors that participate in and define the international system. Exercises 4, 5, and 6 examine explanations of international events that are derived from the nature of the international system, the interests of nation-states, and the decisions of individuals respectively. Exercises 7 through 11 examine instruments of international relations including power, the use of force, international law and organization, and the global economy. Finally, Exercise 12 examines the problems of environmental policy in the international system as a way to apply what you learned about how international relations works.

There are many people who greatly helped the creation of this book. David Smetters, formerly of MicroCase Inc., provided us with encouragement, guidance, support, and thorough reviews of our initial chapters. Julie Aguilar edited the entire manuscript for content and helped us with some important rewrites. The data were gathered from many sources. The core variables of the NATIONS file were taken from the Nations of the World file in the MicroCase Archive. Thanks are owed to the technical staff at MicroCase Inc. and Wadsworth Publishers for their help in preparing the data for use with the text. Renée Marlin-Bennett, Walter Seabold, and Eric Belgrad provided us with encouragement, advice, and instructive reviews. The comments of the anonymous reviewers were invaluable. Finally, we must thank our students who suffered through three versions of the manuscript. We hope they found the exercises to be informative.

This book is dedicated to our wives, Elaine L. Vaurio and Kris Rosenblatt, without whose support it would not have been completed.

GETTING STARTED

INTRODUCTION

International relations is grounded in the real world. We may refer to theories that seem far removed from reality, but in the end, we must return to the laboratory of the real world. This book is intended to do three things. First, it examines some of the more common and more important concepts, theories, and phenomena in international relations. Second, the book grounds your exploration of international relations in the laboratory of the real world by providing you with real data about international relations. Finally, and perhaps most important, it provides you with a tool for exploring international relations on your own. Yes, we will guide you through a series of presentations and exercises, but you can easily venture out on your own to see how international relations works by using the Student ExplorIt software and the data provided with it.

Each exercise in the book focuses on a set of concepts or theories in international relations through examples drawn from data on international relations. You can follow along with the examples using the Student ExplorIt guides embedded in the text. Worksheets at the end of each exercise give you an opportunity to explore the examples and concepts on your own.

SYSTEM REQUIREMENTS

- Windows 95 (or higher)
- 8 MB RAM
- CD-ROM drive
- 3.5" disk drive
- 15 MB of hard drive space (if you want to install it)

NETWORK VERSIONS OF STUDENT EXPLORIT

A network version of Student ExplorIt is available at no charge to instructors who adopt this book for their course. It is worth noting that Student ExplorIt can be run directly from the CD and diskette on virtually any computer network—regardless of whether a network version of Student ExplorIt has been installed.

INSTALLING STUDENT EXPLORIT

If you will be running Student ExplorIt directly from the CD-ROM and diskette—or if you will be using a version of Student ExplorIt that is installed on a network—skip to the section "Starting Student ExplorIt."

To install Student ExplorIt to a hard drive, you will need the diskette and CD-ROM that are packaged inside the back cover of this book. Then follow these steps in order:

1. Start your computer and wait until the Windows desktop is showing on your screen.

2. Insert the diskette into the A drive (or B drive) of your computer.

3. Insert the CD-ROM disc into the CD-ROM drive of your computer.

4. On most computers the CD-ROM will automatically start and a welcome menu will appear. If the CD-ROM doesn't automatically start, do the following:

   Click [Start] from the Windows desktop, click [Run], type **D:\SETUP**, and click [OK]. (If your CD-ROM drive is not the D drive, replace the letter D with the proper drive letter.)

5. To install Student ExplorIt to your hard drive, select the second option on the list: "Install Student ExplorIt to your hard drive."

6. During the installation, you will be presented with several screens, as described below. In most cases you will be required to make a selection or entry and then click [Next] to continue.

The first screen that appears is the **License Name** screen. (If this software has been previously installed or used, it already contains the licensing information. In such a case, a screen confirming your name will appear instead.) Here you are asked to type your name. It is important to type your name correctly, since it cannot be changed after this point. Your name will appear on all printouts, so make sure you spell it completely and correctly! Then click [Next] to continue.

A **Welcome** screen now appears. This provides some introductory information and suggests that you shut down any other programs that may be running. Click [Next] to continue.

You are next presented with a **Software License Agreement**. Read this screen and click [Yes] if you accept the terms of the software license.

The next screen has you **Choose the Destination** for the program files. You are strongly advised to use the destination directory that is shown on the screen. Click [Next] to continue.

The Student ExplorIt program will now be installed. At the end of the installation, you will be asked if you would like a shortcut icon placed on the Windows desktop. It is recommended that you select [Yes]. You are now informed that the installation of Student ExplorIt is finished. Click the [Finish] button and you will be returned to the opening Welcome Screen. To exit completely, click the option "Exit Welcome Screen."

INSTALLING STUDENT EXPLORIT TO A LAPTOP COMPUTER

If you are installing Student ExplorIt to a hard drive on a laptop that has both a CD-ROM drive and a floppy disk drive, simply follow the preceding instructions. However, if you are installing Student ExplorIt to a hard drive on a laptop where you cannot have both the CD-ROM drive and floppy disk drive attached at the same time, follow these steps in order:

1. Attach the CD-ROM drive to your computer and insert the CD-ROM disc.

2. Start your computer and wait until the Windows desktop is showing on your screen.

3. On most computers the CD-ROM will automatically start and a welcome menu will appear. If it does, click Exit.

4. Click [Start] from the Windows desktop, select [Programs], and select [Windows Explorer].

5. Click the drive letter for your CD-ROM in the left column (usually D:\). A list of folders and files on the CD-ROM will appear in the left column.

6. From the Windows Explorer menu, click [Edit] and [Select All]. The folders and files on the CD-ROM will be highlighted. Using your mouse, right click (use your right mouse button) on the list of folders and files. From the box that appears select [Copy].

7. In the left column of the Windows Explorer menu, right click once on your C drive (do NOT select a folder) and select [Paste] from the box that appears.

8. Close Windows Explorer by clicking the [X] button on the top right corner.

9. Remove the CD-ROM and CD-ROM drive from your computer and attach the floppy disk drive. Place the floppy disk drive from your workbook in the drive.

10. Click [Start] from the Windows desktop, click [Run], type C:\SETUP and click [OK].

11. Select the first option from the Welcome menu: **Run Student ExplorIt from the CD-ROM**. Within a few seconds Student ExplorIt will appear on your screen.

STARTING STUDENT EXPLORIT

There are three ways to run Student ExplorIt: (1) directly from the CD-ROM and diskette, (2) from a hard drive installation, or (3) from a network installation. Each method is described below.

Starting Student ExplorIt from the CD-ROM and Diskette

Unlike most Windows programs, it is possible to run Student ExplorIt directly from the CD-ROM and diskette. To do so, follow these steps:

1. Insert the 3.5" diskette into the A or B drive of your computer.

2. Insert the CD-ROM disc into the CD-ROM drive.

3. On most computers the CD-ROM will automatically start and a welcome menu will appear. (Note: If the CD-ROM does **not** automatically start after it is inserted, click [Start] from the Windows desktop, click [Run], type D:\SETUP and click [OK]. If your CD-ROM drive is not the D drive, replace the letter D with the proper drive letter.)

4. Select the first option from the Welcome menu: **Run Student ExplorIt from the CD-ROM**. Within a few seconds Student ExplorIt will appear on your screen.

Starting Student ExplorIt from a Hard Drive Installation

If Student ExplorIt is installed to the hard drive of your computer (see earlier section "Installing Student ExplorIt"), it is **not** necessary to insert either the CD-ROM or floppy diskette. Instead, locate the Student ExplorIt "shortcut" icon on the Windows desktop, which looks something like this:

To start Student ExplorIt, position your mouse pointer over the shortcut icon and double-click (that is, click it twice in rapid succession). If you did not permit the shortcut icon to be placed on the desktop during the install process (or if the icon was accidentally deleted), you can alternatively follow these directions to start the software:

Click [Start] from the Windows desktop.

Click [Programs].

Click MicroCase.

Click Student ExplorIt.

After a few seconds, Student ExplorIt will appear on your screen.

Starting Student ExplorIt from a Network

If the network version of Student ExplorIt has been installed to a computer network, you must insert the floppy diskette (not the CD-ROM) that comes with your book. Then double-click the Student ExplorIt icon that appears on the Windows desktop to start the program. (Note: Your instructor may provide additional information that is unique to your computer network.)

MAIN MENU OF STUDENT EXPLORIT

Student ExplorIt is extremely easy to use. All you do is point and click your way through the program. That is, use your mouse arrow to point at the selection you want, then click the left button on the mouse.

The main menu is the starting point for everything you will do in Student ExplorIt. Look at how it works. Notice that not all options on the menu are always available. You will know which options are available at any given time by looking at the colors of the options. For example, when you first start the software, only the OPEN FILE option is immediately available. As you can see, the colors for this option are brighter than those for the other tasks shown on the screen. Also, when you move your mouse pointer over this option, it is highlighted.

EXPLORIT GUIDES

Throughout this workbook, "ExplorIt Guides" provide the basic information needed to carry out each task. Here is an example:

➤ *Data File:* **NATIONS**
➤ *Task:* **Mapping**
➤ *Variable 1:* **5) AGE15–64**
➤ *View:* **Map**

Each line of the ExplorIt Guide is actually an instruction. Let's follow the simple steps to carry out this task.

Step 1: Select a Data File

Before you can do anything in Student ExplorIt, you need to open a data file. To open a data file, click the OPEN FILE task. A list of data files will appear in a window (e.g., DEVELOP, EUROPE, etc.). If you click on a file name *once*, a description of the highlighted file is shown in the window next to this list. In the ExplorIt Guide shown above, the ➤ symbol to the left of the Data File step indicates that you should open the NATIONS data file. To do so, click NATIONS and then click the [Open] button (or just double-click NATIONS). The next window that appears (labeled File Settings) provides additional information about the data file, including a file description, the number of cases in the file, and the number of variables, among other things. To continue, click the [OK] button. You are now returned to the main menu of Student ExplorIt. (You won't need to repeat this step until you want to open a different data file.) Notice that you can always see which data file is currently open by looking at the file name shown on the top line of the screen.

Step 2: Select a Task

Once you open a data file, the next step is to select a program task. Seven analysis tasks are offered in this version of Student ExplorIt. Not all tasks are available for each data file, because some tasks are appropriate only for certain kinds of data. Mapping, for example, is a task that applies only to ecological data, and thus cannot be used with survey data files.

In the ExplorIt Guide we are following, the ➤ symbol on the second line indicates that the MAPPING task should be selected, so click the MAPPING option with your left mouse button.

Step 3: Select a Variable

After a task is selected, you will be shown a list of the variables in the open data file. Notice that the first variable is highlighted and a description of that variable is shown in the Variable Description window at the lower right. You can move this highlight through the list of variables by using the up and down cursor keys (as well as the <Page Up> and <Page Down> keys). You can also click once on a variable name to move the highlight and update the variable description. Go ahead—move the highlight to a few other variables and read their descriptions.

If the variable you want to select is not showing in the variable window, click on the scroll bars located on the right side of the variable list window to move through the list. See the following figure.

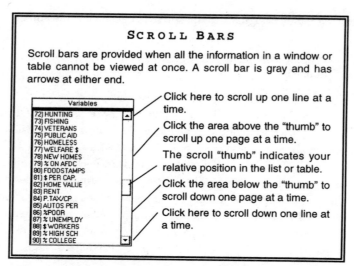

SCROLL BARS

Scroll bars are provided when all the information in a window or table cannot be viewed at once. A scroll bar is gray and has arrows at either end.

Variables

72) HUNTING
73) FISHING
74) VETERANS
75) PUBLIC AID
76) HOMELESS
77) WELFARE $
78) NEW HOMES
79) % ON AFDC
80) FOODSTAMPS
81) $ PER CAP.
82) HOME VALUE
83) RENT
84) P.TAX/CP
85) AUTOS PER
86) %POOR
87) % UNEMPLOY
88) $ WORKERS
89) % HIGH SCH
90) % COLLEGE

Click here to scroll up one line at a time.

Click the area above the "thumb" to scroll up one page at a time.

The scroll "thumb" indicates your relative position in the list or table.

Click the area below the "thumb" to scroll down one page at a time.

Click here to scroll down one line at a time.

By the way, you will find an appendix at the back of this workbook that contains a list of the variable names for key data files provided in this package.

Each task requires the selection of one or more variables, and the ExplorIt Guides indicate which variables you should select. The ExplorIt Guide example here indicates that you should select 5) AGE15–64 as Variable 1. On the screen, there is a box labeled Variable 1. Inside this box, there is a vertical cursor that indicates that this box is currently an active option. When you select a variable, it will be placed in this box. Before selecting a variable, be sure that the cursor is in the appropriate box. If it is not, place the cursor inside the appropriate box by clicking the box with your mouse. This is important because in some tasks the ExplorIt Guide will require more than one variable to be selected, and you want to be sure that you put each selected variable in the right place.

To select a variable, use any one of the methods shown below. (Note: If the name of a previously selected variable is in the box, use the <Delete> or <Backspace> key to remove it—or click the [Clear All] button.)

- Type the **number** of the variable and press <Enter>.

- Type the **name** of the variable and press <Enter>. Or you can type just enough of the name to distinguish it from other variables in the data—AGE would be sufficient for this example.

- Double-click the desired variable in the variable list window. This selection will then appear in the variable selection box. (If the name of a previously selected variable is in the box, the newly selected variable will replace it.)

- Highlight the desired variable in the variable list, then click the arrow that appears to the left of the variable selection box. The variable you selected will now appear in the box. (If the name of a previously selected variable is in the box, the newly selected variable will replace it.)

Once you have selected your variable (or variables), click the [OK] button to continue to the final results screen.

Step 4: Select a View

The next screen that appears shows the final results of your analysis. In most cases, the screen that first appears matches the "view" indicated in the ExplorIt Guide. In this example, you are instructed to look at the Map view—that's what is currently showing on the screen. In some instances, however, you may need to make an additional selection to produce the desired screen.

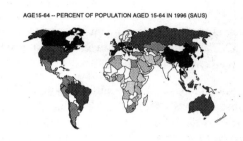

AGE15-64 -- PERCENT OF POPULATION AGED 15-64 IN 1996 (SAUS)

(OPTIONAL) Step 5: Select an Additional Display

Some ExplorIt Guides will indicate that an additional "Display" should be selected. In that case, simply click on the option indicated for that additional display. For example, this ExplorIt Guide may have included an additional line that required you to select the Legend display.

Step 6: Continuing to the Next ExplorIt Guide

Some instructions in the ExplorIt Guide may be the same for at least two examples in a row. For instance, after you display the map for AGE15–64 in the example above, the following ExplorIt Guide may be given:

> Data File: **NATIONS**
> Task: **Mapping**
> ➤ Variable 1: **10) ALIGN CW**
> ➤ View: **Map**

Notice that the first two lines in the ExplorIt Guide do not have the ➤ symbol in front of the items. That's because you already have the data file NATIONS open and you have already selected the MAPPING task. With the results of your first analysis showing on the screen, there is no need to return to the main menu to complete this next analysis. Instead, all you need to do is select ALIGN CW as your new variable. Click the [[⊡]] button located in the top left corner of your screen and the variable selection screen for the MAPPING task appears again. Replace the variable with 10) ALIGN CW and click [OK].

To repeat: You need to do only those items in the ExplorIt Guide that have the ➤ symbol in front of them. If you start from the top of the ExplorIt Guide, you're simply wasting your time.

If the ExplorIt Guide instructs you to select an entirely new task or data file, you will need to return to the main menu. To return to the main menu, simply click the [Menu] button at the top left corner of the screen. At this point, select the new data file and/or task that is indicated in the ExplorIt Guide.

That's all there is to the basic operation of Student ExplorIt. Just follow the instructions given in the ExplorIt Guide and point and click your way through the program.

ON-LINE HELP

Student ExplorIt offers extensive on-line help. You can obtain task-specific help by pressing <F1> at any point in the program. For example, if you are performing a scatterplot analysis, you can press <F1> to see the help for the SCATTERPLOT task.

If you prefer to browse through a list of the available help topics, select **Help** from the pull-down menu at the top of the screen and select the **Help Topics** option. At this point, you will be provided a list of topic areas. Each topic is represented by a closed-book icon. To see what information is available in a given topic area, double-click on a book to "open" it. (For this version of the software, use only the "Student ExplorIt" section of help; do not use the "Student MicroCase" section.) When you double-click on a book graphic, a list of help topics is shown. A help topic is represented by a graphic with a piece of paper with a question mark on it. Double-click on a help topic to view it.

If you have questions about Student ExplorIt, try the on-line help described above. If you are not very familiar with software or computers, you may want to ask a classmate or your instructor for assistance.

EXITING FROM STUDENT EXPLORIT

If you are continuing to the next section of this workbook, it is *not* necessary to exit from Student ExplorIt quite yet. But when you are finished using the program, it is very important that you properly exit the software—do not just walk away from the computer or remove your diskette. To exit Student ExplorIt, return to the main menu and select the [Exit Program] button that appears on the screen.

Important: If you inserted your diskette and/or CD-ROM disc before starting Student ExplorIt, remember to remove it before leaving the computer.

EXERCISE 1

INTERNATIONAL RELATIONS IN PERSPECTIVE

Tasks: Univariate, Historical Trends, Mapping
Data Files: HISTORY, NATIONS, FPSURVEY

Why study international relations? It seems, at times, that the affairs of diplomats, multinational corporations, international organizations, and the like are distant interferences in our daily lives. Perhaps the most compelling reason to study international relations is the nature of the subject itself. As a social science, international relations is not some abstract phenomenon separated from human life. We create and define international relations with all of the actions we take that cross borders. International relations is the study of international events. International events are actions taken by one actor (government, corporation, group, or individual) that are targeted at another actor. What makes these events international is that the two actors reside in different nation-states. This means that the subject of international relations is bound up with the existence of the nation-state system and changes as that system changes. Unlike chemistry that studies the molecule or biology that studies the cell, the thing we study in international relations is constantly changing. The modern nation-state system had its birth in 17th-century Europe with the fall of feudalism and the development of centralized kingdoms. Since that time the nation-state system has changed and grown. Certainly the factors that affected international relations in 1650 are different from those that affect international relations today. We must also recognize that today's understandings of international relations will probably not apply to human political, social, and economic life 350 years from now.

Thus, international relations is a phenomenon that is constructed out of our daily lives. We create international relations and, in some ways, international relations creates us—at least it creates the world in which we live and work. To understand why we should study international relations we first must answer two other questions: How does international relations affect us in our daily lives, and how do our actions affect international relations? Questions like these are not easy to answer and this text does not offer the answers. Rather, it provides a means for you to explore information about the world so that you can find your own answers. To help you do this, you will use the Student ExplorIt software and data files that accompany this workbook. The software is easy to learn and the data will help you pose and answer questions as you explore your world. Student ExplorIt software will create tables, graphs, and analyses to enable you to explore questions and hypotheses about international relations on your own. No, you do not need to know mathematics or statistics to use this program. You do not even need to know much about computers. The program allows you to "point and click" on commands. That is, you need only know what you want to explore, point at the proper command buttons to examine the data, and be able to interpret some simple tables and graphs. The book will pose some of the questions and help you interpret the results. The real value of a text like this is that it permits you to examine your own questions at your own pace. The data we prepared for you are drawn from the international sources and major research programs that helped define the study of international relations over the last 30 years. This exercise will get you started on your exploration of international relations, how it affects you and how you affect it.

WHAT DO PEOPLE THINK ABOUT INTERNATIONAL RELATIONS?

Do people believe that international relations affects their daily lives? We can explore this question by examining the results of a survey of the American public (FPSURVEY) and elites (FPELITES) conducted by the Chicago Council on Foreign Relations in 1998.[1] The survey investigators questioned a random sample of 1507 people from the general population in the U.S. and 383 people who were identified as opinion leaders—including members of the U.S. Congress, business leaders, educators, interest group leaders, and officials in the executive branch of the U.S. government.[2] We can explore what the general population thinks about the impact of international affairs on their lives by using the UNIVARIATE task in Student ExplorIt. UNIVARIATE produces a percentage table and pie chart to show how the respondents to the survey answered this question.

Below you will see the ExplorIt Guide that lists the steps to obtain this pie chart. If you do not understand this guide, reread the *Getting Started* section at the beginning of this book. When you see ExplorIt Guides in this and all other exercises in the book, you are strongly advised to actually do the steps at a computer. This procedure will help you learn how to use Student ExplorIt and become more familiar with the program. It will also help prepare you to complete the worksheets at the end of each exercise.

➤ *Data File:* **FPSURVEY**
➤ *Task:* **Univariate**
➤ *Primary Variable:* **18) IMPECON**
➤ *View:* **Pie**

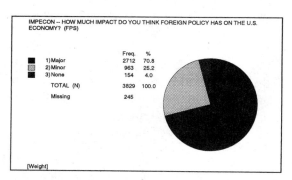

If you want to reproduce this graphic on your computer screen using ExplorIt, read the instructions in the *Getting Started* section of this book. For this example, you would open the file named FPSURVEY, select the UNIVARIATE task, and select 18) IMPECON as the primary variable. (Remember, the ➤ symbol indicates which steps you need to perform if you conduct the examples in order as you follow along in the book. So, in the next example, you only need to identify a new variable because Student ExplorIt will remember the data file and task.)

---

[1] The *American Public Opinion and U.S. Foreign Policy, 1998* study is one of nine data files that will be used in conjunction with this text. Information about each of these data files is contained in the Appendix.

[2] The tables and analyses will show more than 1,507 respondents to the survey. This is because the survey methodology used "weighting," a process whereby undersampled groups are estimated by applying a multiplier to boost their numbers.

As you can see, 2,712 or 70.8% of the 3,829 people in the survey who responded to this question believe that U.S. foreign policy has a "major impact" on the U.S. economy. You can also see that 245 people did not provide a response to this question. When this happens, they are counted as "missing" for this variable and are not included in the final analysis.

One way that international relations affects people's lives is through the unemployment rate. Foreign competition can drive U.S. workers out of their jobs as U.S. companies move their factories overseas or use overseas labor for their production. By looking at variable 19) IMPEMPL, we can see how much influence the public thinks U.S. foreign policy has on the U.S. unemployment rate.

<table>
<tr><td>Data File: FPSURVEY</td></tr>
<tr><td>Task: Univariate</td></tr>
<tr><td>➤ Primary Variable: 19) IMPEMPL</td></tr>
<tr><td>➤ View: Pie</td></tr>
</table>

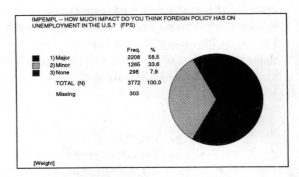

If you are continuing from the previous example, return to the variable selection screen. Select variable 19) IMPEMPL as the new Primary Variable.

Here we can see that 58.5% of the respondents believe that U.S. foreign policy has a major impact on domestic unemployment. However, it is important to note that what this analysis doesn't tell us is what *kind* of impact respondents feel foreign policy has on unemployment—only how *much* impact. Yet, people's attitudes often change when looking at other aspects of international affairs. "All politics is local," as former U.S. House of Representatives Speaker Tip O'Neill once said.

<table>
<tr><td>Data File: FPSURVEY</td></tr>
<tr><td>Task: Univariate</td></tr>
<tr><td>➤ Primary Variable: 20) IMPLIVING</td></tr>
<tr><td>➤ View: Pie</td></tr>
</table>

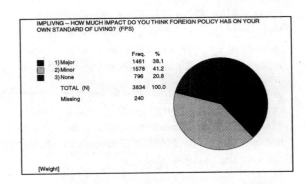

While a majority of the public realizes that foreign policy affects the economy and unemployment, a much smaller proportion (38.1%) thinks that foreign policy has a major impact on their overall quality of life. This is well understood by U.S. politicians who often downplay their involvement in foreign affairs because they believe that the public views this activity as frivolous. President George H. Bush, who enjoyed the highest presidential approval ever recorded after the Persian Gulf War in 1991, was defeated in the 1992 election by Bill Clinton. Clinton's chief campaign strategist, James Carville, kept a sign in large letters over his desk that read "It's the economy stupid" to keep the Clinton campaign focused on domestic economic issues. Nevertheless, in a world where bank transfers can be made from Hong Kong to New York in seconds and where nuclear terror is ever present, there are many ways that international relations affects our daily lives.

INTERNATIONAL RELATIONS AND YOU

One of the most dramatic ways that international relations can affect your life is through warfare. All male U.S. citizens are required to register for the draft upon their 18th birthday. While the majority of events in the international system are peaceful events, wars have long dominated the study and practice of international relations. One way to explore the amount of warfare in the system is to examine the number of nation-months of war. A nation-month is one month spent at war by one nation. If two nations are at war for three months, the system accumulates six nation-months of war. The HISTORICAL TRENDS task graphs the level of a variable across time. This allows us to analyze changes in data. The HISTORY file contains information on 61 variables from the years 1900–1999. The variable 32) NATION_MO shows the total nation-months of war in the international system from 1900 to 1980.

➤ *Data File:* **HISTORY**
  ➤ *Task:* **Historical Trends**
  ➤ *Variable:* **32) NATION_MO**

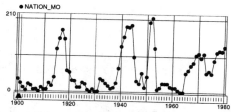

Nation—months of war under way in the year

The ➤ symbol on the DATA FILE line indicates that you must return to the main menu and open a new data file—HISTORY.

There are three key peaks of warfare during the 20th century. They correspond with World War I (1914–1918), World War II (1939–1945), and the Korean War (1949–1953). The graph also shows that the world was not free of warfare between and after these major wars. The period 1965–1980 accounted for over 1,424 nation-months of war. This was the height of the "cold war." One study estimated that over 29 million people were killed in wars between nation-states from 1900 to 1980.[3]

War has been very unevenly distributed across the nation-states since 1945. Most states have experienced no international warfare. To see which states have been in the most wars, we can use the MAPPING task in Student ExplorIt and the NATIONS file, which contains data on the 174 largest nation-states. The MAPPING procedure allows us to view the data using a map of the world, or by ranking the nation-states.

---

[3] The estimates here are taken from summaries of the data from the *Correlates of War* study conducted by J. David Singer and Melvin Small that examined 118 wars between 1815 and 1980. *The Correlates of War* study defined an interstate war as a military conflict where at least one of the participants is a recognized nation-state with at least 500,000 population in which there were at least 1,000 battle-related deaths. For further readings see Small and Singer, (1982).

➤ *Data File:* **NATIONS**
     ➤ *Task:* **Mapping**
➤ *Variable 1:* **116) WARS 45–92**
     ➤ *View:* **Map**
   ➤ *Display:* **Legend**

WARS 45-92 -- NUMBER OF INTERNATIONAL WARS ENTERED INTO FROM 1945-1992 (COW)

Category	N
None	(118)
One	(27)
Two+	(25)
Missing Data	(4)

The ➤ symbol on the DATA FILE line indicates that you must return to the main menu and open a new data file—NATIONS. Remember to select Legend from the menu on the left.

Throughout this book, the darkest color represents the "most" of a variable while the lightest color represents the "least." Here, those nation-states that entered into two or more wars between 1945 and 1992 are the darkest red. The next darkest nation-states (orange) entered into one war since 1945, and the lightest colored states (yellow) entered into no interstate wars between 1945 and 1992. If you click on a nation-state, Student ExplorIt will highlight the nation-state in green and display its value for the variable. If you click on France, you will see that it is in the highest category with 2+ interstate wars between 1945 and 1992. You can also display the values of the variable for each nation-state by using the RANK view for a map. The 115) WARS variable shows the number of wars that a nation-state entered into between 1815 and 1991.[4]

    Data File: **NATIONS**
       Task: **Mapping**
➤ *Variable 1:* **115) WARS**
     ➤ *View:* **List: Rank**

RANK	CASE NAME	VALUE
1	United Kingdom	52
2	France	44
3	Turkey	27
4	Russia	25
5	China	17
6	Italy	15
7	Spain	13
8	Japan	9
8	Austria	9
8	United States	9

The ranking shows that the great powers in Europe (United Kingdom, France, Turkey, Russia, Italy, Spain) and the imperial powers in Asia (China and Japan) entered into the greatest number of wars.

Nation-states vary significantly in how much they spend on defense. Understandably, those states that are threatened or that have ongoing disputes with their neighbors are likely to spend large portions of their national income on defense. The variable 34) DEFENSE PC in the NATIONS file shows the differences in per-capita defense expenditures in 1994 across the globe.[5]

---

[4] Country comparisons on this ranking may not be valid. Many current countries, like those in Africa, did not gain independence until late in the 20th century.

[5] Per capita expenditures are found by dividing the total expenditure by the size of the population. This gives a per-person expenditure. The data are in dollars per capita.

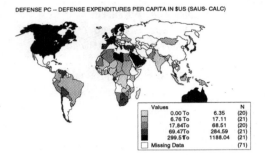

DEFENSE PC -- DEFENSE EXPENDITURES PER CAPITA IN $US (SAUS- CALC)

Values			N
	0.00 To	6.35	(20)
	6.76 To	17.11	(21)
	17.84 To	68.51	(20)
	69.47 To	284.59	(21)
	299.5 To	1188.04	(21)
☐ Missing Data			(71)

Here we see that the industrialized states of Europe and North America and the Middle Eastern states tend to spend the most per capita on defense. Note that the data for Russia and China are missing. If we switch to the RANK view of the expenditures per capita, we can see the actual amounts spent by each nation-state.

RANK	CASE NAME	VALUE
1	United States	1188.04
2	Kuwait	1174.81
3	Saudi Arabia	1039.63
4	Oman	913.76
5	Libya	757.75
6	Sweden	752.72
7	United Kingdom	726.62
8	France	630.59
9	Singapore	559.39
10	Denmark	533.33

In 1994, the United States spent the most per capita on defense—approximately $1,188 per person. Why was a small nation-state like Kuwait ranked second with $1,174 per person? In 1994, Kuwait was rebuilding its military after the 1990–91 Gulf War with Iraq and, as a major oil producer, Kuwait had the necessary funds.

Economists measure the difference between total imports and total exports as the merchandise balance of trade. If a nation-state sells (exports) more than it buys (imports), there is a balance of trade surplus. On the other hand, if a nation-state exports less than it imports, there is a balance of trade deficit. A trade surplus tends to increase the value of the national economy (as measured by the gross national product, or GNP) and indicates that production is increasing and jobs are being created. Trade deficits are a burden on the national economy and indicate that jobs may be lost to foreign competition. The United States ran a trade surplus until about 1970. We can use the HISTORICAL TRENDS task to see the effect of U.S. exports and imports on the balance of trade by graphing these three variables together.

> *Data File:* **HISTORY**
> > *Task:* **Historical Trends**
> *Variables:* **4) BAL TRADE**
> > > **18) EXPORTS**
> > > **30) IMPORTS**

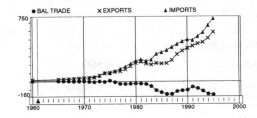

Notice that this task uses a new data file. Also notice that up to four variables can be selected for use at once with the HISTORICAL TRENDS task.

The trends graph shows that while both exports and imports rose since 1960, beginning in the mid-1970s, the rate of increase for imports was greater than the rate of increase for exports. By 1995, the U.S. balance of trade was –$160 billion, meaning that the U.S. imported $160 billion more goods than it exported. What are some of the events that led to the balance of trade deficits after 1970? There is an interactive chronology of events on the computer screen at the bottom of the historical trends graph. You can move through this chronology by clicking your mouse pointer on the up and down arrows on the right side of the events window.

Although there are many causes of trade deficits, and there are many events in this list, it is important to realize not all items in this list cause trade deficits. However, with this said, there are two international events that are notable. In August 1971, President Nixon announced a "New Economic Policy" for the United States. Click on that event, and its date will be highlighted on the trends graph. Until that time, the value of the dollar had been pegged against the price of gold. This put the U.S. at a disadvantage when other countries could manipulate the value of their currencies. The New Economic Policy allowed the dollar to "float" on the international market and placed a 10% tariff surcharge on many imports. This means that, beginning in 1971, the value of the U.S. dollar was determined by the currency market place, not the official policy of the government. The second event occurred in 1973 with the Yom Kippur war. As a protest against U.S. support for Israel during that war, the Arab oil-producing states embargoed oil sales to the U.S. and other Western nation-states. The price of oil rapidly increased as U.S. suppliers sought other sources. These two events illustrate how both economic and political international affairs can directly affect the domestic economy and thereby directly affect you. How does the trade balance affect your life? Although there are other causes, the balance of trade is one factor that contributes to unemployment.

> *Data File:* **HISTORY**
> > *Task:* **Historical Trends**
> *Variables:* **5) BAL TRADE2**
> > > **50) UNEMPLOYMT**

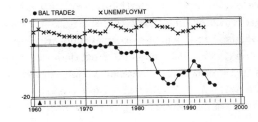

Click the [Clear All] button to delete your variable selections from the previous example.

Note that we are using a different variable for balance of trade (BAL TRADE2). This variable is scaled differently (in 10 billions of U.S. dollars) so that it can be displayed well on the same graph as the unemployment rate. Beginning in about 1970, the U.S. trade balance started to fluctuate and fall. At the same time, the U.S. unemployment rate rose erratically. If a state imports more than it exports, its consumers are paying the wages of foreign workers with their purchases, not the wages of its own workers. Trade deficits place pressures on domestic production of goods and services through foreign competition. While total production may remain healthy or even increase, individual industries may be devastated by the foreign competition.

We all affect international relations through the collective actions of our daily lives. For example, when we choose to vacation abroad, we transfer money earned at home to hotels and restaurants in other nation-states.

Data File: **HISTORY**
Task: **Historical Trends**
➤ *Variables:* **47) FORTRAVEL$**
48) USTRAVEL$

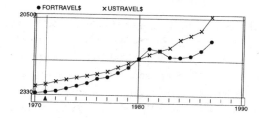

Travel is big business. From 1970 to 1987, the dollar value of American travel abroad (USTRAVEL$) rose from about $2.4 billion per year to over $20 billion per year. In the same period, expenditures by foreign travelers in the United States (FORTRAVEL$) rose from $2.3 billion per year to about $15 billion per year. Although these payments and receipts represent only a small proportion of the U.S. economy, tourism is an important source of revenue for many smaller nation-states and can have a significant impact on foreign relations with those states.

Most governments, including the United States, control the travel of their citizens. The United States Department of State maintains a list of travel restrictions and warnings. Travel to most states is not affected by the list. The State Department issues a "public announcement" when travel to a state or region of a state is dangerous because of some short-term problem. The problem can be political (such as an upcoming election that is likely to spawn local violence), environmental (such as earthquake damage, weather alerts, or erupting volcanoes), or social (such as a high incidence of crime in a particular area of a country). If the problem is severe, as in the case of the ongoing political conflict in Bosnia-Herzegovina, the Department of State will issue a "travel warning," which means that the U.S. government recommends that Americans not travel to that state. States that are in direct political conflict with the United States will suffer "travel restrictions." At the time this book was written, only three states had restricted travel—Iraq, Libya, and Cuba. Travel to these states was illegal without a license, and licenses were issued only for specified purposes. The variable TRAV REST in the NATIONS file contains information on travel announcements, warnings, and restrictions issued by the U.S. Department of State as of August 2000.

➤ *Data File:* **NATIONS**
  ➤ *Task:* **Mapping**
➤ *Variable 1:* **98) TRAV REST**
  ➤ *View:* **Map**
  ➤ *Display:* **Legend**

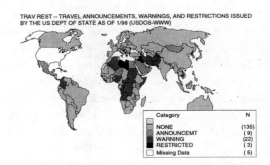

TRAV REST -- TRAVEL ANNOUNCEMENTS, WARNINGS, AND RESTRICTIONS ISSUED BY THE US DEPT OF STATE AS OF 1/98 (USDOS-WWW)

Category	N
NONE	(135)
ANNOUNCEMT	(9)
WARNING	(22)
RESTRICTED	(3)
Missing Data	(5)

To reopen quickly a previously used data file, return to the main menu, click [File] in the upper left corner, and select NATIONS from the list.

It is clear from the map that the travel "hot spots" in August 2000 were concentrated in Africa, the Middle East, and the Balkan Peninsula in southwestern Europe. At that time, there had been recent coups, civil war, or ethnic violence in Algeria, Burundi, the Congo (formerly Zaire), Angola, Lebanon, Liberia, Nigeria, Central African Republic, Cambodia, Bosnia, Somalia, the Solomon Islands, and Afghanistan. Travel warnings were issued for Colombia, Iran, and Pakistan, because of outstanding threats against American lives.

The aggregation of our individual decisions to purchase goods and services has a direct and significant impact on imports and exports. Our tastes for foreign-made goods have increased imports in some key manufacturing sectors to the point where U.S. production is nearly nonexistent.

➤ *Data File:* **HISTORY**
  ➤ *Task:* **Historical Trends**
➤ *Variables:* **27) IMP CARS**
            28) IMP ELEC
            29) IMP SHOES

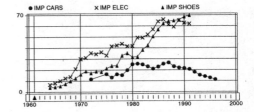

● IMP CARS   ✕ IMP ELEC   ▲ IMP SHOES

Notice this task uses a new data file.

The graph shows the "import penetration" of three products. That is, the graph shows the percentage of the total sales of the product in the U.S. that are imports. Since 1963, the proportions of imports in shoes and consumer electronics (TV's, radios, CD players, etc.) have risen to the point where foreign-made products clearly dominate the U.S. market. By 1991, imports made up well over 60% of the total U.S. sales in these goods. Imports in the motor vehicle industry rose through the 1960s, 1970s and 1980s to a high of 26.7% in 1987. Since then, the percentage of imported motor vehicles fell to about 11% of the U.S. market in 1996. Are you responsible for the falling domestic share of these industries? Of course there are many reasons why people buy imported shoes or electronics, and we will examine these reasons in Exercise 10. Foreign-made products may be less expensive, better made, or better designed. Yet, in the end, we choose to buy the foreign products freely, and the collective result of these decisions affects international relations.

STUDYING INTERNATIONAL RELATIONS IS STUDYING HOW THE WORLD WORKS

International relations is a multidisciplinary field of study. We use theories from politics, economics, anthropology, geography, sociology, and psychology to explain international events. This book is meant to be a tool that will help you navigate the difficult terrain of this complex subject. One of the best ways to learn is to explore. The exercises that follow will introduce conceptual frameworks for understanding events within the context of worksheets that allow you to explore how those frameworks help you answer questions. We begin by defining the nature of international relations and its major fields of thought in Exercise 2. Exercise 3 explores the nation-state system as it is created by sovereignty. Exercises 4, 5, and 6 examine the three major levels of analysis—system level analysis, state level analysis, and individual level analysis. Exercises 7 through 11 introduce various instruments of international relations—power, warfare, international law and organization, and the international economy. Exercise 12 explores how theories and instruments are applied in the area of the international environment. At the end of each exercise is a set of worksheets that allow you to explore questions we pose and questions you may have about international relations. We begin by using the Student ExplorIt software to explore some more questions about how international relations affects our lives and how we affect international relations in the worksheets for Exercise 1.

WORKSHEET

NAME:

COURSE:

DATE:

Workbook exercises and software are copyrighted. Copying is prohibited by law.

EXERCISE

1

REVIEW QUESTIONS

Based on the first part of this exercise, answer True or False to the following items:

The period of the cold war, from 1945 through 1989, was a period of relatively peaceful international relations as measured by nation-months of war.   T   F

The merchandise balance of trade is the difference between the value of all economic transactions (imports, exports, loans, grants, etc.) that enter a nation-state and all the economic transactions that exit a nation-state in a given year.   T   F

A balance of trade surplus tends to add value to the gross national product of a nation-state.   T   F

The United States has consistently had a balance of trade deficit since the mid-1970s.   T   F

The United States spent a larger proportion of the total federal budget on defense during the Reagan administration (1981–1988) than it did during the Kennedy-Johnson administration (1961–1968).   T   F

The democratic, industrialized states of Europe and North America spend less per capita on national defense than do most nation-states in other regions of the world.   T   F

Imports of shoes and consumer electronics now make up more than 60% of the total sales of these goods in the United States.   T   F

International relations is the study of international events.   T   F

According to the data from the 1998 American Public Opinion and U.S. Foreign Policy Survey, most Americans do not believe that U.S. foreign policy has a major impact on their standard of living.   T   F

International events necessarily involve actions taken by an actor directed at a target where the actor and target are in different nation-states.   T   F

EXPLORIT QUESTIONS

You will need to use the ExplorIt software and data that came with this book for the following worksheets. You need to go through the *Getting Started* section of this book before you begin the worksheets. The Student ExplorIt tasks used in these worksheets are the same that were used in the preliminary section of Exercise 1. If you have any difficulties using the software to obtain the appropriate information, or if you want to learn additional features of the tasks, use the on-line help [F1].

1. We saw in the preliminary section of Exercise 1 that most people believed that foreign policy has a major impact on the U.S. economy and on individuals' jobs. We also saw that a small percentage of the respondents thought that foreign policy has a major impact on individuals' standard of living. Do these beliefs translate into support for foreign affairs? You can use the ExplorIt UNIVARIATE task to examine this question in different ways.

> ➤ *Data File:* **FPSURVEY**
> ➤ *Task:* **Univariate**
> ➤ *Primary Variable:* **34) USACTIVE**
> ➤ *View:* **Pie**

a. Fill in the blanks below with the percentages from the pie chart table.

1) Active   _____%

2) Stay Out   _____%

b. Do Americans generally support an active U.S. role in world affairs? Yes No

Does this support translate into support for increased U.S. defense spending? We saw in Exercise 1 that the United States ranked first among the nation-states in defense spending per capita.

> *Data File:* **FPSURVEY**
> *Task:* **Univariate**
> ➤ *Primary Variable:* **2) DEFENSE**
> ➤ *View:* **Pie**

c. Fill in the blanks below with the percentages from the pie chart table.

Expand defense spending   _____%

Keep defense spending the same   _____%

Cut defense spending   _____%

d. In your own words, from the data, do you think the American people support increasing, maintaining, or cutting the defense budget?

2. We saw in Exercise 1 that trade balances impact your life by affecting the unemployment rate in the domestic economy. What other ways does the trade balance affect the domestic economy? To answer this question, we can look at some other economic variables.

What is the relationship between the trade balance and foreign exchange? The exchange rate of a foreign currency (such as the Japanese yen) is the "price" of that currency in your currency. For instance, how many dollars does it take to buy 1,000 Japanese yen? The price of currency fluctuates in response to many factors that are related to the health of an economy, including the trade balance. When the demand for a currency goes up, the exchange rate increases. We would expect that if a state has a trade deficit, the value of the currency of one of its main trading partners will rise because a trade deficit means there is an increased demand for the other country's goods. Look at the value of the Japanese yen over time and compare it to the U.S. trade balance. To make the graph that plots the value of the yen in US$ with the U.S. merchandise balance of trade over time, do the following:

> ➤ *Data File:*   **HISTORY**
> ➤ *Task:*   **Historical Trends**
> ➤ *Variables:*   **59) $/1000YEN**
>   **5) BAL TRADE2**

The graph shows the dollar cost of purchasing 1,000 yen and the U.S. balance of trade in 10 billions of dollars (e.g., for 1990, the graph shows a balance of trade deficit of about "–10," which translates to a deficit of about –$100 billion).

a. About what year does the U.S. merchandise balance of trade begin to fall?   _____

b. About what year does the value of the Yen begin to rise dramatically?   _____

c. In your own words, describe what you can conclude about the relationship between trade deficits and exchange rates. For example, when the value of the U.S. merchandise trade balance falls, what happens to the value of the yen?

3. The U.S. government recognizes that your actions define and affect international relations—especially economic relations. The ongoing trade deficit with Japan was the subject of a series of negotiations that began in September 1989 called the Structural Trade Initiative but were commonly known as the "Lifestyle Talks." These negotiations focused not on trade barriers such as tariffs or quotas but on the consumer behavior of the residents of the United States and Japan. The theory was that U.S. residents spend too much and save too little while Japanese residents spend too little and save too much. This means that Americans demand Japanese products more than the Japanese demand American products. The negotiations were concluded in April 1990. Among other things, Japan agreed to streamline its retail distribution and shorten its government employees' work week while the United States agreed to set up tax-free family savings accounts.

> Data File: **HISTORY**
> Task: **Historical Trends**
> ➤ Variables: **39) SAVE JAPAN**
> **40) SAVE USA**

a. Do Americans save less of their income than the Japanese?   Yes   No

> ➤ Data File: **NATIONS**
> ➤ Task: **Mapping**
> ➤ Variable 1: **89) SAVINGS**
> ➤ View: **List: Rank**

b. What is the United States' rank in gross domestic savings as a % of GDP?   _____

c. What percentage of gross domestic product does the United States save?   _____%

d. What percentage of gross domestic product does Japan save?   _____%

EXERCISE 2

APPROACHING INTERNATIONAL RELATIONS

Tasks: Historical Trends, Cross-tabulation, Mapping, Univariate
Data Files: HISTORY, NATIONS, FPELITES

INTERNATIONAL RELATIONS AND INTERNATIONAL EVENTS

International relations is the study and practice of international events. An international event is an action taken by an actor that is directed toward another actor, called the target, where the actor and the target are in different nation-states. The actors and the targets can be international organizations, agencies and agents of national governments, sub-national governments (such as state, provincial, or city governments), corporations and businesses, groups (such as Greenpeace, labor unions, or the Red Cross), or individuals. An actor can also be a target, and a target can be an actor. That is, in one event the actor, the United States government, might take an action toward a target, the government of Iraq. In the next event, the actor may be the government of Iraq and the target may be the government of the United States. Actions are either verbal or physical. Verbal actions include such things as indicating support or opposition, making promises, or making threats. Physical actions include, for example, warfare, lending money, confiscating property, or signing a treaty. The actor acts in order to influence some behavior, attitude, or belief of the target. Although there are many unintended consequences of actions, actors act with intent. The actor attempts to influence the target by affecting something that is important to the target such as its security, economic well-being, or prestige. Actions can be classified by their issue. For example, there can be economic actions, military actions, or diplomatic actions, to name only a few of the categories.

Since *international* events must occur across borders, international relations depends on the existence of the international system of nation-states. This does not mean that other types of social and political interactions are uninteresting or irrelevant to international relations. It merely means that international relations extracts international events from the universe of all interactions as its subject of study and practice. This also situates international relations in history. The nation-state has not always existed in the form we know it now, and we cannot assume that the international system will persist in the future. Thus, descriptions and explanations of international events are necessarily specific to the historical period in which those events occurred. Although we can learn much from history, we must always be wary of how the system of states has changed. By limiting our analysis to describing and explaining international events, we try to identify a subject that we can study with some universal application.

Formally limiting our study to the international event is also the first step in being "scientific." Although there are many paths to understanding international relations, we choose a scientific path when we follow a prescribed scientific process. The process starts with theory; that is, it starts with a naive understanding of the world about us. From that theory we assert what we expect to find in observing the world, if the theory is true. These assertions are hypotheses about how international relations works. Hypotheses must be falsifiable. If there is no way to falsify a claim, it cannot be a scientific hypothesis. The hypotheses must be verified through observation or reasoning. We learn about international relations through both the success and the failure of this validation, and we use this knowledge to refine our theories. Scientific theories cannot be proven, as such. Theories are explanations. They help us understand unknown phenomena, but since they must be based on falsifiable hypotheses, they are useful only until someone comes up with a better explanation. It is assumed that the scientific method is both replicable and objective. It is replicable if the methods are standardized and made public. Objectivity is more difficult. It is impossible in any social science to be fully objective since we bring our political and social biases to the process. Objectivity is replaced instead by "intersubjectivity." That is, scientists usually start from a position of shared subjective understandings of the world because they have been similarly socialized into the process of science and their naive understandings of the world are a result of that process. The problem with this is that the shared intersubjective understandings of the world are often the result of power struggles and political processes themselves. We will follow a scientific approach in this book, but we will stop from time to time to examine our own biases and assumptions.

There are many ways that the scientific method has been applied to the study of international events. Some studies focus on the actors and targets, rather than on the events themselves. Field Theory attempts to explain events by classifying the actors that perform them. These analyses make claims about what types of nation-states are likely to go to war in what situations (see Rummel 1972 for an example of field theory). Cross-national studies look for statistical correlations between characteristics of the actors and the kinds of actions they perform. Other studies focus on the events themselves. Event case studies attempt to describe and explain specific events by examining the history and the characteristics of the actors involved. Events data analyses explore large databases of events to see if there are patterns in the actions of the actors and targets. One of these event data analyses is the Conflict and Peace Data Bank (COPDAB for short). COPDAB is a database that contains records of over 390,000 international events that occurred between 1948 and 1978. The database was created by researchers who read over 70 newspapers and other news sources from all over the world and coded information about international events using a standardized coding method. Some of the COPDAB data are contained in the data files included with this book. COPDAB did not capture all international events since it only coded events that were reported in one of the news sources used by the project. Also, COPDAB only coded events of nation-state actors. It did not, for example, record the international events of Exxon, Greenpeace, or the AFL-CIO. The actions of some nation-states, like France, were more likely to be reported than the actions of a small state like Mauritius. Some actions, like interstate war, are more likely to be reported than the transfer of economic development funds. Nevertheless, COPDAB painted a picture of dense and rising international activity as time progressed. We can explore the COPDAB data to see the scale and scope of international relations from 1948 through 1978.

➤ *Data File:* **HISTORY**
    ➤ *Task:* **Historical Trends**
➤ *Variable:* **17) TOT EVNTS**

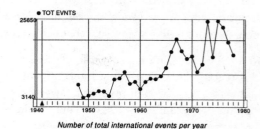

Number of total international events per year

The general trend from 1948 through 1978 was for the number of international events to increase, but there was great variation from year to year during this time. One question we need to ask is, What could have led to this general increase in events or what could have *caused* the increase? One answer is that we would expect the total number of international events to rise as the number of nation-states increase. During this time period many states were created as the former colonial empires withdrew from their territories around the world. We do not have a variable to directly measure the rate at which nation-states were created, but we can measure another aspect of this move toward national independence.

The variable 12) EVENT/ST shows us the number of events per nation-state for the years 1948–1978. We can use this variable to test our hypothesis that as the number of nation-states increases, so will the number of events. After all, if there are more nations interacting, it is logical to assume there will be more incidents of conflict or disagreement.

Data File: **HISTORY**
    Task: **Historical Trends**
➤ *Variable:* **12) EVENT/ST**

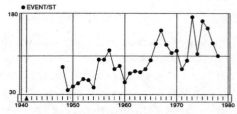

Number of international events per state

Although we can see great variation from year to year, the number of events per nation-state in the international system increased dramatically from a little more than 30 in 1948 to well over 100 in 1978. This shows support for our hypothesis.

What kinds of events were occurring during this time period? We know in 1978 there were not a hundred wars around the world. Since COPDAB classified events by their issue and level of conflict, we can see what types of events occurred each year.

Data File: **HISTORY**
    Task: **Historical Trends**
➤ *Variables:* **15) ECON EVNTS**
            31) MIL EVENTS
            16) POL EVNTS

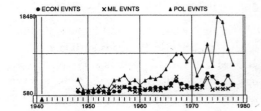

The majority of events in most years were political events—those that involved signing treaties, declaring support or condemnation, and other diplomatic exchanges. Although international events often focus on military conflict, economic events outnumbered military events in most years.

We tend to think of international relations as being composed mostly of conflict between nation-states. It is true that the dangers of international conflict, especially in the age of nuclear weapons, require that states be wary and prepared; nevertheless, cooperative events are more common in international relations than conflictive events. This should not be surprising when one considers that even in conflictive settings, the carrot is often more effective than the stick. The variables 13) CONFL EVNT and 14) COOP EVNT explore the levels of conflict and cooperation respectively in the COPDAB data.

Data File: **HISTORY**

Task: **Historical Trends**

➤ Variables: **13) CONFL EVNT**

14) COOP EVNT

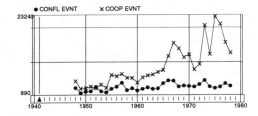

The graph shows that the number of cooperative events rose dramatically in the years from 1948 through 1978 (4,393 to 12,663) while the number of conflictive events remained relatively static (2,415 to 2,961).

APPROACHES TO THE STUDY OF INTERNATIONAL RELATIONS

The study of international relations as a unique subject is relatively new. The first endowed chair of international relations was created at the University of Aberystwyth in Wales in 1919. Even with this short history, approaches to the study of international relations have changed markedly over the years. Although there have been many schools of thought, two approaches have dominated the literature and practice in Western experience. In response to the horrors of World War I, idealist practitioners and scholars of international relations thought that international institutions, like the League of Nations, could create international norms for behavior that would prevent another world war. Idealism should not be equated with a utopian view of world government, even though some idealists proposed this. Idealism instead refers to international relations based on shared norms or ideals that are born of shared interests and implemented through institutional arrangements. These institutions included official governmental organizations, such as the Permanent Court of International Justice, as well as informal institutions like the international marketplace. Recently, this approach has been called neo-liberalism because it focuses less on official governmental institutions, such as the United Nations, and more on norms related to cooperation and competition that arise from shared interests in economic growth in the market or shared democratic ideals.

The second school of thought traces its lineage far back in the history of political relations. Realism asserts that political entities such as nation-states act according to identifiable self-interests. The most general of these interests is survival, and the only way to ensure survival in a competitive world is to obtain and maintain power vis-à-vis the other actors. Realism was dominant after World War II when analysts of international relations pointed to the inter-war years and stated that international relations cannot be based on normative ideals in a world where the pursuit of individual interests takes precedence over behavior shaped by moral values. Perhaps the clearest statement of realism in international relations was the book *Politics Among Nations* by Hans Morgenthau, first published in 1948. Realism throughout the era of the cold war was associated with national chauvinism. It was often used to rationalize the foreign policy of specific nation-states locked in competitive struggles with their opponents. Recent proponents of the realist approach have been called neo-realists. Neo-realism focuses less on the prescriptions for action and more on the characteristics of the nation-state system to which states must respond in order to survive.

Serious critiques have been offered for both the idealist/neoliberal and the realist/neorealist schools of thought. One critique arises from the reliance on the state as the primary actor in the international system. We will explore this critique further in Exercise 3, but the main points are that the sovereignty of the nation-state has been eroded by technology, multinational economic institutions (both public and private), and by the evolution of the nation-state itself to the point where it no longer can be seen as the defining actor in the system. Another critique arises from feminist theory that asserts that while states may act according to their interest in survival, there are many ways to define survival and many ways to achieve it. Feminist theory proposes that the realist reliance on military power is derived from the dominance of a masculine perspective in defining foreign policy.

THE FRAMEWORK FOR UNDERSTANDING INTERNATIONAL RELATIONS: THE LEVEL OF ANALYSIS

The data from the COPDAB project show that international relations is composed of a diverse set of international events. There are patterns to be found in this web of international activity, yet the depth and complexity of these patterns seem to defy explanation. A framework of analysis is needed that can place the explanation of international events in the context of the institutional structure that makes up international relations. One such framework is sometimes called the "level of analysis" question. According to this framework, there are three different levels of analysis. Some patterns in the events are best explained by understanding how individuals behave. Although actors may be nation-states, corporations, or international organizations, all events are the result of individuals making decisions. The *individual level of analysis* attempts to explain international events by examining the factors that affect individual decision-making. Some patterns in international events can be explained by understanding the characteristics of group actors such as nation-states. The *state level of analysis* assumes that different nation-states have different interests and different processes for implementing foreign policy. By understanding these interests and processes, one can understand international relations. Individuals and nation-states exist within an international system with characteristics and forces of its own. The *system level of analysis* proposes that international events are responses to the nature of the system itself. We will examine each of these three levels of analysis—individual, state, and system—in depth in Exercises 4, 5, and 6, but we will explore some of the basic ideas now.

THE INDIVIDUAL LEVEL OF ANALYSIS: PEOPLE MAKING DECISIONS

All international events are the result of people making decisions. Some of those people act on behalf of a nation-state, but they are all influenced by the same factors that affect how you and I make decisions in our daily lives. These factors include our knowledge, ideology, personal interests, human nature, and mental and physical health. It is interesting to examine the differences between the opinions of elite decision-makers and the opinions of the general public on issues related to international relations. Do you think there is a difference in how members of Congress, members of the executive branch, and the general population view American defense spending? We can look at what members of Congress think about the level of spending by using ExplorIt's subset variable capability.

➤ *Data File:* **FPELITES**
➤ *Task:* **Univariate**
➤ *Primary Variable:* **2) DEFENSE**
➤ *Subset Variable:* **9) SAMPLE**
➤ *Subset Categories:* **Include: 4) Congress**
➤ *View:* **Pie**

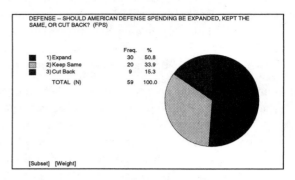

The option for selecting a subset variable is located on the same screen you use to select other variables. For this example, select 9) SAMPLE as a subset variable. A window will appear that shows you the categories of the subset variable. Select 4) Congress as your subset category and choose the [Include] option. Then click [OK] and continue as usual.

With this particular subset selected, the results will be limited to Congress. The subset selection continues until you exit the task, delete all subset variables, or clear all variables.

When we look only at members of Congress, we see that 50.8% think American defense spending should be expanded and 33.9% believe that it should be kept the same. Next, we can look at members of the executive branch.

Data File: **FPELITES**
Task: **Univariate**
Primary Variable: **2) DEFENSE**
Subset Variable: **9) SAMPLE**
➤ *Subset Categories:* **Include: 5) Exec. Br.**
➤ *View:* **Pie**

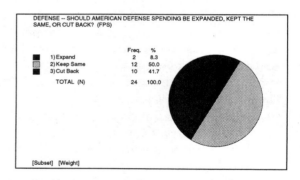

The easiest way to change the subset category to Exec. Br. (from Congress) is to first delete the subset variable 9) SAMPLE. Then reselect 9) SAMPLE as the subset variable. Include 5) Executive as your subset category. Then click [OK] and continue as usual.

When we look just at members of the executive branch, we find that only 8.3% believe that American defense spending should be expanded and 50% think it should be kept the same. Finally, we can look at the general public.

Data File:	**FPELITES**
Task:	**Univariate**
Primary Variable:	**2) DEFENSE**
Subset Variable:	**9) SAMPLE**
➤ *Subset Categories:*	**Include: 7) Gen. pop.**
➤ *View:*	**Pie**

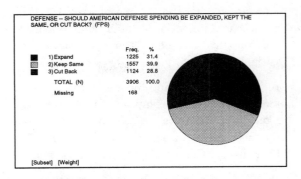

Here we see that of the general public, 31.4% believe that defense spending should be expanded and 39.9% believe that defense spending should be kept the same.

To see the differences and similarities between these three groups, we used a three-step process that involved obtaining three univariate distributions. Student ExplorIt includes a one-step procedure for obtaining the same result. This procedure is called a ***cross-tabulation*** and yields a table including the same data you saw in the three univariate distributions. Here is how it looks.

Data File:	**FPELITES**
➤ *Task:*	**Cross-tabulation**
➤ *Row Variable:*	**2) DEFENSE**
➤ *Column Variable:*	**9) SAMPLE**
➤ *Subset Variable:*	**9) SAMPLE**
➤ *Subset Categories:*	**Include: 4) Congress,**
	5) Exec. Br., 7) Gen. Pop.
➤ *View:*	**Table**
➤ *Display:*	**Column %**

DEFENSE   by   SAMPLE

Weight Variable: WEIGHT
Cramer's V: 0.047 **

		SAMPLE			
		Congress	Exec. Br.	Gen. Pop.	TOTAL
D E F E N S E	Expand	30	2	1225	1257
		50.8%	8.3%	31.4%	31.5%
	Keep Same	20	12	1557	1589
		33.9%	50.0%	39.9%	39.8%
	Cut Back	9	10	1124	1143
		15.3%	41.7%	28.8%	28.7%
	Missing	0	0	168	168
	TOTAL	59	24	3906	3989
		100.0%	100.0%	100.0%	

> To construct this table, return to the main menu and select the CROSS-TABULATION task. Then select 2) DEFENSE as the row variable, 9) SAMPLE as the column variable, and 9) SAMPLE as the subset variable. Include 4) Congress, 5) Exec. Br., and 7) Gen. Pop. as your subset categories. When the table is showing, select the [Column %] option.

In the table, 33.9% of Congress, 50% of the executive branch, and 39.9% of the general public think spending should be kept the same. This matches the univariate results obtained above, as it should.

However, you must be somewhat careful with this comparison. There are only 59 members of Congress and 24 members of the executive branch included in this analysis, while there are 3,906 members of the general population. Therefore, the responses for the general public are more representative than those for the other two groups. So, do these results reflect an actual difference in these groups, or are they merely due to random chance? To determine if observed results reflect real relationships or if they are merely due to random chance, statisticians use tests of statistical significance. Differences observed in a random sample are said to be *statistically significant* when these differences are high enough that they are not likely to be due to random chance.

In international relations, we assume that any observed difference in a sample is significant when it occurs fewer than 5 times out of 100 by chance alone. When we say that a difference is statistically significant, we infer that it reflects a real relationship between the variables. If a difference would occur more than 5 times out of 100 by chance alone (a probability level of .05), we say that the difference is not statistically significant, and we conclude that it does not reflect a real relationship between the variables.

In addition to knowing the statistical significance of a relationship, we also want to understand the strength of a relationship. That is, once we know that the differences we observe in a table are not likely to be due to chance, we then want to know how much one variable affects another variable. In the table above, this means we want to know how much knowing the category a person is in (Congress, Executive, or General Population) helps us understand his or her views on defense spending.

To see the strength of the relationship between 9) SAMPLE and 2) DEFENSE, look above the table where it reads "Cramer's V: 0.047." The Cramer's V statistic indicates the *strength* of a relationship in cross-tabulations. The closer it is to 1.0 the stronger the relationship is. A Cramer's V of .045 shows a weak relationship between the two variables. Next, we can look at the summary view of this table.

Data File:	**FPELITES**
Task:	**Cross-tabulation**
Row Variable:	**2) DEFENSE**
Column Variable:	**9) SAMPLE**
Subset Variable:	**9) SAMPLE**
Subset Categories:	**Include: 4) Congress,**
	5) Exec. Br., 7) Gen. Pop.
➤ View:	**Summary**

DEFENSE   by   SAMPLE

Nominal Statistics

Chi-Square: 17.400 (DF = 4; Prob. = 0.001)

V:	0.047	C:	0.066		
Lambda:(DV=9)	0.000	Lambda:(DV=2)	0.004	Lambda:	0.004

Ordinal Statistics

Gamma:	0.142	Tau-b:	0.023	Tau-c:	0.006
s.error	0.091	s.error	0.015	s.error	0.004
Dyx:	0.093	Dxy:	0.006		
s.error	0.060	s.error	0.004		
Prob. =	0.122				

There is a lot of information shown on this screen, most of which we will not use in this book. These calculations are covered in a statistics course. However, we are interested in one result, the chi-square test. We are interested only in the probability of the chi-square test, not its value. Here we see that the probability of the chi-square test is .001. That means there is a 1 in 1000 chance that a random distribution of the cases would have produced these results. If the probability of chi-square is less than .05, statisticians say the relationship is "significant."

Student ExplorIt makes it easy to test for significance. If you switch back to the table view and look again at Cramer's V, you will see two asterisks to the right of the value. If V is followed by one asterisk, the difference it represents is statistically significant at the .05 level of probability. That is, it would be expected to occur fewer than 5 times out of 100 by chance alone. If two asterisks follow V, the difference it represents is statistically significant at the .01 level of probability; it would be expected to occur less than 1 time out of 100 by chance alone. Whether V has one or two asterisks after it, we conclude the difference in the sample is statistically significant and thus is not likely to be due to random chance. If no asterisks follow V, the difference it represents is not statistically significant, and we conclude that there is no difference in the population.

Notice that the V of .047 in our table is followed by two asterisks. This means the differences between Congress, the executive branch and the general population would occur by chance fewer than 1 time out of 100. We can conclude there is a small, but significant, difference between the views of the Congress, the executive branch, and the public about spending on the defense budget.

How do the differences between Congress, the executive branch and the general population affect international relations and how can they be explained? Clearly, U.S. military expenditure is an important variable in understanding international events. The United States is a major power. If it increases its defense expenditures, other nation-states may do the same. In the American political system, the Congress has an important role in setting the military priorities of the United States through the defense budget. Why do the views of Congress members differ from the views of the public? Individual-level analysis tells us to look for characteristics of the key decision-makers to explain international events. In this case, the important characteristic is embedded in U.S. politics. Congress members favor increasing defense spending because it garners support from key contributors that can aid their reelection. While this factor alone does not fully explain U.S. defense expenditures, using the individual-level of analysis does help us understand some of the reasons why events occur.

THE STATE LEVEL OF ANALYSIS CHARACTERISTICS OF THE NATION-STATES

The state level of analysis focuses on the differences between nation-states. States differ in terms of resources, location, geography, culture, history, language, religion, political system, and ideology, just to name a few. The state level of analysis presumes that some of the patterns we see in international events are caused by these differences. It also presumes that the motivating factor behind a nation-state's behavior is its national interest. Defining and describing the national interest is often difficult and may not be a fruitful analytical tool, as we shall see later. Nevertheless, explanations of international events are derived by identifying the differences between nation-states that affect their national interest. One state-level theory is that democracies are more cooperative and less warlike than non-democratic forms of government. This is not easy to test. Some democratic states may be the target of conflictive events initiated by non-democratic states. Evaluation of the theory must take into account the context of the interaction. The COPDAB data may provide us with insight on this theory by comparing the proportion of conflictive events initiated by the state (CONFLICT) across categories of the nation-state's type of political system. If the theory is correct, we should find that democratic nation-states have lower levels of conflict than other types of nation-states.

> Data File: **NATIONS**
> Task: **Cross-tabulation**
> Row Variable: **26) CONFLICT**
> Column Variable: **36) DEMOCRACY2**
> View: **Table**
> Display: **Column %**

CONFLICT   by   DEMOCRACY2
Cramer's V: 0.178 *

		DEMOCRACY2			
		Low	High	Missing	TOTAL
CONFLICT	Low	29	35	0	64
		41.4%	59.3%		49.6%
	High	41	24	0	65
		58.6%	40.7%		50.4%
	Missing	25	17	3	45
	TOTAL	70	59	3	129
		100.0%	100.0%		

The value of Cramer's V (0.178) with an asterisk (*) indicates that there is a weak, but statistically significant, relationship between type of political system and the proportion of a nation-state's events that are conflictive. We can see this by comparing the column percentages across the columns. 58.6% of the nation-states with low levels of democratic freedoms had high proportions of conflictive events. This compares to only 40.7% of the highly democratic states having high proportions of conflictive events. One must be careful not to infer too much about the relationship between type of political system and conflict. The measures used here are crude at best, and there are many other factors that might explain the observed data. Nevertheless, it seems that the state level of analysis helps us understand some of the variables that affect international conflict by looking at the characteristics of the nation-states themselves.

The System Level of Analysis: The Setting for International Events

The system level of analysis requires that one be able to see the whole of international relations as a system, rather than a mere collection of parts. The international political system is typically characterized by the number of "poles." A system pole, like a magnetic pole, is a nation-state with enough influence to attract or repel the interests of other nation-states in a way that affects the entire system. The last half of the 19th century was characterized by a "multipolar" system because there were a number of "great powers" (Great Britain, France, Russia, Germany, Austria, Italy, and some others) that could attract or repel the interests of other states. The period between 1945 and 1991 was the era of the cold war, which was also called the bi-polar system. During this period, the international system was strongly influenced by the political interests of two superpowers—the United States of America (USA) and the Union of Soviet Socialist Republics (USSR).

The system level of analysis assumes that events can be explained, at least in part, by the characteristics of the international system in which they are initiated. For example, one of the "rules" of the bipolar system is that the superpowers avoid direct military confrontation. They compete for the support of "client" states which are usually smaller, less developed countries. Wars are fought in and between these states that act as surrogates for direct superpower military competition. If this theory is valid, we should see distinct differences between regions in the proportion of conflictive events. We begin by simply looking at a map of the distribution of conflictive events.

Data File: **NATIONS**
➤ Task: **Mapping**
➤ Variable 1: **27) CONFLICT %**
➤ View: **Map**

CONFLICT % -- PERCENT OF EVENTS INITIATED THAT ARE CONFLICTIVE (COPDAB)

On the map, states with darker colors initiated a higher proportion of conflictive events than states with lighter colors. It appears that the two superpowers (USA and USSR) initiated high proportions of conflictive events. It also appears that states in the Middle East and Asia also initiated high proportions of conflictive events. The map shows that conflict during the cold war was concentrated in some of the less developed countries, which supports the system-level hypothesis that surrogate conflict does explain some international events. More analysis is needed. Without knowing more about why these specific conflict events occurred, it is impossible to say that system characteristics caused the conflict. The system-level of analysis does, however, tell us that some events occur because of the nature of the international system itself.

Much of system-level theory seeks those explanations in the rules that states follow in various international systems. These rules are not legal restrictions but, rather, are guides for policy makers. Policy makers understand the nature of the system in which they exist, and they understand that certain behaviors are likely to succeed in a given system while others are not. In addition to these rules, system-level theory tells us to explain international events by looking at variables that are global in nature. Two of these variables are very important as we enter the 21st century. World population is increasing rapidly. No nation-state can individually control world population, yet its effects may have devastating impact on all states. This is also true of effluent pollution, such as CO_2.

➤ *Data File:* **HISTORY**
    ➤ *Task:* **Historical Trends**
➤ *Variable:* **58) WORLD POP**

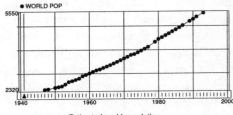

Estimated world population

At the turn of the 21st century, total world population is over 6 billion. How much longer can the growth rate shown in the graph above be sustained without depleting the Earth's ability to regenerate food and energy supplies? This is a system-level variable because it is a characteristic of the system as a whole.

Data File: **HISTORY**
    Task: **Historical Trends**
➤ *Variable:* **9) CO2**

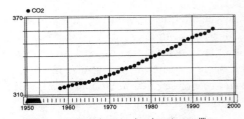

CO_2 concentration in the atmosphere in parts per million

Here we can see the level of carbon dioxide found in the upper atmosphere in parts per million. The measurements were taken at Mauna Loa Observatory, high atop a mountain in Hawaii. It is apparent that CO_2 levels have been rising since the late 1950s. There is much debate, which we will examine in Exercise 12, about whether or not this rise in CO_2 indicates an increasing problem with the greenhouse effect. Certain carbon-based chemicals, like CO_2, can act like the glass on a greenhouse—letting the electromagnetic radiation from the sun in but not letting radiant heat escape back into space. If the greenhouse effect is real, the rising levels of CO_2 could mean that average temperature will rise on Earth. This "global warming" could affect crops, industry, water availability, and other key variables. While variables like population and CO_2 levels are not directly political variables, the system level of analysis tells us to examine how characteristics of the global condition affect the politics among nation-states.

THE MAJOR THEMES OF INTERNATIONAL RELATIONS

What are the major themes and questions of international relations? The answer to this question is always changing. That is due, in part, to the changing nature of the nation-state system and of the nation-state itself. Many forces have affected the nation-state through history. The state has evolved in response to changes in technology, population, culture, and economics. The system as a whole has also changed. The bipolar system that existed during the cold war was significantly different from the multipolar system that existed at the end of the nineteenth century. One of the key questions that must be addressed in international relations is, What will be the nature of the next international system? Will a new form of multipolar system arise, will the United States become the dominant actor? Will China or Russia rise to challenge U.S. hegemony? Since many of the explanations of international relations are specific to the type of system, these questions are very important.

Other questions bridge the gap between system-level theory and state-level theory. Threats to the human ecology from population growth, rising industrial pollution, and depletion of natural resources arise at the level of the system but are embedded in the activities of the private individuals within the bounds of the sovereign nation-state. Sovereignty, as we shall see in the next exercise, defines the system of states by providing legal and customary basis for autonomous actions. That is, in international relations, the sovereign state does not answer to any higher authority. It is autonomous. Pollution that crosses borders and population growth that consumes valuable world resources are problems that demand action by the international community. Such problems challenge the social basis of sovereignty itself. Nation-states also face challenges to their autonomy from the changing nature of economic relations. In a globally competitive market, many nation-states have voluntarily surrendered some of their autonomy to regional economic regimes such as the European Union or the North American Free Trade Agreement. It is probably premature to predict the end of the autonomous state, but a major question for students of international relations is, How does the state respond to these pressures and how do these responses affect international events?

Many of the questions facing international relations arise from the international economy. As we saw earlier, the volume of international economic events has increased dramatically since 1948. Since the fall of the Soviet Union in 1991, the world economy has become more uniformly capitalistic. At times, the world economy needs management to prop up failing national economies or to stimulate international economic growth. Who, or what, will provide that management? It is generally thought that the United States did much to manage the world economy from the end of World War II to sometime in the 1970s. Since that time, what management exists has come from multilateral institutions such as the International Monetary Fund, the Group of Seven, or the World Bank. What are the effects of these multilateral institutions on individuals, groups, and nation-states, and how do they affect international events? These are questions that we face as the world economy grows and matures. The benefits of world economic growth have not been evenly distributed among or within nation-states. Economic development conditions are actually worse off in many parts of Africa today compared to 20 years ago. Other questions facing international relations are, Why is underdevelopment so persistent and what can be done about it? Official development assistance (foreign aid) was often used as a tool of systemic politics during the cold war. What are the incentives for giving aid now that the cold war is over?

Disparities in economic benefits often exacerbate existing ethnic and racial tensions. Some analysts of the late 1970s thought that the importance of the nation-state was withering in international relations due to the erosion of sovereignty by international institutions such as multinational corporations. But the "nation" of nation-state is alive and well. Ethnic conflicts in the emergent states of the former Yugoslavia and the former Soviet Union emphasize the importance of understanding ethnic relations in explaining international events. Religion, too, is an increasingly important variable in international relations. One question that international relations must address is how relations between ethnically and religiously diverse nation-states can proceed without conflict.

NAME:

COURSE:

DATE:

REVIEW QUESTIONS

Based on the first part of this exercise, answer the following items:

The realist approach to the study of international relations is better than the idealist approach because realism deals only with what really happened.   T   F

Because international events must take place across borders, only nation-states can be actors or targets in international events.   T   F

The most common type of events in international relations is military events.   T   F

The COPDAB data files are more likely to document events between major powers than events that involve the smaller nation-states.   T   F

The system level of analysis asserts that the nature of the international system can help explain international events.   T   F

The scientific method requires all of the following except (circle one):

    a.   falsifiable hypotheses.

    b.   shared intersubjective understandings.

    c.   proof that a theory is true.

    d.   reproducible results.

Neo-liberalism is an approach to international relations that encourages a socialist view of the world.   T   F

The individual level of analysis assumes that (circle one):

    a.   individual nation-states are the primary actors in international relations.

    b.   patterns in international events are, to some extent, explained by knowing how people make decisions.

    c.   the most important phenomenon in international relations is how events affect the lives of individuals.

    d.   only international events where individuals are the actors are worth studying.

The study of international relations as a unique field of study only began in the early 20th century.   T   F

The number of conflictive international events far exceeds the number of cooperative events in most years since 1948.   T   F

EXPLORIT QUESTIONS

If you have any difficulties using the software to obtain the appropriate information, or if you want to learn additional features of the tasks, refer to the online help [F1].

1. The individual, state, and system levels of analysis are related to each other in many ways. Two of the factors that affect how a person makes a decision are religion and cultural heritage. The religious and cultural distribution within and between nation-states also affects the formulation of national interest and the events that states initiate. What is the distribution of the major world religions? Create a map that explores this question by following these instructions:

> ➤ *Data File:* **NATIONS**
> ➤ *Task:* **Mapping**
> ➤ *Variable 1:* **86) RELIGION**
> ➤ *View:* **Map**
> ➤ *Display:* **Legend**

   a.   What regions of the world are majority Christian?

   b.   List five majority Christian nation-states. (Hint: Click on a nation-state on the map to see its name or use the RANK view of the MAPPING procedure.)

        _____   _____

        _____   _____

        _____

   c.   What regions of the world are majority Islamic?

   d.   List five primarily Islamic states:

        _____   _____

        _____   _____

        _____

e.   How might a person's religion affect the decisions that he or she makes in performing international events?

2.   The modern nation-state was born from cultural self-determination in Europe in the 17th century. We will explore this more in Exercise 3, but the European model of the nation-state implies that nation-states are organized around common culture and history. Many states are multicultural. Which states have the highest levels of cultural diversity? A variable in the NATIONS data file (MULTI-CULT) measures cultural diversity by determining the odds that any two people differ in their race, ethnicity, religion, tribal group, or language group. Use the mapping function of Student ExplorIt to see which states have the highest levels of cultural diversity. On the map, darker shades mean more cultural diversity.

> Data File: **NATIONS**
>   Task: **Mapping**
> ➤ Variable 1: **68) MULTI-CULT**

a.   What regions of the world have the highest level of cultural diversity?

b.   What regions have the lowest level of cultural diversity?

c.   Use the RANK view in the ExplorIt MAPPING function to see the rank ordering of the states by their level of cultural diversity. What are the 10 countries that rank highest on this measure of cultural diversity?

1. _____   6. _____

2. _____   7. _____

3. _____   8. _____

4. _____   9. _____

5. _____   10. _____

Exercise 2: Approaching International Relations

Can you see anything that these states have in common? If so, what?

d.   The state level of analysis assumes that the behavior of nation-states is based on their national interest. What are the problems that a multicultural state faces in identifying and acting on its national interest? Write a short paragraph that discusses your answer.

3.   The system level of analysis assumes that characteristics of the system help explain international events. We will explore the system level in detail in Exercise 4. There are many characteristics of the system as a whole that can affect the behavior of actors. One is the distribution of economic capability and another is the systemic problem of air pollution. These two systemic variables are not unrelated. As we discussed in the preliminary section of Exercise 2, CO_2 emissions are a problem for the entire system, especially if they lead to global warming, as some scientists contend. While all states may be affected by CO_2, not all contribute equally and not all have the economic resources to address the problem adequately. What states contribute the most to CO_2 emissions? Follow the instructions below to answer this question.

> *Data File:* **NATIONS**
> *Task:* **Mapping**
> ➤ *Variable 1:* **57) GREENHOUSE**

a.   Looking at the map, what regions seem to have the highest level of greenhouse gas emissions per capita? (Darker shades mean more greenhouse gas emissions.)

b.   Use the RANK view on the map to see the names of the states with the highest greenhouse emissions per capita. Then list the top five producers per capita of greenhouse gasses.

        1._____   4. _____

        2._____   5. _____

        3._____

c.   Looking at this list, what can you conclude about the types of countries that have the highest emissions?

ACTORS IN THE INTERNATIONAL SYSTEM: STATES, SOVEREIGNTY, AND INDIVIDUALS

If the nation state is seen as the sole actor in the system, one may lose sight of the human beings for whom and by whom the game is supposed to be played.

If one sees only the mass of individual humans of whom mankind is composed—the power game of states appears as an inhuman interference with the lives of ordinary people

ARNOLD WOLFERS (1959:83)

Tasks: Mapping, Univariate, Historical Trends, Cross-tabulation, Scatterplot
Data Files: HISTORY, NATIONS, FPSURVEY

International relations was described in the previous exercise as a science that attempts to describe and explain international events. International events are actions taken by an actor directed toward a target where the actor and the target are in different nation-states. That is, the action necessarily crosses a border. This does not mean, however, that all the actors and targets have to be nation-states. It merely means that the actor has to be in a different nation-state than the target in order for the event to be *international*. The actors and targets can be governments, groups (such as the United Nations or Greenpeace), or even individual people (such as Bill Gates, Yasir Arafat, or you).

Some analysts claim that only nation-states should be considered in international events since only nation-states define the borders and only they have enough power to affect change within the system as a whole. To these analysts, all individuals are citizens of some nation-state and their actions are performed under the jurisdiction of a state. To other analysts, the collection of individuals in a state is arbitrary. All actions attributed to the nation-state are, in fact, performed by individuals or groups of individuals (such as the United States Secretary of State or the British Parliament). Thus, international events can be explained only by understanding how individuals make choices and decisions.

So, which actors are primary—states or individuals? The answer lies somewhere along the middle path. Yes, all decisions are made by individuals and groups of individuals, so it is important that we understand how these decisions are made. For these decisions to affect *international* events, however, they must be made in the context of a system of territorial nation-states that is defined by sovereignty. This exercise examines sovereignty and the characteristics of nation-states.

DEFINING THE NATION-STATE

It is generally accepted that for a political community to be a nation-state in the international system, it must have territory, population, effective rule over that population (authority), and recognition by other nation-states. A community that achieves these four characteristics is sovereign—that is, it is formally autonomous and equal within the international system. We will examine each of these qualities in turn, starting with territory. The variable AREA in the NATIONS file shows the total land area of each nation-state.

➤ Data File: **NATIONS**
➤ Task: **Mapping**
➤ Variable 1: **12) AREA**
➤ View: **Map**

AREA -- AREA IN SQUARE MILES (SAUS)

The map shows differences in area (total square miles) of each nation-state by the shade of the country. The darker the country, the larger the area. More information is gained by looking at the ranking of the nation-states.

Data File: **NATIONS**
Task: **Mapping**
Variable 1: **12) AREA**
➤ View: **List: Rank**

RANK	CASE NAME	VALUE
1	Russia	6659250
2	China	3600930
3	Canada	3560219
4	United States	3539227
5	Brazil	3265061
6	Australia	2941285
7	India	1147950
8	Kazakhstan	1059630
9	Argentina	1056637
10	Algeria	919591

If you scroll down the ranking (using the scroll arrows on the right), you see that the states vary greatly in the size of their territory. More territory does not make a state more sovereign. Sovereignty means that states like Russia with over 6,600,000 square miles of territory are equal partners in the international system with nation-states like Singapore, which has only 241 square miles.

Territory is formed by borders that are accepted—or at least defended—by the governments of the nation-states. Not all borders are accepted by the states on either side. Territorial disputes are common. Some disputes are long-standing legal disagreements. These disputes can heat up into military action, as was the case when Argentina and Great Britain went to war over the Falkland Islands (known as the Malvinas Islands in Argentina) in 1982. Argentina and Great Britain had conflicting claims to these islands in the southern Atlantic since the 1830s. To see how common territorial disputes have been over the last 20 years, map the variable BORDER.

Data File: **NATIONS**
Task: **Mapping**
➤ Variable 1: **18) BORDER**
➤ View: **Map**
➤ Display: **Legend**

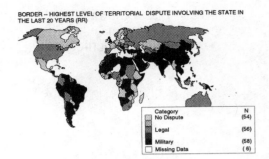

BORDER -- HIGHEST LEVEL OF TERRITORIAL DISPUTE INVOLVING THE STATE IN THE LAST 20 YEARS (RR)

Category	N
No Dispute	(54)
Legal	(56)
Military	(58)
Missing Data	(6)

The map shows states with border disputes sometime during the last 20 years. States with light shading (yellow) had no disputes over territory. States with medium shading (orange) had legal disputes with another state over territory. In dark shaded (red) states, the dispute escalated to military action. We tend to think of the nation-state as a constant. Yet over two-thirds of the states had either a legal or a military dispute with another over territory.

Population is the second characteristic of the nation-state. Clearly, territory without people cannot be a nation-state. Like territory, population varies greatly from state to state, and all sovereign states are formally equal regardless of the size of their population.

Data File: **NATIONS**
Task: **Mapping**
➤ Variable 1: **81) POP96**
➤ View: **List: Rank**

RANK	CASE NAME	VALUE
1	China	1210005
2	India	952108
3	United States	265563
3	Indonesia	206612
5	Brazil	162661
6	Russia	104801
7	Japan	123537
8	Bangladesh	123063
9	Pakistan	113914
10	Nigeria	86488

The NATIONS data file contains only data on states with populations of at least 200,000 which includes most of the world's states. The smallest nation-state at the time this book was written is Nauru, an island community in the South Pacific. Nauru has about 10,000 people living on a small island of 8.1 square miles near the intersection of the equator and the international date line. Though small, Nauru is a member of major international organizations, such as the Universal Postal Union and the International Civil Aviation Organization, with equal status in those organizations to states such as Russia, China, and the United States.

The characteristic of population has more meaning than merely the number of people living within a territory. Population constitutes the "nation" of nation-state. The modern nation-state was conceived in 17th century Europe as feudalism gave way to monarchical states. From the Treaty of Westphalia in 1648 to the Treaty of Versailles in 1919, the principle of national self-determination guided the formation of states. The state (government and territory) should equate with nation (a population's culture, history, and ethnicity) as much as possible. Yet, it is clear that many states are multicultural.

Data File: **NATIONS**
Task: **Mapping**
➤ *Variable 1:* **68) MULTI-CULT**
➤ *View:* **Map**

MULTI-CULT -- MULTI-CULTURALISM:ODDS THAT ANY 2 PERSONS WILL DIFFER IN THEIR RACE, RELIGION, ETHNICITY (TRIBE), OR LANGUAGE GROUP (STARK)

The map shows the odds that any two people will differ in their race, religion, ethnicity, or language group. Darker shades indicate a higher level of multicultural mix. The map indicates that the nation of the modern nation-state is a complex mixture of cultural groups and may not be a cohesive nation at all. This is particularly true in nation-states outside of Europe. We will explore this phenomenon in greater detail later.

The third characteristic of a state is its ability to exercise effective rule over the population within its territory—that is, a state must have authority. It is this characteristic that refers to the apparatus of state control—the government. Not all governments have effective rule. During the 1980s the government of Lebanon did not control large segments of its population and territory. Bosnia-Herzegovina from its inception has been unable to consolidate authority over the people within the boundaries recognized by the international community. Most states do exercise effective rule through a combination of force and threat of force and through socializing their people to believe in the legitimacy of their authority. We can examine the level of civil disorder in the international system as an indicator of effective rule through the variable FIGHT COPS in the NATIONS file. We call this an indicator because it is not a direct measure of state authority, but nation-states where people are willing to fight with the police are likely to be nation-states where state authority has broken down.

Data File: **NATIONS**
Task: **Mapping**
➤ *Variable 1:* **46) FIGHT COPS**
➤ *View:* **Map**

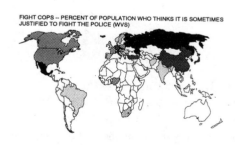

FIGHT COPS -- PERCENT OF POPULATION WHO THINKS IT IS SOMETIMES JUSTIFIED TO FIGHT THE POLICE (WVS)

On the map, the darker the shading the higher percentage of people who believe that it is sometimes justified to fight the police. It is important to note that when these data were collected in 1993, many of the countries with high percentages were having crises of legitimacy. Mexico was addressing a peasant uprising in the state of Chiapas, Czechoslovakia had just split into the Czech and Slovak Republics, and Eastern Europe and the former Soviet states were grappling with dramatic changes in their governments and economies. This suggests that individuals whose sense of national identity and pride are in crisis are more likely to oppose the will of the state. We can explore this by reviewing the previous map and comparing it with the variable NATL PRIDE.

Data File: **NATIONS**
Task: **Mapping**
Variable 1: **46) FIGHT COPS**
➤ Variable 2: **70) NATL PRIDE**
➤ View: **Maps**

FIGHT COPS -- PERCENT OF POPULATION WHO THINKS IT IS SOMETIMES
JUSTIFIED TO FIGHT THE POLICE (WVS)

r = −0.383**

NATL PRIDE -- PERCENT WHO SAY THEY ARE VERY PROUD TO BE (BRITISH,
AMERICAN, ETC) (WVS)

The states with a high proportion of people claiming that they are proud to be citizens of that state have darker shading on the lower map. When we look at the two maps we can see they are different. But how different do two maps have to appear for us to say that they are different? When we just look at the maps visually, it's sometimes difficult to determine precisely how different or similar they are. Fortunately, there is a simple method for determining how similar or different any two maps are. This method is called *regression analysis* and was invented about 100 years ago by English scholar Karl Pearson. Once you see how he did it, you will find it easy to apply. Regression analysis starts by creating a *scatterplot* that plots the values of two variables.

In order to introduce the ideas of regression analysis and scatterplots we will step away, briefly, from our current discussion examining the state's authority over its population. First, look at a map showing the percentage of the population in each nation-state that is between the ages of 15 and 64, and a map showing the mean years of school in the population aged 25 and older.

Data File: **NATIONS**

Task: **Mapping**

➤ Variable 1: **5) AGE 15–64**

➤ Variable 2: **44) EDUCATION**

➤ View: **Map**

AGE15-64 -- PERCENT OF POPULATION AGED 15-64 IN 1996 (SAUS)

r = 0.801**

EDUCATION -- 1990: MEAN YEARS OF SCHOOL AMONG 25 AND OLDER (HDR, 1993)

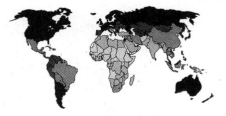

The maps look very similar, but do they represent a close relationship between the age of a nation-state's population and its level of education? To develop a scatterplot we first draw a horizontal line across the bottom of a piece of paper to represent the map showing age and a vertical line to represent the map showing the education level. Uganda was the country with the lowest percentage of its population between the ages of 15 and 64. On the left end of the horizontal line, we will write 48. On the right we will write 71 to represent South Korea, the country with the highest percentage of population between 15 and 64. At the bottom of the vertical line we write 0 to represent average years of schooling for adults, since Burkino Faso had the lowest percent. At the top we will write 13 to represent the United States. The outline of our scatterplot graph looks like this:

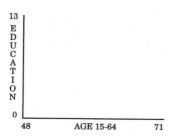

Now that we have a line with an appropriate scale to represent each map, the next thing we need to do is refer to the distributions for each map in order to find the value for each nation-state and then

38

locate it on each line according to its score. We will start with Germany. Germany was fifth lowest for the percentage of its population aged 15–64 at 68.5. So we make a mark on the horizontal line just to the left of the 71 that is already there (for South Korea). Germany was the state with the seventh highest average education at 11.1. So we make a mark on the vertical line slightly below 13 (for the United States). Now we draw a line up from the mark for Germany on the horizontal line and draw another line out from the mark for Germany on the vertical line. Where these two lines intersect we draw a dot. This dot represents the combined map locations of Germany.

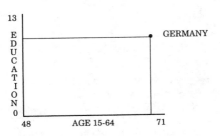

Next, we will locate Madagascar, an island nation-state off the coast of southeastern Africa. Madagascar's percentage of population between 15 and 64 is 51.7%, and its mean years of school among people 25 and older is 2.2. Draw a line up from where 51.7% is to the right of 48 on the horizontal axis (also called the X-axis) and a line right from where 2.2 is above 0 on the vertical axis (also called the Y-axis). The point at the intersection of those two lines represents the values of AGE 15–64 and EDUCATION for Madagascar on the scatterplot.

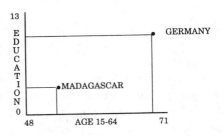

When we have followed this procedure for each nation-state, we will have 70 dots located within the space defined by the vertical and horizontal lines representing the two maps. What we have done is to create a **scatterplot**. Fortunately, you do not have to go through all this trouble. ExplorIt will do it for you. This ExplorIt guide shows you how.

<table>
<tr><td>Data File:</td><td>NATIONS</td></tr>
<tr><td>➤ Task:</td><td>Scatterplot</td></tr>
<tr><td>➤ Dependent Variable:</td><td>44) EDUCATION</td></tr>
<tr><td>➤ Independent Variable:</td><td>5) AGE 15–64</td></tr>
</table>

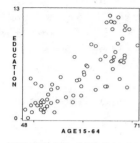

r = 0.801**   Prob. = 0.000   N = 70   Missing = 104

Notice that the Scatterplot task requires two variables.

Special feature: When the scatterplot is showing, you may obtain information on any dot by clicking on it. A little box will appear around the dot, and the values of 5) AGE 15–64 (or the X-axis) and 44) EDUCATION (or the Y-axis) will be shown.

Now that each nation-state is represented by a dot on the scatterplot, we can view the regression line.

<table>
<tr><td>Data File:</td><td>NATIONS</td></tr>
<tr><td>Task:</td><td>Scatterplot</td></tr>
<tr><td>Dependent Variable:</td><td>44) EDUCATION</td></tr>
<tr><td>Independent Variable:</td><td>5) AGE 15–64</td></tr>
<tr><td>➤ View:</td><td>Reg. Line</td></tr>
</table>

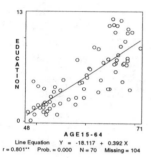

Line Equation   Y = -18.117 + 0.392 X
r = 0.801**   Prob. = 0.000   N = 70   Missing = 104

To show the regression line, select the [Reg. Line] option from the menu.

The *regression line* represents the straight line that best summarizes the trend of the dots. It is the line that comes closest to connecting all the dots. The closer the dots in any scatterplot are to the regression line, the more alike are the two maps represented in the scatterplot. The farther the dots are from the regression line and, thus, the less they resemble a straight line, the less the variables represented by the two maps are related to each other.

To make it simpler to interpret the dots in a scatterplot, Pearson invented a statistic called *correlation coefficient* and used the letter r as the symbol for this coefficient. The absolute value of the correlation coefficient varies from 0.0 to 1.0. When two maps are identical (as when you have two maps of the same variable), the correlation coefficient will be 1.0. When the maps are completely different from each other, the coefficient will be 0.0. The closer the correlation coefficient is to 1.0, then, the more alike are the two maps.

Look at the lower part of the screen above and you will see r = 0.801. This indicates that the maps are very similar. Ignore the asterisks after this figure for now.

Correlation coefficients can be positive or negative. The one we've just seen is positive: When countries have a high proportion of people between age 15 and 64, they are likely also to have high values of average years of education. As one variable goes up, the other variable goes up. But negative correlations are also possible. With a negative correlation, as the value of one variable goes up, the other variable goes down. We will look at one now by returning to our discussion that examines the role authority plays in the stability of a nation-state.

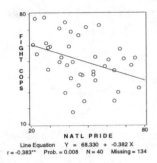

Data File:	**NATIONS**
Task:	**Scatterplot**
➤ Dependent Variable:	**46) FIGHT COPS**
➤ Independent Variable:	**70) NATL PRIDE**
➤ View:	**Reg. Line**

Line Equation Y = 68.330 + -0.382 X
r = -0.383** Prob. = 0.008 N = 40 Missing = 134

Here we see that where less of the population has feelings of national pride, more of the population thinks it is sometimes justified to fight the police. Notice that the regression line now slopes downward from left to right, rather than upward, as in the previous example. This type of slope always indicates a negative correlation. Thus, you'll also notice that a minus sign now precedes the correlation coefficient: r = –0.383.

Some correlations are above zero, but are still too small for us to conclude that two variables are related. When this is the case, we treat the correlations as if they were due to random chance and conclude that the correlation is in effect zero. The software automatically tells you whether the correlation was likely to be due to random chance or whether it was most likely due to a real relationship between the variables. If you look back at the r value on your screen, you will see that two asterisks follow this value (r = –0.383**). Two asterisks mean there is less than 1 chance in 100 that this correlation is due to random chance. One asterisk means there is less than 1 chance in 20 that it is an accident. When no asterisks follow a correlation coefficient, the chances are too high that it could be due to random chance, and we conclude there is no correlation at all. *Treat all correlations without asterisks as zero correlations.*

When r has at least one asterisk, it indicates a statistically significant relationship. In assessing the strength of this correlation, treat an r smaller than .3 (in absolute value) as a weak relationship, an r between .3 and .6 as a moderate relationship, and an r greater than .6 as a strong relationship. Keep in mind, however, that correlation and causation are not the same thing. It is true that without correlation there can be no causation. But correlations often occur between two variables without one being a cause of the other. That is the case here. There is a moderate, but statistically significant, negative correlation between FIGHT COPS and NATL PRIDE. However, does one cause the other? No—what we see here is that there is definitely a *relationship* between these variables, just not causation. Therefore, it appears that developing a sense of national pride is a powerful tool for establishing a state's authority.

While most states do have effective rule over their territory and population, many states have experienced crises of rule over the last 20 years. The Correlates of War (COW) Project collected data on all major interstate and civil wars since 1816.[1] The study defined a major civil war as an internal war where military action was involved, the government was involved, there was effective resistance to the government, and at least 1000 battle deaths occurred on both sides during the war (see Singer and Small, 1994).

The data from COW that you have on the Student ExplorIt disk merely count the number of such wars, without regard for their intensities. With the variable CIVIL WAR in the NATIONS file, we can see how many countries had civil wars that met this definition in the period from 1945 to 1992.

Data File: **NATIONS**
➤ Task: **Univariate**
➤ Primary Variable: **20) CIVIL WAR**
➤ View: **Pie**

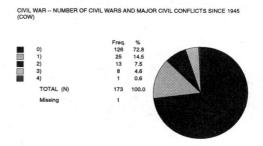

CIVIL WAR -- NUMBER OF CIVIL WARS AND MAJOR CIVIL CONFLICTS SINCE 1945 (COW)

	Freq.	%
0)	126	72.8
1)	25	14.5
2)	13	7.5
3)	8	4.6
4)	1	0.6
TOTAL (N)	173	100.0
Missing	1	

The pie chart shows that 72.8% of the nation-states did not experience any civil wars between 1945 and 1992. That means that 27.2% of the states have experienced major civil war since 1945. Most of these had only one civil war in that period, but some states had as many as three or four major civil wars. Civil unrest is a challenge to a state's sovereignty.

Recognition is the one characteristic of a state that is not in the hands of the nation-state itself. Recognition is conferred by other states. When the government of a nation-state changes, it raises questions about who holds the sovereignty of the state. If the change is legal and orderly, recognition normally passes to the new government. If, however, the change is revolutionary, it is sometimes the case that other states do not recognize the new government as sovereign until it can exhibit authority over its territory and population. Such was the case in 1997 when forces under the control of Laurent Kabila overthrew the government of Mobutu Sesu Seko in Zaire in Africa (now known as the Democratic Republic of Congo). Kabila's government was immediately recognized by other African governments and then cautiously recognized by Western powers after Kabila agreed to hold democratic elections. Chiang Kai-shek's Kuomintang Party formed the recognized government of China after World War II. The Kuomintang retreated to the island of Taiwan during the Chinese civil war, leaving most of China's population and territory in the hands of Mao Tse-tung's Communist Party, which established the People's Republic of China. The majority of other nation-states refused to recognize the People's Republic of China, continuing to recognize the Republic of China on Taiwan as the legitimate government of China. This small island enjoyed the benefits of sovereignty, including China's veto power on the United Nations Security Council, until 1979, when the United States recognized the People's Republic of China as the legitimate government of China.

THE GROWTH OF THE NATION-STATE SYSTEM

It is clear that although territory, population, and authority are necessary requirements for sovereignty, they are not sufficient. Sovereignty is achieved only upon recognition by other nation-states. The number of recognized sovereign nation-states has increased significantly in this century.

---

[1] The Correlates of War project was conducted by J. David Singer and Melvin Small at the University of Michigan. See Singer and Diehl (1990) for a good description of some of their findings.

➤ *Data File:* **HISTORY**
   ➤ *Task:* **Historical Trends**
➤ *Variables:* **41) SOVSTATES**

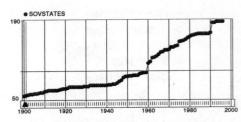

Total number of sovereign states in existence per year

You will notice from the graph that there were three periods of rapid growth in the number of states in the 20th century. The number of states grew by 21% (16 nation-states) in the first ten years after World War II. Most of these nation-states were in the Middle East, South Asia, or Southeast Asia. The second period of rapid growth occurred during the early 1960s when the number of nation-states grew by 43% (42 nation-states). Most of these were in Africa and became sovereign after achieving independence from former colonial powers. The most recent period of growth occurred in the 1990s with the dissolution of the Soviet Union and the changes that accompanied it in Eastern Europe. During this period the number of nation-states grew by 13% (22 nation-states).

THE LEGAL PRINCIPLES OF SOVEREIGNTY

Since sovereignty is ultimately gained through recognition, it is a juridical reality more than an empirical reality. That is, sovereignty is derived from legal principles that create the international system more than from the observable characteristics of the states. Two of these principles are the principle of formal equality and the principle of non-intervention. Formal equality means that all sovereign states enter the international system legally equal—with the same rights and responsibilities under international law. Thus, the Republic of Palau, a collection of 200 mostly uninhabited Pacific Islands with about 17,000 people, has equal vote in the United Nations General Assembly to the People's Republic of China with over 1.2 billion people.

Non-intervention means that sovereign states do not intervene in the internal affairs of other sovereign states. Non-intervention gives rise to the defining condition of the international relations—formal anarchy. Hedley Bull, a British scholar of international relations, said that anarchy is "the central fact of international relations and the starting point of theorizing about it" (1966:35). Anarchy simply means that in a world of sovereign states, there is no higher authority to which a state can appeal for assistance or to enforce international laws. That is, among sovereigns, there is no world government.

There are some significant critiques of the concept of sovereignty in international relations. The first concern arises out of the Eurocentric nature of the nation-state system. Crawford Young, a political scientist at the University of Wisconsin, spoke of the state as a "normative concept" (1977:66). Young points out that what we think of as a state emerged out of medieval Europe. As it has been applied to the rest of the world, the state is more a model of how political life should be organized than how it is organized. We can explore Young's critique by mapping the date when states became sovereign.

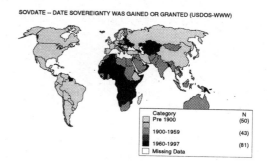

SOVDATE -- DATE SOVEREIGNTY WAS GAINED OR GRANTED (USDOS-WWW)

Category	N
Pre 1900	(50)
1900-1959	(43)
1960-1997	(81)
Missing Data	

On the map, the date of a state's sovereignty is shown by the shade of the country. Darker states became sovereign more recently than lighter states. The state, as we know it, was born in Europe and spread outward—first to the Western Hemisphere, then to Asia and finally to Africa.

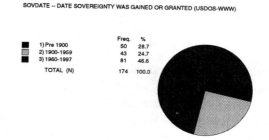

SOVDATE -- DATE SOVEREIGNTY WAS GAINED OR GRANTED (USDOS-WWW)

	Freq.	%
1) Pre 1900	50	28.7
2) 1900-1959	43	24.7
3) 1960-1997	81	46.6
TOTAL (N)	174	100.0

The pie chart and table show that 46.6% of the states became sovereign since 1960 and 71.3% (24.7 + 46.6) became sovereign in the 20th century. Most of the states outside of Europe were, at one time, a colony of one of the European states. The variable COLONY in the NATIONS file indicates which nation-states were colonies of other nation-states.

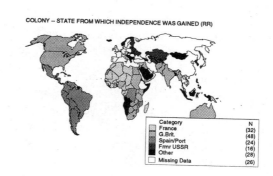

COLONY -- STATE FROM WHICH INDEPENDENCE WAS GAINED (RR)

Category	N
France	(32)
G.Brit.	(48)
Spain/Port	(24)
Frmr USSR	(16)
Other	(28)
Missing Data	(26)

The nation-states of North and West Africa and Southeast Asia were colonies of France. Great Britain had colonies in North America, East Africa, South Asia, and Australia/New Zealand. Spain and Portugal together accounted for most of the colonies in South America. It is perhaps incorrect to say the newly independent states of the former Soviet Union were colonies, but it was from the Soviet Union that they gained their independence in 1991.

Earlier, we noted that many states are multicultural. The degree of multiculturalism is associated with the date of sovereignty. You can see this relationship if you create a cross-tabulation table with the degree of multiculturalism (MULTICULT2) as the row variable and the date of sovereignty (SOVDATE) as the column variable.

Data File: **NATIONS**
➤ Task: **Cross-tabulation**
➤ Row Variable: **69) MULTICULT2**
➤ Column Variable: **92) SOVDATE**
➤ View: **Tables**
➤ Display: **Column %**

MULTICULT2   by   SOVDATE
Cramer's V: 0.254 **

		Pre 1900	1900-1959	1960-1997	TOTAL
	SOVDATE				
0-33%		25	22	14	61
		53.2%	51.2%	17.7%	36.1%
34-66%		12	11	34	57
		25.5%	25.6%	43.0%	33.7%
67-100%		10	10	31	51
		21.3%	23.3%	39.2%	30.2%
Missing		3	0	2	5
TOTAL		47	43	79	169
		100.0%	100.0%	100.0%	

The majority of the nation-states formed before 1960 have low degrees of cultural diversity (less than 34% chance that two people are from different cultural groups). States formed after 1959 have higher levels of multiculturalism. This relationship is statistically significant. Crawford Young's thesis is that the dynamics of cultural pluralism in these new states causes cultural conflicts which challenge the states' ability to achieve effective authority over their population. We can see this in another table.

Data File: **NATIONS**
Task: **Cross-tabulation**
➤ Row Variable: **31) C.CONFLICT**
➤ Column Variable: **69) MULTICULT2**
➤ View: **Tables**
➤ Display: **Column %**

C.CONFLICT   by   MULTICULT2
Cramer's V: 0.570 **

		0-33%	34-66%	67-100%	Missing	TOTAL
	MULTICULT2					
NONE		36	4	0	0	40
		59.0%	7.1%	0.0%		23.8%
POLITICAL		20	29	9	0	58
		32.8%	51.8%	17.6%		34.5%
VIOLENCE		4	15	12	0	31
		6.6%	26.8%	23.5%		18.5%
WARFARE		1	8	30	0	39
		1.6%	14.3%	58.8%		23.2%
Missing		0	1	0	5	6
TOTAL		61	56	51	5	168
		100.0%	100.0%	100.0%		

Fifty-nine percent of the nation-states with low levels of cultural diversity had no cultural conflict while 58.8% of the states with high levels of cultural diversity experienced some kind of cultural war. Young's thesis seems to be supported. The European model of the nation-state does not seem to apply as well in other parts of the world. The problems associated with multicultural governance strains one of the basic qualities of the state—establishing effective authority over population and territory.

Another critique of sovereignty has been raised by feminist authors in international relations. Much of international relations theory and practice is based on the realist point of view that the anarchy which comes from sovereignty leaves the state in a "self-help" system whereby its interests stand in opposition to the interests of others. The result is a system of conflict and tension whereby the state's primary interest is its survival and that survival can be ensured only through power secured with military force. Feminist theorists point out that concepts like power, force, and authority which frame the theory and practice of international relations, are masculine concepts. Since most of the world's leaders are male, the ideals by which international relations are played out are male ideals. Although some argue that a system of sovereignty defined by women might be kinder and gentler, the real focus of the argument is that sovereignty and the resulting anarchy is contextual. That is, the effects of being sovereign are determined by the individuals who make decisions and their ideologies, beliefs, and knowledge. There is little doubt that men are more common among the decision makers today. The variable %FEM.HEADS in the NATIONS file permits us to explore the gender bias of world leadership by examining the proportion of women at government ministerial level around the world.

<table>
<tr><td>Data File: NATIONS</td></tr>
<tr><td>➤ Task: Univariate</td></tr>
<tr><td>➤ Primary Variable: 127) %FEM.HEADS</td></tr>
<tr><td>➤ View: Summary</td></tr>
</table>

%FEM.HEADS -- PERCENT OF WOMEN AT GOVERNMENT MINISTERIAL LEVEL (HDR, 1995)

Mean:	6.476	Std.Dev.:	7.063	N: 164
Median:	5.000	Variance:	49.883	Missing: 10
99% confidence interval +/- mean: 5.051 to 7.901				
95% confidence interval +/- mean: 5.391 to 7.560				

Value	Freq.	%	Cum.%	Z-Score
0	50	30.5	30.5	-0.917
3	12	7.3	37.8	-0.492
4	9	5.5	43.3	-0.351
5	15	9.1	52.4	-0.209
6	13	7.9	60.4	-0.067
7	12	7.3	67.7	0.074
8	5	3.0	70.7	0.216
9	6	3.7	74.4	0.357
10	10	6.1	80.5	0.499
11	6	3.7	84.1	0.641
12	1	0.6	84.8	0.782

Many of the calculations you see here are covered in a statistics course and we will not discuss them in this book. In the summary information at the top right of your screen you will see N and Missing. The value after N is the number of countries included in this analysis; in this case there are 164 countries. The number after Missing is the number of countries missing from this analysis (i.e., there were no data for these countries with this variable).

Looking at the table, you will see five columns: *Value*, *Freq*, %, *Cum.%*, and *Z-Score*. The *Value* in this analysis is the percentage of women at the government ministerial level. The *Frequency* is the number of nation-states with that value. In other words, in the first row where the value is zero, there are 50 nation-states with no women ministers. The percentage (%) column shows the percentage of the total number of nation-states (the N value) that are in this row. Thus 30.5% of nation-states have no women ministers. The *Cumulative* % column adds up the percentages as you go down the table. Look at the row with value 10 (i.e., 10% of the ministers are women). The *Cumulative* % column shows that 80.5% of the nation-states have governments where women hold 10% or less of the minister positions. We will not be using the *Z-Score* in this book. You can learn more about this score in a statistics course.

In review, we have explored the four basic characteristics of states: territory, population, authority, and recognition. While territory, population, and authority are necessary conditions, they are not sufficient for granting sovereignty. Sovereignty is achieved only upon recognition by other states. This means that sovereignty is actually a legal condition that is conferred by the community of states and based on legal principles of non-interference and formal equality. Critiques of sovereignty are raised both because of the Eurocentric model of the state and because of the masculine nature of the concepts it embodies and generates.

WORKSHEET

NAME: _____

COURSE: _____

DATE: _____

EXERCISE

3

REVIEW QUESTIONS

Based on the first part of this exercise, answer the following items:

When a political community is able to secure effective rule over a defined territory
and population, it automatically is considered sovereign within the international system.   T   F

The principle of non-intervention means that no nation-state will ever interfere in
the affairs of another nation-state.   T   F

China has the largest area of any state in the world.   T   F

Only two other countries have a larger population than the United States of America.   T   F

The principle of formal equality means that all nation-states have the same ability
to act in the international system.   T   F

Most of the states in the world became sovereign before the 20th century began.   T   F

States that became sovereign since 1959 tend to be more multicultural than states
that gained sovereignty before 1960.   T   F

Half of the states in the world have no women at the ministerial level in their
government.   T   F

To be sovereign, a political community must have all the following characteristics except (circle
one):

- a.   territory.
- b.   recognition.
- c.   equal power with other nation-states.
- d.   effective rule over its territory and population.

The concept of anarchy in international relations means that, because of the
formal autonomy of sovereign states, there is no world government.   T   F

EXPLORIT QUESTIONS

1.   A sovereign state is autonomous. That is, a sovereign state as an actor in the international system
     does not answer to another authority. Being autonomous is not the same as being independent.
     Many states are not independent due to low economic capabilities. We can explore the differences in
     these capabilities among the sovereign states.

➤ *Data File:* **NATIONS**
➤ *Task:* **Mapping**
➤ *Variable 1:* **49) GNP94**
➤ *View:* **List: Rank**

What states have the highest and lowest gross national product? (Gross national product measures the total annual production of goods and services in a state for a year.)

	State Name	Value of GNP
HIGHEST GNP	_____	_____
LOWEST GNP	_____	_____

India's rank on GNP: _____

2. GNP per capita indicates the total product per person in a state. This is a better measure of total wealth because a large state, like India, will have a large GNP merely because many people are producing. But, if that production is distributed across all the people, it will show that India's economic production is low given its population.

Data File: **NATIONS**
Task: **Mapping**
➤ *Variable 1:* **53) GNPPC94**
➤ *View:* **List: Rank**

	State Name	Value of GNP
HIGHEST GNP	_____	_____
LOWEST GNP	_____	_____

India's rank on GNP per capita: _____

United States' rank on GNP per capita: _____

3. States that have high external debt are dependent upon the lender states and institutions (banks and international organizations). The lender institutions often can intervene into the internal affairs of the state's economy. The International Monetary Fund and the International Bank for Reconstruction and Development (World Bank) often have placed severe restrictions on a state's economy as preconditions for more loans or renegotiating the terms of existing debt payments.

Data File: **NATIONS**
Task: **Mapping**
➤ *Variable 1:* **33) DEBTPCT**
➤ *View:* **List: Rank**

a.   How many nation-states have external debt that exceeds 100% of their
      annual gross national product?   _____

External debt often accumulates in states that receive foreign aid. States that depend greatly on foreign aid for the performance of their economy may not have much chance of ever paying off their
debt.

> Data File: **NATIONS**
> Task: **Mapping**
> ➤ Variable 1: **9) AID PCT**
> ➤ View: **List: Rank**

b.   How many states receive more than 20% of their GDP in foreign
      assistance?   _____

c.   You can illustrate and analyze the relationship between dependence on foreign assistance and
      total external debt by viewing a scatterplot.

> Data File: **NATIONS**
> ➤ Task: **Scatterplot**
> ➤ Dependent Variable: **33) DEBTPCT**
> ➤ Independent Variable: **9) AID PCT**
> ➤ View: **Reg. Line**

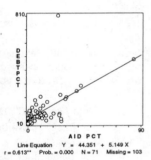

Line Equation   Y = 44.351 + 5.149 X
r = 0.613**   Prob. = 0.000   N = 71   Missing = 103

**Note that the SCATTERPLOT task requires you to choose two variables. Make sure your
screen matches the scatterplot shown above.**

What is the correlation coefficient for these two variables?   _____

Is the correlation coefficient statistically significant?   Yes   No

d.   Considering your answers to 3a–c, write a short paragraph that discusses the meaning of sov-
      ereign autonomy among dependent states.

4. As we stated in the preliminary section of Exercise 3, all sovereign states are formally equal within the international system. This does not mean that all states have the same power and abilities. Some international organizations recognize these differences in power and ability and create states that are first among equals. For example, only five states (China, France, Great Britain, Russia, and the United States) have veto power within the United Nations Security Council. Voting in the World Bank is prorated such that states which provide more capital for the bank have more votes.

> *Data File:* **NATIONS**
> ➤ *Task:* **Mapping**
> ➤ *Variable 1:* **100) TROOPS**
> ➤ *View:* **List: Rank**

a. Major differences exist between states in terms of their military power. What states have the highest and the lowest number of troops in their total armed forces?

	State Name	Number of Troops
HIGHEST # OF TROOPS	_____	_____
LOWEST # OF TROOPS	_____	_____

b. Many states with relatively small armed forces still spend a large proportion of their gross domestic product on the military. Gross domestic product is the value of goods and services produced in a state in a year not including imports and exports.

> *Data File:* **NATIONS**
> *Task:* **Mapping**
> ➤ *Variable 1:* **126) % GDP ARMY**
> ➤ *View:* **List: Rank**

What state spends the largest proportion of its GDP on defense? _____

c. To see if there is a relationship between the total size of the armed forces and the proportion of gross domestic product spent on the military, view a scatterplot.

> *Data File:* **NATIONS**
> ➤ *Task:* **Scatterplot**
> ➤ *Dependent Variable:* **126) % GDP ARMY**
> ➤ *Independent Variable:* **100) TROOPS**
> ➤ *View:* **Reg. Line**

What is the correlation coefficient for these two variables? _____

Is the correlation coefficient statistically significant?   Yes   No

5. In the preliminary section of this exercise, we discussed the feminist critique of sovereignty. The data we looked at showed that there were few women at the ministerial level in most governments of the world. Another part of that critique is that women have different interests in international affairs than do men. It is claimed that women are interested more in cooperation and human needs than in conflict and military dominance. To explore this, we can compare the responses to questions about U.S. foreign policy goals by men and by women.

Use a cross-tabulation to compare each of the variables below with GENDER. Copy the first row of the column percentages from the cross-tabulation table into the spaces provided and write a few sentences to analyze the data.

a. GOALHUNG - Foreign Policy Goal: Combating World Hunger

> *Data File:* **FPSURVEY**
> *Task:* **Cross-Tabulation**
> *Row Variable:* **11) GOALHUNG**
> *Column Variable:* **6) GENDER**
> *View:* **Table**
> *Display:* **Column %**

Open the FPSurvey data file and select the CROSS-TABULATION task. Select 11) GOALHUNG as the row variable and 6) GENDER as the column variable. When the table appears, select the [Column %] option.

Dependent Variable: GOALHUNG   MALE   FEMALE

Column %'s for the Very Important (Very) row   _____   _____

b. GOALPOWR - Foreign Policy Goal: Maintaining World Power

> *Data File:* **FPSURVEY**
> *Task:* **Cross-Tabulation**
> *Row Variable:* **14) GOALPOWR**
> *Column Variable:* **6) GENDER**
> *View:* **Table**
> *Display:* **Column %**

Dependent Variable: GOALPOWR   MALE   FEMALE

Column %'s for the Very Important (Very) row   _____   _____

c. Reviewing your answers to 5a and 5b, write a paragraph that comments on the idea that if women had more access to political power, sovereignty and its effects would be different.

EXPLAINING EVENTS IN THE INTERNATIONAL SYSTEM

Those who cannot remember the past are condemned to repeat it.

GEORGE SANTAYANA

Nothing endures but change.

HERACLEITUS

What is history but a fable agreed upon?

NAPOLEON BONAPARTE

Tasks: Mapping, Univariate, Historical Trends, Scatterplot, Cross-tabulation
Data Files: EUROPE, HISTORY, NATIONS

What is a system? Systems surround us. Computer systems control everything from our cars to our toasters. We exist as part of a biological system that responds to stimuli such as population growth and pollution. Population and pollution are products of demographic and economic systems. How can all these diverse things be called systems? According to the *American College Dictionary*, a system is "an assemblage or combination of things or parts forming a complex or unitary whole" (Barnhart 1966:1230). Thus, systems are composed of elements related to each other by some pattern or scheme. It is sometimes said that in a system, the whole is greater than the sum of its parts. The elements of the international system are its actors (states, groups, or individuals). To be a system, these elements must be related in some pattern of behavior such that the whole takes on an identity of its own.

The system level of analysis is based on two propositions that must be assumed—or better yet—must be proved. The first proposition is that *there are patterns in international events*. If international events are wholly random, then there is little use in trying to explain or understand them. The second proposition is that *these patterns can be explained, at least in part, by understanding the characteristics and operations of the international system*. Exploring the first proposition is the task of this entire book. Exploring the second proposition is the goal of this chapter. Before we can begin, however, we must first be convinced that actors and their actions form identifiable international systems. To do this, we must examine the history of the modern international system.

THE BIRTH OF THE MODERN STATE SYSTEM

The quotations by George Santayana and Heracleitus at the beginning of this exercise frame our approach to historical analysis. While Santayana's advice about learning from the past is important, we must recognize that the international system is constantly changing. Thus, all international relations theory is historically specific. That is, a theory that helps us understand conflict in the multipolar era of the late 19th century may not help us understand conflict today, even if we see similar circumstances. So much has changed in technology, politics, economics, and demographics that lessons learned from history must be regarded with skepticism. Does this mean that we should ignore history? No, while history may not provide the guideposts we want for understanding events, it does tell us much about the characteristics of the current international system. The message we draw from Napoleon's quotation is that the international system is what we collectively have made it to be. It does not exist outside our actions, beliefs, norms, and behaviors. In fact, those actions, beliefs, norms, and behaviors create it. As we saw in Exercise 3, the principles of non-intervention and formal equality create sovereignty, which is the basis of the modern state system. Thus, history is essential for understanding the international system we live in now. Without this understanding, we have no basis for attributing patterns observed in international events to the characteristics of the international system.

The roots of the modern international system can be traced from the fall of European feudalism in the 14th and 15th centuries, through the rise of the absolutist monarchies in the 16th and 17th centuries, to the birth of the modern liberal state at the end of the 18th century and throughout the 19th century. As we saw in Exercise 3, while there are many forms of political organization in the history of the world, the model of the modern state was born in Europe and exported to the rest of the world through imperialism. The feudal state was marked by decentralized authority and feudal property rights. Local lords owed their allegiance to their lords, not to the king or queen. Absolutist states arose in Europe after the Thirty Years' War. The Treaty of Westphalia that ended that war is often cited as the origin of the nation-state system. While this is a bit simplistic, the treaty did establish the basic principles of national self-determination and sovereignty. Absolutist states were marked by the centralized authority of a king or queen, the emergence of standing armies, establishment of bureaucracy, and the rise of professional diplomacy. Foreign policy interests of absolutist states centered around the imperial interests of their kings or queens. Louis XIV of France captured the essence of absolutism when he proclaimed "L'état c'est moi" (I am the state).

THE RISE OF LIBERALISM

The first liberal revolutions occurred in the United States (1776) and in France (1789). Liberalism is based on ideals of freedom and individual choice. These ideals include (1) broadened participation in political decision making through democratic institutions; (2) laissez-faire economics, whereby the government does not interfere with the market; (3) a self-regulating economy whereby the market self-adjusts to the pressures of supply and demand, thus ensuring economic efficiency; and (4) the primacy and protection of individual property rights. Capitalism and liberalism are highly associated. As liberalism matured, an expanding elite was able to invest its resources and have the rights to enjoy the returns on that investment. This elite demanded that the role of the king or queen be diminished to ensure that the state's interests conformed to their interests. "L'état c'est moi" was replaced by "We, the people. . . ." At the turn of the 21st century, most states have embraced the liberal ideals. The fall of the Soviet bloc in 1991 led one historian to proclaim the "end of history" due to the "remarkable consensus concerning the legitimacy of liberal democracy as a system of government" (Fukuyama, 1992:xi) .

Yet liberalism is a recent phenomenon, even in Europe. One measure of a state's acceptance of liberalism is its acceptance of universal adult suffrage in the political process. Universal suffrage is achieved when there are no barriers to adults (men and women) voting. These barriers include requirements for property ownership, poll taxes, or literacy requirements. The United States achieved universal adult suffrage in 1965 with the passage of the Voting Rights Act. Universal suffrage was achieved in the

Western European nation-states as recently as 1978. In most nation-states, men achieved universal suffrage long before women did.

➤ Data File: **EUROPE**
➤ Task: **Mapping**
➤ Variable 1: **7) VOTE**
➤ View: **Map**

VOTE – DATE OF UNIVERSAL SUFFRAGE FOR ADULT MEN AND WOMEN (RR)

On the map, states that achieved universal adult suffrage more recently are shown in darker hues. You can see the dates of enfranchisement by using the RANK view on the previous map.

Data File: **EUROPE**
Task: **Mapping**
Variable 1: **7) VOTE**
➤ View: **List: Rank**

RANK	CASE NAME	VALUE
1	Moldova	1978
2	Portugal	1976
3	Switzerland	1971
4	Hungary	1953
5	Greece	1952
6	Bosnia	1949
7	Italy	1948
7	Belgium	1948
9	Bulgaria	1947
10	Romania	1946

Moldova (1978), Portugal (1976), and Switzerland (1971) were the last European nation-states to achieve universal suffrage. None of the European states had universal suffrage until the 20th century. Many nation-states have adopted more liberal governments in the last 25 years. Latin America made significant moves away from military regimes toward more democratic forms of government in the 1970s and 1980s. West Africa is making a similar transition, with fragile democracies replacing military and one-party regimes now. The fall of the Soviet bloc has radically changed Eastern Europe and Eurasia. You can see these changes by comparing two variables on government type in 1970 and 1995 in the NATIONS data file.

➤ Data File: **NATIONS**
➤ Task: **Mapping**
➤ Variable 1: **55) GOVTYPE70**
➤ Variable 2: **56) GOVTYPE95**
➤ Views: **Map**
➤ Display: **Legend**

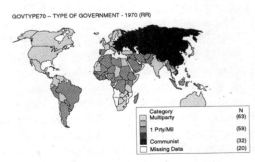

GOVTYPE70 -- TYPE OF GOVERNMENT - 1970 (RR)

Category	N
Multiparty	(63)
1 Prty/Mil	(59)
Communist	(32)
Missing Data	(20)

r = 0.235**

GOVTYPE95 -- TYPE OF GOVERNMENT - 1995

Category	N
Multiparty	(132)
1 Prty/Mil	(33)
Communist	(5)
Missing Data	(4)

In the map, the lightest shaded nation-states have formally embraced liberal democracy, the medium shaded states are military or one-party regimes, and the darkest shaded nation-states are communist regimes. While there are still authoritarian and communist states in Central Africa, the Middle East, and in Asia, it is clear from the map that liberal democracy is becoming a norm for the elements of the international system. Liberal states have different interests in international relations than absolutist, authoritarian, or communist states. Because of the broadened participation base and because of the increased importance of market capitalism, liberal states are interested in protecting assets (at home and abroad) and in furthering the interests of individual citizens and corporations.

INTERNATIONAL ORDER AMIDST ANARCHY

The international system of states is defined not only by the nature of its elements, but also by the nature of the interactions among those elements. These relationships constitute the patterns that give the system its identity. Kenneth Waltz (1979), an American scholar of international relations, characterized the nation-state system as a "self-help" system. Sovereign nation-states, as we discussed in Exercise 3, do not defer to a higher authority. They are autonomous. This establishes the formal anarchy of international relations because there is no world government. Waltz points out that in this anarchy, each state must be responsible for its own well-being and security—thus it is a self-help system. The absence of a higher authority does not mean that there is no order in international relations. Order is achieved by the rules and norms of behavior that constitute the system. These rules differ depending on the characteristics of the system itself. System characteristics include the number of poles (major actors), the number and characteristics of the actors, and the effects of technology, economic structures, and demographic distributions. Political systems are usually classified by the number of major political actors, called system poles, that influence them. Historically, we have observed only multipolar (four or more poles) and bipolar systems (two system poles). In theory, there could also be unipolar or tripolar systems.

During the 19th century, especially the second half, the international system was a multipolar system. In this system a small number of major powers dominated international relations. Interactions were fluid and competitive. While it was in the interest of individual states to ensure their security vis-à-vis other states, it was not in their interests to engage in direct military conflict since the major powers were roughly equal in capability. The competitiveness was played out by shifting alliances to maintain a balance of power that would ensure system stability. The bipolar system emerged from the devastation of World War II. In the bipolar system, two actors dominated the system (the United States and the Soviet Union). These actors built spheres of influence by aligning with other nation-states to form two opposing blocs. Although there was much tension in the system, the two major powers never came into direct conflict. Instead, conflicts were played out in competition for the non-aligned states or as attempts to shift the alignment of a state. These local conflicts have been called surrogate wars because the local fighters were acting as surrogates for the competition between the US and the USSR. The bipolar, cold-war system came to an end in 1991 with the disintegration of the Soviet bloc.

What is the current, or the next, international system? This is one of the major questions that faces students of international relations today. It is a vitally important question and the answer is not now known. The last system transition from the 19th-century multipolar to the post–World War II bipolar system took 30 years and included two world wars. The current transition may not be so violent, but conflicts in the former Yugoslavia, Africa, and the Middle East indicate that although systems may institutionalize relations of dominance and control, they do provide stability for the major actors.

THE RISE AND FALL OF EUROPE'S BALANCE-OF-POWER SYSTEM

In 1870, there was no Germany. Instead, there was a collection of 30 German states and principalities connected by common culture, language, and history. This collection was the remnant of earlier feudalism and of the dissolution of the Holy Roman Empire ruled by the Austrian Hapsburg family. The largest and most powerful of these states was Prussia, occupying much of the territory around Berlin. During the middle 19th century, Prussia had pressured many of the smaller German states to join with it to form a German empire. In 1870, France and Prussia went to war over a dispute about the succession of the Spanish crown. The Franco-Prussian War was a turning-point in the development of the multipolar balance-of-power international system. Although France was considered to be the most powerful state in Europe, Prussia won the war in six weeks. In the years following the war, Prussia forced the rest of the smaller German states into the German Empire, which was declared in 1872. German Chancellor Otto von Bismarck faced a difficult task. He had to consolidate the recently created empire into a viable nation-state while keeping a wary eye on a defeated but still powerful France. His solution was to engineer a series of fluid, dynamic alliances to balance the power in Europe. We can explore these alliances with a series of maps using the EUROPE file.[1]

In 1870, Central Europe was dominated by the great powers, countries like France that were militarily on an equal par with others and that individually had great influence on European politics. In 1873, Bismarck forged the Three Emperors League between Germany, Russia, and the Austro-Hungarian Empire to stand against France. This alliance was shaky due to territorial disputes between Austria and Russia. In 1882, Bismarck forged a second alliance between Germany, Italy, and the Austro-Hungarian Empire. The Triple Alliance would stand until World War I. The mapping function in Student ExplorIt allows you to illustrate the shifting alliances during this period by comparing alliance variables in the EUROPE file.

---

[1] The following maps are approximate. The EUROPE file shows boundaries of the European states as they exist today. The boundaries of many states have changed radically since the end of the 19th century. While the following maps are not precise, they do show the approximate boundaries of the alliances discussed. Poland did not exist as an independent nation-state during this period. Northern and western Poland was part of Germany while eastern and southern Poland was part of Russia. The map shows the outline of modern-day Poland, but the shading will include it as part of Germany throughout the following discussions.

> *Data File:* **EUROPE**
>   *Task:* **Mapping**
> *Variable 1:* **2) ALLY 1870**
> *Variable 2:* **3) ALLY 1882**
>   *Views:* **Map**
>   *Display:* **Legend**

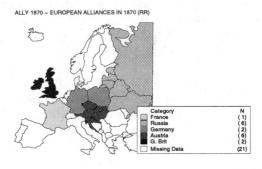

ALLY 1870 – EUROPEAN ALLIANCES IN 1870 (RR)

r = 0.960**

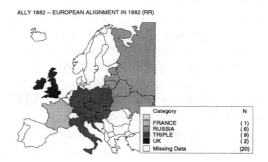

ALLY 1882 – EUROPEAN ALIGNMENT IN 1882 (RR)

France first signed an alliance with Russia in 1894 as an agreement to aid Russia with its railroads. With this agreement, most of the powers of Central Europe were committed, with the exception of Great Britain. From 1870 to 1904, Great Britain was considered to be the balancer in the balance of power. It was not party to an alliance. If France and Germany should go to war, neither side could count on British support, nor could they guarantee that Britain would not aid their foes. This changed in 1904 when Britain entered a secret alliance with France known as the Entente Cordiale. In 1907 Russia was added to form the Triple Entente. By comparing the ALLY 1870 variable with ALLY 1907, you can see that Europe went from five independent great powers to two opposing blocs. This change in the European international system set the stage for World War I.

> *Data File:* **EUROPE**
>   *Task:* **Mapping**
> *Variable 1:* **2) ALLY 1870**
> *Variable 2:* **4) ALLY 1907**
>   *Views:* **Map**
>   *Display:* **Legend**

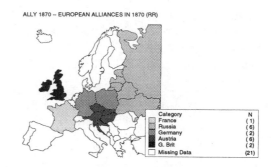

ALLY 1870 – EUROPEAN ALLIANCES IN 1870 (RR)

r = 0.504*

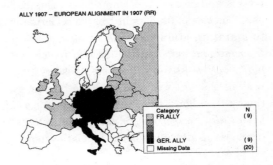

ALLY 1907 – EUROPEAN ALIGNMENT IN 1907 (RR)

The multipolar system secured peace between the major powers through mutual cooperation in a competitive system. Although there was substantial tension between individual actors and between alliances, actors turned to other actors for security through alliances. Much of the competition among actors was played out in colonial holdings outside of Europe where direct conflict could have led to war between the major powers. Most of the Latin American colonies achieved independence in the 1820s. Africa, on the other hand, had not been heavily colonized by European powers, and it was nearby. European claims in Africa rapidly increased during the second half of the 19th century. By the 1880s these claims began to overlap. The major powers met in Berlin in 1885 to divide up Africa to avoid conflicts that could destabilize the system. Of course, the Africans themselves had no voice in this conference. We can explore European claims in Africa in the second half of the 19th century by comparing maps created by the variables AFRICA1880 and AFRICA1914 in the NATIONS data file.

> *Data File:* **NATIONS**
> *Task:* **Mapping**
> *Variable 1:* **3) AFRICA1880**
> *Variable 2:* **4) AFRICA1914**
> *Views:* **Map**

AFRICA1880 -- EUROPEAN CLAIMS IN AFRICA AS OF 1880 (RR)

r = 0.511**

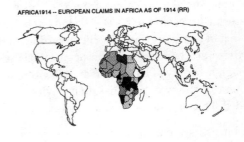

AFRICA1914 -- EUROPEAN CLAIMS IN AFRICA AS OF 1914 (RR)

The multipolar system diminished after World War I. The devastation of the war left the great power system in disarray. The Great Depression of the 1930s further exacerbated the decline of the great powers and created the conditions in Europe for the rebirth of German militarism and imperial interests. The rise of fascism in Italy and Germany challenged the ability of a waning international system to maintain stability. This brings us to one of the basic propositions of system-level analysis. *International systems, like the multipolar system, tend to stabilize international relations between the major actors*. At the same time, these systems may destabilize the relations between lesser actors, as we will see when we examine the bipolar system below. A second major proposition of system-level theory that flows from the first is that *periods of system change tend to be inherently unstable and potentially dangerous for the major actors*. This is something we should take to heart as we live through the aftermath of the bipolar system.

THE BIPOLAR SYSTEM OF THE 20TH CENTURY

The bipolar system arose from the ravages of World War II. Two superpowers emerged from the end of the war. The United States, due to its geographic separation from Europe and Asia, emerged with its industrial base intact. Due to wartime military building, the American industrial capability was at an all-time high. France, Germany, and the other continental European states suffered tremendous losses of both population and industry during the war. While Great Britain was not invaded, aerial bombardment ravaged its industrial capability. Although the Soviet Union suffered grievous loss of life (more than 20 million), much of its industrial base east of the Ural Mountains was not destroyed. In addition, in 1944 and 1945 forces of the United States, Great Britain, and France swept across Europe from the west while Soviet forces swept across from the east leaving a de facto divided Europe at the end of the war. This can be seen on a map in the EUROPE file created by the OCCUPIED variable.

➤ *Data File:* **EUROPE**
➤ *Task:* **Mapping**
➤ *Variable 1:* **6) OCCUPIED**
➤ *View:* **Map**
➤ *Display:* **Display**

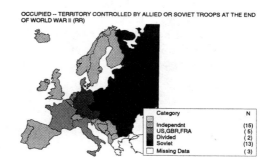

OCCUPIED -- TERRITORY CONTROLLED BY ALLIED OR SOVIET TROOPS AT THE END OF WORLD WAR II (RR)

Category	N
Independnt	(15)
US,GBR,FRA	(5)
Divided	(2)
Soviet	(13)
Missing Data	(3)

The map shows that forces from the United States, Great Britain, and France controlled most of Western Europe and parts of Germany and Austria, while Soviet forces controlled Eastern Europe and the rest of Germany and Austria. According to the terms of the Yalta and Potsdam conferences in 1945, all these states were to have open elections to determine their post-war governments. By 1949, through a variety of legitimate and illegitimate means, most of the states controlled by Soviet forces at the end of the war had installed Soviet-style communist governments while Germany remained divided. Thus began the bipolar system.

The bipolar system was characterized by two rigidly opposing blocs of states aligned with either one superpower (the United States) or the other (the Soviet Union). The two superpowers were evenly matched in power capabilities. They did not want to face each other directly. Instead, the bipolar system was marked by competition for other nation-states to be won over to or retained in one's bloc. This competition was played out initially in Europe and then spread to the less developed nation-states in Latin America, Asia, the Middle East, and Africa. Alignment was initially institutionalized by economic and security pacts. The first of these was the Marshall Plan, initiated in 1947, which offered economic assistance from the United States for post-war reconstruction, and the second was the Council for Mutual Economic Assistance (known as COMECON), initiated in 1949, which provided close economic ties between the Soviet Union and its allies. Participation in these two economic regimes can be seen by mapping the variable ECON ASST in the EUROPE file.

Data File: **EUROPE**
Task: **Mapping**
➤ Variable 1: **5) ECON ASST**
➤ View: **Map**
➤ Display: **Display**

The lightest shaded nation-states on the map did not participate in either regime. The medium shaded (brown) states received Marshall Plan assistance. The dark red states were members of COMECON. Germany is shown as a divided state because the map shows current state borders after German reunification in 1989. We can view the relationship between ECON ASST and the earlier OCCUPIED variable by adding OCCUPIED to the map.

Data File: **EUROPE**
Task: **Mapping**
Variable 1: **5) ECON ASST**
➤ Variable 2: **6) OCCUPIED**
➤ Views: **Map**
➤ Display: **Legend**

r = 0.851**

It is not surprising that these two variables are strongly correlated (r = 0.851**). Military occupation led to political change, which led to economic alignments.

The two superpowers also institutionalized their alignments with a series of multilateral and bilateral security treaties. The United States created the North Atlantic Treaty Organization (NATO) in Europe, the Baghdad Pact and Central Treaty Organization (CENTO) in the Middle East, the South East Asian Treaty Organization (SEATO), the ANZUS Treaty in Asia, and the Rio Pact in the Western Hemisphere. To counter the U.S. treaties, the Soviet Union created the Warsaw Pact in Europe and entered into a series of bilateral security agreements in Asia and Africa. You can see the alignments created by these treaties by mapping the variable CW TREATY in the NATIONS file.

➤ Data File: **NATIONS**
➤ Task: **Mapping**
➤ Variable 1: **30) CW TREATY**
➤ View: **Map**
➤ Display: **Legend**

CW TREATY -- MULTILATERAL & BILATERAL TREATY MEMBERSHIP DURING THE COLD WAR (RR)

Category	N
Multilat W	(39)
Bilat W	(3)
Divided	(3)
Bilat E	(15)
Multilat E	(7)
Missing Data	(107)

The map shows the nation-states that were aligned with the United States and the Soviet Union through either multilateral or bilateral treaties. A multilateral treaty is one that includes many nation-states as parties to the treaty. A bilateral treaty is an agreement between only two nation-states. The lighter shades on the map were aligned with the United States while the darker shades were aligned with the Soviet Union.

ALIGNMENT AND NON-ALIGNMENT

We have been using the word *alignment* to describe relationships in the bipolar system while we described these arrangements in the multipolar system as alliances. Although the bipolar system was more rigid, it was less formal. The superpowers promoted their ideologies and catered to the interests of other states to entice them into their blocs. Since alignments were not formalized in signed treaties, it is difficult to observe which nation-state was aligned with which bloc. One measure of bipolar alignment was the source of a nation-state's armaments. Most of the world's arms were made in the United States, Western Europe, or the Soviet bloc countries. The variable ALIGN CW codes the percentage of arms imported from the Eastern or Western Blocs during the period 1964–1973. States that imported more than 90% of their arms from the United States and its NATO allies were coded as Aligned West, while states that imported more than 90% of their arms from Soviet bloc states were coded Aligned East. Other states were coded Neutral.

Data File: **NATIONS**
Task: **Mapping**
➤ Variable 1: **10) ALIGN CW**
➤ View: **Map**
➤ Display: **Legend**

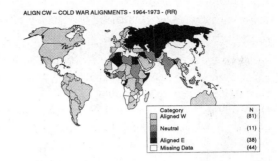

ALIGN CW -- COLD WAR ALIGNMENTS - 1964-1973 - (RR)

Category	N
Aligned W	(81)
Neutral	(11)
Aligned E	(38)
Missing Data	(44)

There are two notable findings in the map. First, the alignments follow the security pact memberships shown above very closely. This is not surprising, but it does tend to validate arms sales as a measure of alignment. Second, there are very few non-aligned states on the map. It seems that if a state bought arms from the United States it did not buy arms from the Soviet bloc, and vice versa. We can explore this further by creating a univariate distribution of the variable ALIGN CW.

Data File: **NATIONS**
➤ Task: **Univariate**
➤ Primary Variable : **10) ALIGN CW**
➤ View: **Pie**

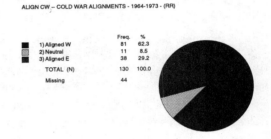

ALIGN CW -- COLD WAR ALIGNMENTS - 1964-1973 - (RR)

	Freq.	%
1) Aligned W	81	62.3
2) Neutral	11	8.5
3) Aligned E	38	29.2
TOTAL (N)	130	100.0
Missing	44	

Only 8.5% of the states bought less than 90% of their arms from one of the two superpower blocs. Very few states were in the middle. Either they bought from the East or they bought from the West. Thus, alignment was real.

In 1955, twenty-nine states from Africa and Asia met in Bandung, Indonesia, to promote unity among the developing countries in the face of cold-war competition. In 1961, Josip Tito of Yugoslavia, Gamal Abdel Nassar of Egypt, Sukarno of Indonesia, and Jawaharlal Nehru of India called for the formation of an organization of nation-states that formally rejected alignment to either of the two blocs. The Non-Aligned Movement (NAM) began with 25 members and has grown to over 100. It has met regularly since 1961 to promote the independence of the less developed countries and to provide a forum for Third-World issues. As the cold war ends the NAM continues to meet, but it now must redefine its mission. Use the MAPPING tool in Student ExplorIt to see the members of the NAM in the early 1970s.

Data File: **NATIONS**
➤ Task: **Mapping**
➤ Variable 1: **72) NONALIGNED**
➤ View: **Map**

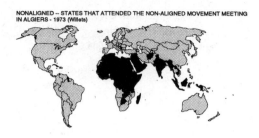

NONALIGNED -- STATES THAT ATTENDED THE NON-ALIGNED MOVEMENT MEETING IN ALGIERS - 1973 (Willets)

From the beginning, the United States opposed the formation of the NAM. Throughout the 1960s and 1970s the United States claimed that the NAM was a tool of Soviet influence. Membership in the NAM was open to any state that was not a member of NATO, CENTO, SEATO, and the Warsaw Pact. Nevertheless, states were barred from membership if they were seen as being too highly aligned with one of the superpowers. This policy, however, was unevenly applied. South Korea and the Philippines were barred from membership because of their ties to the United States while Cuba, North Korea, and North Vietnam were permitted to be members even though they were closely linked to the Soviet Union (Hastedt and Knickrehm, 1991:99).

One of the maxims of the bipolar system is that the two superpowers should not come into direct military conflict because of the threat of nuclear devastation that could result from a direct confrontation. The system itself provided for stable relationships between the major actors. This stability, however, did not extend to the rest of the world. It was among the newly independent and less developed states in Africa, Asia, Latin America, and the Middle East that many East-West conflicts came to blows. Many wars were fought where one side was supported by the United States and the other side was supported by the Soviet Union. These conflicts were called surrogate wars because each side was acting as the surrogate for one of the superpowers. You can view states where surrogate wars occurred with the variable SURROGATE on the NATIONS file.

Data File: **NATIONS**
Task: **Mapping**
➤ Variable 1: **94) SURROGATE**
➤ View: **Map**
➤ Display: **Legend**

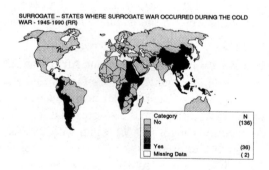

SURROGATE -- STATES WHERE SURROGATE WAR OCCURRED DURING THE COLD WAR - 1945-1990 (RR)

Category	N
No	(136)
Yes	(36)
Missing Data	(2)

For this variable, a surrogate war is defined as an armed conflict in which there were at least 1000 violent deaths and it was either an ideological war where one side was supported by a superpower or any war where both sides were supported by one of the superpowers. The civil war in El Salvador during the 1980s was an ideological conflict where the government of El Salvador was directly supported by the United States. The 1973 Yom Kippur War in the Middle East was not fundamentally an ideological war (communist vs. capitalist), but actors on both sides of the conflict were supported by opposing superpowers.

International Relations

We will explore the effects of alignment in the worksheets for this exercise. Before we turn to those worksheets, it is important to examine system characteristics and system change. As we stated before, systems provide stability for the major actors and the absence of a system is often associated with instability.

SYSTEM CONTINUITY AND CHANGE

There is much speculation about what the next international system may be like. Some analysts see the United States emerging as the single dominant actor in a unipolar system, others see a unified Europe contributing to a new multipolar system. Beyond the number of poles, systems are also affected by the scale of international activity and by the technologies that affect transportation, communications, and warfare. Another oft-quoted phrase by Heracleitus, the 4th century B.C. Greek historian, is "You can never step in the same river twice," meaning that similar situations are different enough that they cannot be wholly the same. Even if a new multipolar system emerges from the end of the cold war, it will be a different system from the balance of power system that existed in 1870. The number of actors has increased dramatically. Recalling the map in Exercise 3, over 70% of the current sovereign states gained sovereignty during the 20th century. The second figure in Exercise 2 showed that the international system is a much busier place than it was 50 years ago. Other measures of international activity show marked increase in the last 100 years. One such measure is the total volume of world trade as measured by the total value of exports.

> *Data File:* **HISTORY**
> > *Task:* **Historical Trends**
> *Variables:* **46) TRADE**

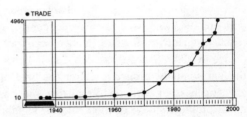

The value of world exports in billions of current U.S. dollars

This figure shows that the total value of world trade has risen steadily from 18.3 billion dollars (US) in 1935 to nearly 5 trillion dollars in 1995. That is a 270-fold increase in 60 years. Another indicator of the level of economic transactions that affects the system is the volume of rail traffic. The variable RAIL TRAF measures the total volume of freight shipped over the world's railroads.

Data File: **HISTORY**
Task: **Historical Trends**
> *Variables:* **38) RAIL TRAF**

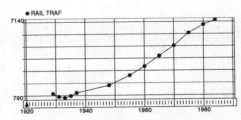

Railfreight traffic in billions of ton-kilometers

This graph shows that rail freight has increased from 1030 billion ton-kilometers[2] in 1930, with a slight dip during the Depression, to over 7 trillion ton-kilometers in 1984.

---

[2] A ton-kilometer is measured as 1 ton of freight being moved 1 kilometer. Thus 100 ton-kilometers could result from moving 1 ton 100 kilometers or from moving 2 tons 50 kilometers.

Paralleling these changes in international activity and transportation have been radical changes in the technology of communications and warfare. On August 2, 1990, military forces from Iraq invaded Kuwait. On August 6, the United States received permission from the Saudi Arabian government to send troops and fighter aircraft to defend the Saudi border. By August 8, the 2nd Brigade of the 82nd Airborne Division of the United States Army was on the ground in Saudi Arabia. Communication in today's world is instantaneous in most parts of the globe. One good measure of the change in telecommunications is the number of active phone lines in the world.

Data File: **HISTORY**
Task: **Historical Trends**
➤ Variables: **35) PHONES**

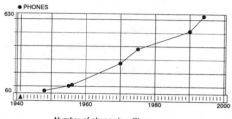

Number of phones in millions

The number of end-user telephone lines has increased by 10-fold from 1948 to 1994. It is not difficult to see how the United States was able to respond so quickly to the Kuwait crisis in 1990.

Perhaps the most important technological change that affected system development in the last 100 years was the technology of nuclear weapons. The United States detonated the first nuclear device on July 16, 1945 and used nuclear weapons on Japan on August 6 and 9, 1945. The Soviet Union began a crash program to develop nuclear weapons at the end of World War II and tested its first nuclear device in 1949. Since that time, Great Britain, France, and China have developed publicly announced nuclear weapons programs. After the breakup of the Soviet Union, Kazakhstan, Ukraine, and Belarus gave up nuclear weapons programs and destroyed their weapons. In 1998, both India and Pakistan made public displays of their nuclear capability. The variable NUCLEAR in the NATIONS file can be mapped to show the nation-states that have nuclear programs, those that are suspected to have nuclear weapons programs—even though the state has not acknowledged it—and those states that have dismantled nuclear weapons programs.

➤ Data File: **NATIONS**
➤ Task: **Mapping**
➤ Variable 1: **73) NUCLEAR**
➤ View: **Map**
➤ Display: **Legend**

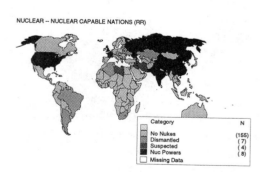

Nuclear weapons had an important role in defining the bipolar system, for without them, the United States and the Soviet Union could not have extended their influence across the globe. More importantly, the two superpowers were kept at bay by what has been called the balance of terror—the fear of retaliation against aggression. The potential consequences of direct superpower warfare were so terrible that an uneasy peace existed between the United States and the Soviet Union.

Other military technologies also affected the international system. At the beginning of the 20th century, the most important weapon in a nation-state's arsenal for extending its power across the globe was the battleship. World War II demonstrated the importance of aircraft carriers in global competition. During the post-war era, submarines were the naval weapon of choice for direct superpower competition. This was particularly true beginning in the mid-1950s when technology was developed that would permit nuclear-powered submarines to sit off an enemy's coastline and deliver nuclear missiles to targets thousands of miles inland in a few minutes. Variables in the HISTORY file permit us to explore the changing composition of naval forces and arms races in the bipolar system.

➤ *Data File:* **HISTORY**
   ➤ *Task:* **Historical Trends**
➤ *Variables:* **6) BATTLESHIP**
   7)CARRIERS
   42) SUBS USA

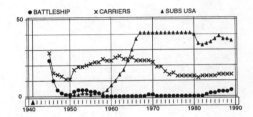

The graph shows that the number of battleships in the United States Navy fell after World War II from 23 in 1945 to none by 1958. Battleships saw a small revival in the mid-1980s as platforms for cruise missile launches and coastal bombardment. The prime naval weapon for delivering a U.S. presence in many of the smaller disputes that occurred during the cold war was the aircraft carrier. The above graph also shows that the U.S. attack carrier fleet declined after World War II from 28 to 11 in 1950, but rose again to between 22 and 26 during the 1960s in response to a perceived need for a versatile naval weapons system during the bipolar system. Ballistic missile nuclear submarines, however, grew rapidly from 1 in 1951 to 41 in 1967. The arms race between the United States and the Soviet Union was particularly evident in the competition for ballistic missile submarines.

Data File: **HISTORY**
   Task: **Historical Trends**
➤ *Variables:* **42) SUBS USA**
   43) SUBS USSR

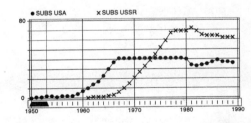

The graph clearly shows an arms race between the two superpowers in the area of ballistic missile nuclear submarines. The number of American ballistic missile submarines rose rapidly during the 1960s to a cap of 41 in 1967 that was negotiated as part of the Strategic Arms Limitations Talks I (SALT I). The first Soviet ballistic missile nuclear submarine was launched in 1962, eleven years after the first American vessel, but the Soviets rapidly caught up and passed the U.S. Navy with 72 ballistic nuclear submarines in service by 1981. The Soviet fleet then fell slowly to the 62 boats required by SALT I in 1987.

International systems can be classified by characteristics such as the number of system poles, density of international activity, and geography. They are distinguished, however, by their effect on the events of the actors in the system. These effects are born from rules of conduct that informally emerge from the interaction of competing nation-states. The rules are instructions or understandings about how to achieve the goals of the actor under the constraints of the system. In the following worksheets, you will explore how systems affect the actions of individual actors and try to identify and understand some of these rules.

WORKSHEET

NAME:

COURSE:

DATE:

EXERCISE

4

REVIEW QUESTIONS

Based on the first part of this exercise, answer True or False to the following items:

It is important that we study history because what has happened in the past always guides us in the present.	T	F
A system is classified as multipolar if it has two or more system poles.	T	F
A bipolar system is characterized by competition based on ideology.	T	F
System-level analysis is based on the idea that patterns in international events are due in part to the characteristics and operations of the international system.	T	F
Periods of system change are marked by instability.	T	F
The bipolar system tended to stabilize international relations for all the actors in the international system.	T	F
Liberalism is based on an ideal of keeping the government out of the operation of the economy.	T	F
By 1996, most states had established some form of liberal government.	T	F
The international system that existed at the end of the 19th century was the bipolar system.	T	F
The bipolar system was more formal than the multipolar system—requiring that international agreements be stated in formal treaties.	T	F

EXPLORIT QUESTIONS

1. Did arms sales really indicate alignment during the cold war? In the preliminary section of Exercise 4 we saw that there were few states that bought significant proportions of their arms from both sides. If a nation-state bought from the United States, it was unlikely to buy from the Soviet Union. We can explore this finding. Create a scatterplot using the value of arms imports from Warsaw Pact countries and the value of arms imports from NATO countries.

> ➤ *Data File:* **NATIONS**
> ➤ *Task:* **Scatterplot**
> ➤ *Dependent Variable:* **14) ARMS EAST**
> ➤ *Independent Variable:* **15) ARMS WEST**

Exercise 4: Explaining Events in the International System

69

Look at the graph. The dots tend to line up along the two axes. Dots that line up along the vertical axis (ARMS EAST) represent nation-states that bought arms from the Eastern Bloc (Soviet Union, etc.) but did not buy arms from the Western Bloc (United States, etc.). Dots that line up along the horizontal axis represent nation-states that bought arms from the Western Bloc but did not buy arms from the Eastern Bloc. The few dots in the middle of the graph represent states that bought arms from both East and West. If you use the mouse to point to a dot and press the left mouse button, ExplorIt will tell you which nation-state that dot represents. Using the mouse, fill in the blanks below.

List three states with the highest level of arms imports only from the East (i.e., that line up along the vertical axis).   _____

_____

_____

List three states that imported arms from both the East and the West (i.e., that are not lined up along either axis but are in the middle of the graph).   _____

_____

_____

List three states with the highest level of arms imports only from the West (i.e., that line up along the horizontal axis).   _____

_____

_____

2. The bipolar system provided a period of 46 years when there was no open warfare directly between the forces of the United States and the Soviet Union. These tense but generally stable relations did not extend to the rest of the world, as we discussed in Exercise 4. Was conflict during this period associated with alignment?

> *Data File:* **NATIONS**
> ➤ *Task:* **Cross-tabulation**
> ➤ *Row Variable:* **26) CONFLICT**
> ➤ *Column Variable:* **10) ALIGN CW**
> ➤ *View:* **Table**
> ➤ *Display:* **Column %**

a. Fill in the table below to explore this question.

	TYPE OF COUNTRY		
	ALIGNED WEST	**NEUTRAL**	**ALIGNED EAST**
% WITH HIGH CONFLICT	_____%	_____%	_____%

Use the SUMMARY view to fill in the following:

Prob. of chi-square: _____

Value of Cramer's V: _____

Write a short paragraph that discusses your findings.

b.   These conflicts, as we stated in Exercise 4, were known as surrogate wars. Since they represent-
     ed conflicts over states that were not rigidly aligned with one of the superpowers, it makes sense
     that they took place primarily in the developing world outside of Europe. Was there a relationship
     between the level of economic development and surrogate war during the cold war?

          Data File: **NATIONS**
               Task: **Cross-tabulation**
     ➤ Row Variable: **94) SURROGATE**
     ➤ Column Variable: **40) ECON DEVEL**
          ➤ View: **Tables**
          ➤ View: **Column %**

Fill in the table below to explore this question.

| | TYPE OF COUNTRY | | |
	LEAST DEV.	DEVELOPING	INDUSTRIALIZED
SURROGATE WAR– YES	_____%	_____%	_____%

Use the SUMMARY view to fill in the following:

Prob. of chi-square: _____

Value of Cramer's V: _____

Write a short paragraph that discusses your findings.

3. During the cold war, members of the non-aligned movement voted as a bloc in the U.N. General Assembly and that bloc tended to vote against U.S. interests. The bipolar system was managed by incentives and penalties issued by the system pole. That is, if the U.S. wanted states to agree with it, the U.S. had to offer incentives. Two incentives are reasonably easy to measure—arms sales and economic aid.

    a. Create a scatterplot of the relationship between the amount of economic aid given and agreement with the United States in U.N. votes.

> | Data File: | **NATIONS** |
> | ----------------------: | ----------- |
> | ➤ Task: | **Scatterplot** |
> | ➤ Dependent Variable: | **6) AGREEUS85** |
> | ➤ Independent Variable: | **109) USAID85** |
> | ➤ View: | **Reg. Line** |

    What is the correlation coefficient?   r = _____

Notice that most of the cases are clustered down in the lower left quadrant of the plot. This is because two states, Israel and Egypt, accounted for over 63% of the total U.S. aid budget in 1985. While these states are important, we can see what happens if we exclude them from the analysis. If you use the mouse to point to a dot on the graph, Student ExplorIt will show you which state the dot represents and will allow you to remove the case.

    b. Follow the instructions below to see the effect of eliminating Israel and Egypt from the analysis.

    Locate Israel on the above plot (upper right corner) by pointing the dot and click the left mouse button.

    REMOVE Israel from the plot.

    What is the correlation coefficient with ISRAEL removed?   r = _____

    Locate EGYPT on the above plot (far right side) by pointing the dot and click the left mouse button.

    Remove EGYPT from the plot.

    What is the correlation coefficient with EGYPT removed?   r = _____

    The independent variable (horizontal axis) is the amount of aid given by the United States in 1985. The dependent variable (vertical axis) is the percentage of votes by a state that agreed with the U.S. vote in the U.N. General Assembly. After reviewing the plot with Israel and Egypt removed, write a short paragraph below that discusses how United States aid affected other nation-states' voting practices in the United Nations.

4. The analysis in question 3 seems to show that foreign aid was an effective tool at generating support for U.S. positions in the United Nations. Arms sales were even more effective tools. You can see this by creating a plot that shows the percentage of agreement with the United States votes in the United Nations (AGREEUS85) and the percentage of a state's arms imports that came from the United States (USARMS%).

Data File:	**NATIONS**
Task:	**Scatterplot**
Dependent Variable:	**6) AGREEUS85**
➤ Independent Variable:	**110) USARMS%**
➤ View:	**Reg. Line**

    a. What is the direction of the relationship? (Circle one.)

        1. Positive (line goes from lower left upward to upper right)
        2. Neutral (line is flat)
        3. Negative (line goes from upper left downward to lower right)

    b. What is the correlation coefficient for this relationship?   r = _____

    c. Write a short paragraph below that discusses this scatterplot.

STATES AND FOREIGN POLICY

Tasks: Mapping, Cross-tabulation, Univariate, Scatterplot
Data Files: NATIONS

FOREIGN POLICY OR INTERNATIONAL RELATIONS?

Until now, we have avoided using the term *foreign policy*. This is a book about international relations, not foreign policy, as such. How is foreign policy different from international relations? As you now know, international relations is the description and explanation of international events and international events are actions taken by actors directed at targets across borders. Foreign policy is a subset of these descriptions and explanations. Foreign policy is the set of values that guide a national government combined with the procedures and strategies it uses to pursue its goals in international relations. Foreign policy is part of the state level of analysis. Like the system level of analysis, the state level presumes that there are patterns in international events. The state level of analysis assumes that these patterns can be explained, at least in part, by the characteristics of the major actors that comprise the international system, nation-states.

There are three general approaches to the state level of analysis. The first approach attempts to identify *characteristics of the nation-state* that are associated with certain actions. These theories are sometimes termed environmental theories because they focus on how the characteristics of the states form the environment within which international events occur. International relations scholars Harold and Margaret Sprout (1965) stated that this environment consists of both tangible factors such as physical geography and intangible factors such as culture and economics. The Sprouts termed this complex environment the milieu of international relations. Are landlocked states more confrontational with their neighbors than states with access to the high seas? Are less economically developed states more likely to go to war than more developed states? Questions like these are answered by examining the relationships between geographic, social, economic, and political characteristics of states and their actions in international relations.

The second approach to the state level of analysis attributes patterns in international events to the *process of foreign policy formation*. For example, a long-standing hypothesis in international relations is that liberal democracies are less likely to go to war against each other than are states with more authoritarian forms of government because they share common goals and interests. This approach is sometimes referred to as comparative foreign policy because it attempts to compare how different states formulate and implement foreign policy and find patterns in their behaviors.

The third approach to the state level of analysis is the *national interest approach*. This approach assumes that, like people, national governments are rational decision-makers[1] that are able to define a national interest and decide on courses of action that are most likely to satisfy that interest. Identification of the national interest is difficult, as we will see in Exercise 6 where we explore how individuals affect international relations. If the national interest is defined broadly enough to achieve a consensus, such as "survival," it becomes meaningless as a guide for specific actions. If the national interest is defined narrowly enough to be a guide for action, it loses its claim to be "national" because it lacks a national consensus. This exercise explores the first two approaches to the state level of analysis. The third approach will be discussed in the next exercise as we explore how the national interest is formed by the interests of individual people.

CHARACTERISTICS OF THE NATION-STATE AND INTERNATIONAL EVENTS

Perhaps the most obvious difference between nation-states is geographic difference. Geographic differences include terrain, proximity to conflictive situations, number of states sharing a border, strategic value (control over mountain passes or naval straits), and natural resources. Conflictive events tend to be concentrated in certain regions of the world. The REGION variable in the NATIONS file classifies nation-states according to the scheme used by the United Nations Development Program (UNDP).

➤ Data File: **NATIONS**
➤ Task: **Mapping**
➤ Variable 1: **84) REGION**
➤ View: **Map**
➤ Display: **Legend**

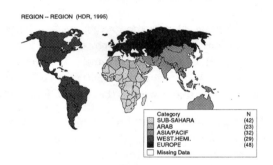

REGION -- REGION (HDR, 1995)

Category	N
SUB-SAHARA	(42)
ARAB	(23)
ASIA/PACIF	(32)
WEST.HEMI.	(29)
EUROPE	(48)
Missing Data	

Regional categories are essentially arbitrary. They are based on history, location, and common culture. For example, in the map above, the nation-states of North and South America are very different on many dimensions including culture, economics, politics, and geography. While they share a common experience of colonization by Europe in the 15th and 16th centuries (albeit by different imperial powers), they are all categorized in the Western Hemispheric category. Given that regional classification is somewhat arbitrary, one might think that REGION is not an important variable. Look at the relationship between REGION and the level of a nation-state's conflictive events.[2]

---

[1] Do not confuse rationality with sanity. An actor is rational if it can identify its preferred outcomes in a situation and choose the one that it believes will provide the greatest utility or satisfaction. Technically, these preferences must be both complete and transitive. Completeness means that for any two choices, A or B, the actor prefers A to B, prefers B to A, or is indifferent between A and B. Transitivity means that for any three choices, A, B and C, if A is preferred to B and B is preferred to C, then A will be preferred to C. While these conditions may be easy to meet in individuals, they are difficult, if not impossible, to guarantee in choices by groups of people (like governments).

[2] Throughout this exercise, we will measure conflict by the level of conflictive events. These data are taken from the COPDAB study. The level of conflict variables record the percentage of conflictive events in the total events in which the nation-state is an actor in the period 1948–1978. Two variables will be used. CONFLICT% is merely the percentage itself. CONFLICT collapses the CONFLICT% variable at its median (middle point). That is, nation-states with CONFLICT% below the median (13.8%) are considered low-conflict states and those above the median are considered high-conflict states.

Data File:	**NATIONS**
➤ Task:	**Cross-tabulation**
➤ Row Variable:	**26) CONFLICT**
➤ Column Variable:	**84) REGION**
➤ Views:	**Table**
➤ Display:	**Column %**

CONFLICT by REGION
Cramer's V: 0.397 **

<table>
<tr><td colspan="2"></td><td colspan="6">REGION</td></tr>
<tr><td colspan="2"></td><td>SUB-SAHARA</td><td>ARAB</td><td>ASIA/PACIF</td><td>WEST.HEMI.</td><td>EUROPE</td><td>TOTAL</td></tr>
<tr><td rowspan="8">C O N F L I C T</td><td>Low</td><td>25</td><td>4</td><td>6</td><td>17</td><td>12</td><td>64</td></tr>
<tr><td></td><td>69.4%</td><td>23.5%</td><td>24.0%</td><td>68.0%</td><td>46.2%</td><td>49.6%</td></tr>
<tr><td>High</td><td>11</td><td>13</td><td>19</td><td>8</td><td>14</td><td>65</td></tr>
<tr><td></td><td>30.6%</td><td>76.5%</td><td>76.0%</td><td>32.0%</td><td>53.8%</td><td>50.4%</td></tr>
<tr><td>Missing</td><td>6</td><td>6</td><td>7</td><td>4</td><td>22</td><td>45</td></tr>
<tr><td></td><td></td><td></td><td></td><td></td><td></td><td></td></tr>
<tr><td>TOTAL</td><td>36</td><td>17</td><td>25</td><td>25</td><td>26</td><td>129</td></tr>
<tr><td></td><td>100.0%</td><td>100.0%</td><td>100.0%</td><td>100.0%</td><td>100.0%</td><td></td></tr>
</table>

There appears to be a difference in the amount of conflict from region to region. In the Arab, Asia/Pacific, and Europe regions, the majority of the nation-states were high-conflict states (76.5%, 76.0%, and 53.8% respectively). If you show the SUMMARY view of this table, the chi-square probability of .0000 and the Cramer's V statistic of 0.397 shows a strong statistically significant relationship between REGION and CONFLICT. This relationship is dramatically illustrated if you use the BAR STACK view of the above table.

Data File:	**NATIONS**
Task:	**Cross-tabulation**
Row Variable:	**26) CONFLICT**
Column Variable:	**84) REGION**
Views:	**Table**
➤ Display:	**Bar - Stack**

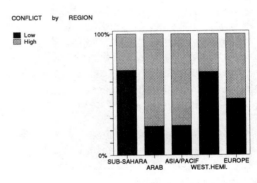

It is clear from these analyses that certain regions of the world had more conflict than others. The Western Hemisphere and Sub-Saharan African region were less conflictive in the period 1948–1978 than were the Asia/Pacific, Arab, and European regions.

Lewis F. Richardson was a pioneer in the statistical analysis of the causes of war. In his book, *Statistics of Deadly Quarrels* (1960), he found a statistical relationship between the number of close neighbors a nation-state has and that state's level of international conflict. Countries with more neighbors on their border are more likely to engage in conflict. We can create a SCATTERPLOT using our data to replicate his analysis.

Data File:	**NATIONS**
➤ Task:	**Scatterplot**
➤ Dependent Variable:	**27) CONFLICT %**
➤ Independent Variable:	**71) NEIGHBORS**
➤ View:	**Reg. Line**

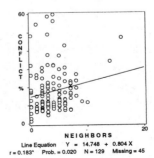

The correlation coefficient (r = 0.183) shows a weak relationship between these two variables, but the asterisk indicates that the relationship is statistically significant meaning that it is unlikely to be due to chance. You must be careful not to place too much confidence in findings like the one above. While it does show that conflict is related to the number of nation-states on the borders, the relationship is dramatically affected by the values of just one nation-state. If you remove China from the analysis, the relationship between the two variables vanishes. Click on OUTLIER and the dot representing China will be highlighted. Click on REMOVE and you will see the relationship between the number of nation-states on the border and the level of conflict without China.

Data File:	**NATIONS**
Task:	**Scatterplot**
Dependent Variable:	**27) CONFLICT %**
Independent Variable:	**71) NEIGHBORS**
View:	**Reg. Line**
➤ Find:	**Outlier/Remove**

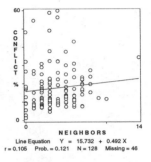

Line Equation   Y = 15.732 + 0.492 X
r = 0.105   Prob. = 0.121   N = 128   Missing = 46

The regression line in the new SCATTERPLOT is much flatter. The value of the correlation coefficient (r) dropped from 0.183 to 0.105, and the significance probability rose from 0.020 to 0.121. Without China, the SCATTERPLOT does not show a relationship between the number of states on the border and the level of conflict. It seems that China, which has an exceptional number of nation-states on its border (16), also had an exceptionally high level of interstate conflict.

Another geographic difference between states that can help explain behavior is their stocks of vital natural resources. In today's world, the most important natural resource is probably oil. The variable OIL on the NATIONS file shows the estimated proved oil reserves of each nation-state in millions of barrels as of January 1997.

Data File:	**NATIONS**
➤ Task:	**Mapping**
➤ Variable 1:	**74) OIL**
➤ View:	**Map**

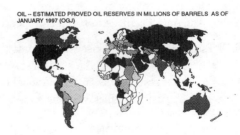

OIL -- ESTIMATED PROVED OIL RESERVES IN MILLIONS OF BARRELS AS OF JANUARY 1997 (OGJ)

The map shows that major oil fields are found in the Middle East, the North Sea, the United States (Alaska and Texas), Venezuela, Nigeria, Angola, Russia, and China. These fields vary significantly in their reserves. Use the RANK option on the above map to see which countries have the largest reserves.

Data File:	**NATIONS**		
Task:	**Mapping**		
Variable 1:	**74) OIL**		
➤ View:	**List: Rank**		

RANK	CASE NAME	VALUE
1	Saudi Arabia	259000.0
2	Iraq	112500.0
3	United Arab Emirates	97800.0
4	Kuwait	94000.0
5	Iran	93000.0
6	Venezuela	71688.9
7	Russia	48573.0
8	Mexico	40000.0
9	Libya	29500.0
10	China	24000.0

Saudi Arabia, by far, has the largest reserves of oil with an estimated 259 billion barrels of oil. Iraq is second with 112.5 billion barrels of oil.[3] The variable OIL3 shows the percentage of total world reserves held by each country.

Data File:	**NATIONS**		
Task:	**Mapping**		
➤ Variable 1:	**76) OIL3**		
➤ View:	**List: Rank**		

RANK	CASE NAME	VALUE
1	Saudi Arabia	25.5
2	Iraq	11.1
3	United Arab Emirates	9.6
4	Kuwait	9.3
5	Iran	9.2
6	Venezuela	7.1
7	Russia	4.8
8	Mexico	3.9
9	Libya	2.9
10	China	2.4

The major Middle East oil producers (Saudi Arabia, Iraq, United Arab Emirates, Kuwait, and Iran) account for over 64% of the estimated world oil reserves. When Iraq invaded Kuwait in 1990, it controlled 20.4% of the world reserves and threatened an additional 25.5% in Saudi Arabia. It is no surprise that the other nation-states responded with warfare when Iraq refused to withdraw.

Physical size is another geographic variable that can affect a state's actions. Larger states typically have more access to natural resources, more arable farmland, and more access to the sea—all of which affect a state's ability to act. Early theorists of international relations believed that control of territory was a key determinant of power and a key determinant of international behavior. British geographer Sir Halford Mackinder believed that the heartland of the Euro-Asian continent was the "pivot region" of world politics. Control of this vast territory meant control of the geographic hub of transportation. It also meant control of large areas with potentially great natural resources. As Mackinder stated, "Who rules East Europe commands the Heartland. Who rules the Heartland commands the World Island Eurasia. Who rules the World Island commands the World" (1904:150). Mackinder predicted in 1904 that both Germany and Russia could become hegemonic powers because of their strategic position to control great territories (see Dougherty and Pfaltzgraf, 1997:154–155). In Exercise 3, we looked at dif-

---

[3] Reserves and production of crude oil are usually measured in barrels. A barrel contains approximately 42 gallons or 159 liters of oil. Thus, Saudi Arabia's reserves are approximately 10.9 trillion gallons, or 41.2 trillion liters, of crude oil.

ferences in territorial size (see the first two maps in that exercise). Are larger states more prone to conflict than smaller states? We can explore this question by examining the physical size of the nation-state and the amount of conflict the state has experienced.

Data File: **NATIONS**
➤ Task: **Cross-tabulation**
➤ Row Variable: **26) CONFLICT**
➤ Column Variable: **13) AREA2**
➤ Views: **Table**
➤ Display: **Column %**

CONFLICT by AREA2
Cramer's V: 0.274 **

		AREA2		
		Low	High	TOTAL
CONFLICT	Low	35	29	64
		66.0%	38.2%	49.6%
	High	18	47	65
		34.0%	61.8%	50.4%
	Missing	34	11	45
	TOTAL	53	76	129
		100.0%	100.0%	

The cross-tabulation shows that 61.8% of the large nation-states (high area) also initiated a high proportion of conflictive events. This compares with only 34.0% of the small nation-states that had a high proportion of conflictive events. As you can see, the relationship is statistically significant. The SUMMARY view shows that chi-square probability is less than .0005.

So, nation-states with more area are more conflictive than smaller states. We can think of many reasons why this might be the case. Perhaps they have more diverse populations that generate conflicting interests. Or they may be engaged in more complex relationships than smaller states. It may be that they have more access to resources that give them the power needed to seek their wills in international relations. Physical area, however, is only one way we can measure the size of a state. Size can also be measured by the population and by the size of the economy. The size of the economy is measured by a nation-state's gross national product (GNP). The GNP is a sum of the value of all the economic transactions within the state in a given year. States with larger populations tend to have larger GNP's because more people are buying, selling, working, and paying taxes. Because of this, GNP by itself is not a good measure of the economic well-being of an economy. It is, however, a good measure of the size of the economy.

Data File: **NATIONS**
➤ Task: **Mapping**
➤ Variable 1: **49) GNP94**
➤ View: **Map**

GNP94 -- GROSS NATIONAL PRODUCT IN BILLIONS OF US DOLLARS - 1994 (HDR97)

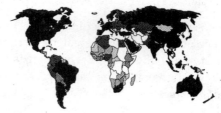

The map above shows that the states with higher GNP are either the states with the largest populations (such as India or China) or the states with the highest level of economic development (such as Great Britain or France). GNP is usually reported for a specific year (our variable is for 1994). It is initially calculated in the local currency (such as British pounds or Indian rupees) but must be converted via exchange rates to a common currency (such as U.S. dollars) to compare across countries. Our variable is recorded in billions of U.S. dollars. You can see the actual distribution of gross national product by using the RANK view from the map above.

Data File:	**NATIONS**
Task:	**Mapping**
Variable 1:	**49) GNP94**
➤ View:	**List: Rank**

RANK	CASE NAME	VALUE
1	United States	6737.4
2	Japan	4321.1
3	Germany	2075.5
4	France	1355.0
5	Italy	1101.3
6	United Kingdom	1069.5
7	China	630.2
8	Canada	569.9
9	Brazil	536.3
10	Spain	525.3

The total value of all economic activity in the United States in 1994 was $6,737,400,000,000, or over 6 trillion dollars. The smallest GNP shown on the list the list was approximately $200,000,000 for Maldives, Comoros, and Equatorial Guinea. The gross size of a nation-state's economy has a significant effect on its international relations. Larger economies initiate more international events. This hypothesis can be tested by looking at a scatterplot between GNP and the number of events initiated by the state. Since the data on events span the years from 1948 to 1978, it would be better if we use a measure of GNP in a year closer to that range.

Data File:	**NATIONS**
➤ Task:	**Scatterplot**
➤ Dependent Variable:	**2) ACTOR EVTS**
➤ Independent Variable:	**47) GNP 77**
➤ View:	**Reg. Line**

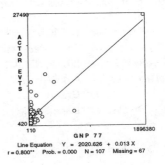

Line Equation   Y = 2020.626 + 0.013 X
r = 0.800**   Prob. = 0.000   N = 107   Missing = 67

This scatterplot shows a very strong positive relationship. However, looking at the scatterplot, we see one case in the top right corner that may be having a strong influence on these results. If you select Outlier, you will see this dot represents the United States, and that our results will change from r = 0.800 to r = 0.402. By removing the United States, our results are still significant, just not as strongly so. Remove the United States and view the new scatterplot.

Data File:	**NATIONS**
Task:	**Scatterplot**
Dependent Variable:	**2) ACTOR EVTS**
Independent Variable:	**47) GNP77**
View:	**Reg. Line**
➤ Find:	**Outlier/Remove**

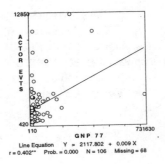

Line Equation   Y = 2117.802 + 0.009 X
r = 0.402**   Prob. = 0.000   N = 106   Missing = 68

It does seem that nation-states with larger economies are more active in international events.

In an earlier figure in this exercise we found that there was a weak relationship between physical area and conflict. Is there a similar relationship when we measure size economically? This relationship is best seen by using a cross-tabulation table in which the variables for the percentage of conflictive events and GNP in 1977 have been collapsed into high-low categories.

Data File: **NATIONS**
➤ Task: **Cross-tabulation**
➤ Row Variable: **26) CONFLICT**
➤ Column Variable: **48) GNP 77B**
➤ Views: **Table**
➤ Display: **Column %**

CONFLICT   by   GNP 77B
Cramer's V: 0.523 **

		GNP 77B			
		Low	High	Missing	TOTAL
C O N F L I C T	Low	42	16	6	58
		80.8%	28.6%		53.7%
	High	10	40	15	50
		19.2%	71.4%		46.3%
	Missing	7	0	38	45
	TOTAL	52	56	59	108
		100.0%	100.0%		

This table shows that 80.8% of the nation-states with low GNP in 1977 initiated a low level of conflictive events. Only 28.6% of the high-GNP countries initiated a low level of conflictive events. We can see there is a strong and significant association (V = 0.523**) that is not likely to be due to chance. The SUMMARY view shows that the probability of chi-square is .0000. The BAR STACK view of this relationship clearly illustrates that nation-states with large economies initiate a higher percentage of conflictive events.

Data File: **NATIONS**
Task: **Cross-tabulation**
Row Variable: **26) CONFLICT**
Column Variable: **48) GNP 77B**
Views: **Graph**
➤ Display: **Bar - Stack**

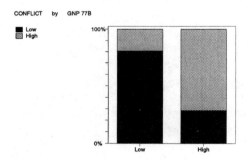

The other way to measure size, besides area and GNP, is population. We looked at differences in population size in Exercise 3. Here, we want to know how those differences affect international events. Are nation-states with larger populations more conflictive than those with smaller populations? Again, a cross-tabulation of the variables on population and percentage of conflict events can answer this question.

Data File: **NATIONS**
Task: **Cross-tabulation**
Row Variable: **26) CONFLICT**
➤ Column Variable: **80) POP77B**
➤ Views: **Table**
➤ Display: **Column %**

CONFLICT   by   POP77B
Cramer's V: 0.532 **

		POP77B			
		Low	High	Missing	TOTAL
C O N F L I C T	Low	42	16	6	58
		80.8%	27.6%		52.7%
	High	10	42	13	52
		19.2%	72.4%		47.3%
	Missing	7	0	38	45
	TOTAL	52	58	57	110
		100.0%	100.0%		

The table above shows that only 19.2% of the nation-states with low populations (below the median) initiated a high percentage of conflictive events. This compares to 72.4% of the high population countries that initiated a high proportion of conflictive events. As you can see, there is a strong association that is unlikely due to chance (V = 0.532**). Once again, size matters. The larger a state's population, the higher its percentage of conflictive events overall.

POLITICAL CHARACTERISTICS AND POLITICAL BEHAVIOR

We noted in the third map in Exercise 4 that the political systems of the world have changed dramatically since 1970. Most of the former communist states of Eastern Europe have embraced some form of market reform and have instituted democratic reforms. During the last 25 years, the authoritarian states in Latin America have also become more democratic.

The shift in types of government can be dramatically illustrated by looking at two variables.

> *Data File:* **NATIONS**
> ➤ *Task:* **Univariate**
> ➤ *Primary Variable :* **55) GOVTYPE70**
> ➤ *View:* **Pie**

GOVTYPE70 -- TYPE OF GOVERNMENT - 1970 (RR)

	Freq.	%
1) Multiparty	63	40.9
2) 1 Prty/Mil	59	38.3
3) Communist	32	20.8
TOTAL (N)	154	100.0
Missing	20	

Here we see that 40.9% of nation-states had multiparty governments while 38.3% of nation-states were single-party/military states and 20.8% were communist.

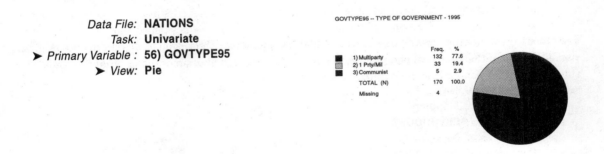

> *Data File:* **NATIONS**
> *Task:* **Univariate**
> ➤ *Primary Variable :* **56) GOVTYPE95**
> ➤ *View:* **Pie**

GOVTYPE95 -- TYPE OF GOVERNMENT - 1995

	Freq.	%
1) Multiparty	132	77.6
2) 1 Prty/Mil	33	19.4
3) Communist	5	2.9
TOTAL (N)	170	100.0
Missing	4	

In just 25 years, we see a major change in that 77.6% of nation-states now have multiparty governments, while there has been a corresponding reduction in communist and single-party or military states. The question that this raises in comparative foreign policy at the state level of analysis is, Do different types of governments behave differently in international relations? For example, are democratic states less likely to initiate wars or are authoritarian states more likely to engage in conflictive events?

Exercise 5: States and Foreign Policy

A long-standing theory in international relations is that democracies are more peaceful than are authoritarian forms of government. There are many reasons for this. It tends to be harder to generate the consensus of public opinion for war that a democratic government may require. The diversity of interests represented in a democracy may create conflicting policies. We can examine whether or not democratic forms of government have fought fewer wars since World War II.

Data File: **NATIONS**
➤ Task: **Cross-tabulation**
➤ Row Variable: **116) WARS 45–92**
➤ Column Variable: **55) GOVTYPE70**
➤ Views: **Graph**
➤ Display: **Bar - Stack**

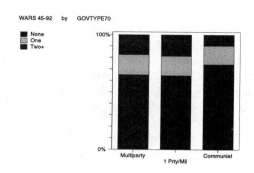

Comparing the three bars above, it appears that there is little difference between the number of wars entered into by democracies and by one-party or military regimes. The small apparent difference between democracies and communist states is not statistically significant; that is, the difference may only be due to random chance (chi-square prob. = .838 — well above our standard of 0.05). So, it appears that democracies were not more peaceful than other forms of government. But surely this is not surprising. Most theorists believe that democracies are more peaceful with each other. That is, democracies do not fight other democracies, but they are not necessarily more peaceful when facing other types of governments. We will explore this theory further in Exercise 8 when we examine why nation-states go to war.

The relationship between the characteristics of a nation-state and its behavior in international relations can be very complex. In the early 1960s, newly independent states in Africa and Asia felt that their interests were not being addressed in international forums such as the United Nations. A group of 77 states joined together to express the interests of the less developed states. The Group of 77 has become a voting bloc and lobbying group for the interests of the less developed nation-states. It still exists today, although in 1998, the Group of 77 had 133 members. The Group of 77 retained its original name because of the historical significance. Take a look at the distribution of the original 77 states.

Data File: **NATIONS**
➤ Task: **Mapping**
➤ Variable 1: **58) GROUP77**
➤ View: **Map**

The map shows that the original 77 members were distributed throughout the less developed world in Latin America, Africa, and southern Asia. Typically, these were the least powerful states that individually could do little to persuade institutions like the United Nations. As a group, however, the 77 states formed a majority voting bloc in the UN General Assembly. In 1964, they used this majority to call a special meeting of all the members of the United Nations under the title "the United Nations Conference on Trade and Development" (UNCTAD) to explore the interests of the Group of 77. This meeting was confrontational, if not acrimonious. Its agenda included proposals to reorganize the world economy to provide special rights and privileges for the developing countries. Clear voting blocs emerged where the economically developed states opposed the less developed states. These blocs also reflected the nature of the bipolar international system at the time since the communist countries supported the proposals of the less developed states in opposition to the Western industrial countries. Given the nature of the agenda, we would expect to observe some differences in voting behavior associated with the state's level of economic development. Should we also expect differences associated with the state's type of government?

The first UNCTAD meeting began with votes on a series of general principles that specified the concerns and some of the desires of the Group of 77. General Principle Eight stated that in the area of international trade "developed countries should grant concessions to all developing countries . . . and should not, in granting these or other concessions, require any concessions in return from the developing countries" (UNCTAD, 1964:20). Voting on this proposal was divided by both the level of economic development at the time and the state's type of government.

Data File: **NATIONS**
➤ *Task:* **Cross-tabulation**
➤ *Row Variable:* **101) UNCTAD1**
➤ *Column Variable:* **50) GNPPC65b**
➤ *Views:* **Graph**
➤ *Display:* **Bar - Stack**

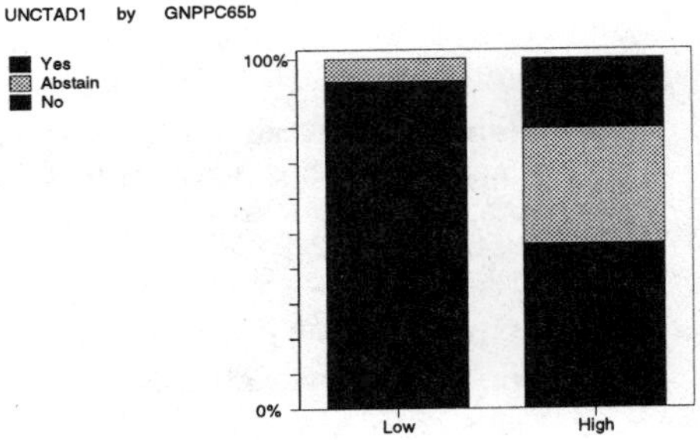

The graph dramatically illustrates that voting behavior on this proposal in UNCTAD was related to the gross national product per capita of the nation-state. The SUMMARY view of this relationship shows a strong statistically significant relationship between the two variables (chi-square probability = .000 and Cramer's V = 0.512). The system level of analysis discussed in the previous exercise implied that during the bipolar era, government type, a characteristic of the nation-state, should be related to voting behavior in UNCTAD. If this analysis is valid, then we should see that the multiparty democracies voted differently than the communist states on the proposal to give developing states trade concessions.

Data File: **NATIONS**
Task: **Cross-tabulation**
Row Variable: **101) UNCTAD1**
➤ *Column Variable:* **55) GOVTYPE70**
➤ *Views:* **Tables**
➤ *Display:* **Column %**

UNCTAD1 by GOVTYPE70
Cramer's V: 0.344 **
Warning: Potential significance problem. Check row and column totals.

UNCTAD1	GOVTYPE70 Multiparty	1 Prty/Mil	Communist	Missing	TOTAL
Yes	21	44	12	0	77
	47.7%	88.0%	92.3%		72.0%
Abstain	13	6	1	0	20
	29.5%	12.0%	7.7%		18.7%
No	10	0	0	0	10
	22.7%	0.0%	0.0%		9.3%
Missing	19	9	19	20	67
TOTAL	44	50	13	20	107
	100.0%	100.0%	100.0%		

This table shows a significant difference in the UNCTAD vote associated with government type. Nearly all of the communist states (12 of the 13 states, or 92.3%) voted for the proposal. Less than half of the multiparty democracies voted for the proposal (47.7%). You should also note that a large majority (88.0%) of the one-party or military governments voted for the trade preferences for the developing countries. A legitimate criticism of this finding could be that one-party and military governments in 1964 generally had low GNP per capita. If this is true, it could be that government type is just another measure of economic development for these states, and it should not be surprising that such governments supported the proposal. We need to find out if government type affected the vote independent of the level of GNP per capita. To do this, we must look at the relationship between the vote and government type within each category of GNP per capita. This is called "controlling" for a variable and is done with the following Student ExplorIt commands:

Data File: **NATIONS**
Task: **Cross-tabulation**
Row Variable: **101) UNCTAD1**
Column Variable: **55) GOVTYPE70**
➤ Control Variable: **50) GNPC65b**
➤ Views: **Tables (Low)**
➤ Display: **Column %**

UNCTAD1   by   GOVTYPE70
Controls: GNPPC65b: Low
Cramer's V: 0.576 **
Warning: Potential significance problem. Check row and column totals.

		GOVTYPE70				
		Multiparty	1 Prty/Mil	Communist	Missing	TOTAL
UNCTAD1	Yes	13	30	0	0	43
		100.0%	93.8%	0.0%		93.5%
	Abstain	0	2	1	0	3
		0.0%	6.3%	100.0%		6.5%
	Missing	10	2	0	6	18
	TOTAL	13	32	1	6	46
		100.0%	100.0%	100.0%		

The option for selecting a control variable is located on the same screen you use to select other variables. For this example, select 50) GNPPC65b as a control variable and then click [OK] to continue as usual. Separate tables for each of the 50) GNPPC65b categories will now be shown for the 101) UNCTAD1 and 55) GOVTYPE70 cross-tabulation.

The table you see here is the cross-tabulation between the vote in UNCTAD and the government type only for low-GNP per capita states. Note first that there is only one communist state in the low-GNP per capita category (mostly because of missing data). Next, note that among low-GNP per capita states, all the multiparty states and nearly all the one-party/military states (93.8%) voted in favor of the proposal. Thus, for the low GNP per capita states, government type made no difference in voting behavior.[4] If you click on the arrow under CONTROL on the Student ExplorIt output screen, you can move the table to those states with high-GNP per capita in 1965.

Data File: **NATIONS**
Task: **Cross-tabulation**
Row Variable: **101) UNCTAD1**
Column Variable: **55) GOVTYPE70**
Control Variable: **50) GNPC65b**
➤ Views: **Tables (High)**
➤ Display: **Column %**

UNCTAD1   by   GOVTYPE70
Controls: GNPPC65b: High
Cramer's V: 0.409 **
Warning: Potential significance problem. Check row and column totals.

		GOVTYPE70				
		Multiparty	1 Prty/Mil	Communist	Missing	TOTAL
UNCTAD1	Yes	8	13	2	0	23
		25.8%	81.3%	100.0%		46.9%
	Abstain	13	3	0	0	16
		41.9%	18.8%	0.0%		32.7%
	No	10	0	0	0	10
		32.3%	0.0%	0.0%		20.4%
	Missing	7	3	0	4	14
	TOTAL	31	16	2	4	49
		100.0%	100.0%	100.0%		

Click the appropriate button at the bottom of the task bar to look at the second (or "next") partial table for 50) GNPPC65b.

---

[4] When the single communist state is dropped from the low-GNP per capita category, the summary statistics confirm that there is no significant relationship between these variables (probability of chi-square = 0.356). You can replicate this by selecting 55) GOVTYPE70 as a subset variable and excluding 3) COMMUNIST.

While government type made no difference in the UNCTAD vote for low-GNP per capita states, the above table shows that it did make a difference among high-GNP per capita states. Among these states, only 25.8% of the multiparty democracies voted in favor of the proposals compared to 81.3% of the one-party/military governments. If the two communist states are dropped from the table,[5] the SUMMARY statistics show a strong statistically significant relationship between these two variables (probability of chi-square = .000 and Cramer's V = 0.547). Thus, among less developed countries, economic interests dominate the voting behavior, regardless of the type of governments. Among the more developed countries, type of government did affect the the UNCTAD vote.

These analyses illustrate that state-level characteristics do help explain some of the patterns we see in international events. They also point out that there are connections between the state level of analysis and the system level of analysis we discussed in Exercise 4. Geography, size, and level of economic development all affect a state's behavior in international events.

---

[5] This can also be replicated by selecting 55) GOVTYPE70 as a subset variable and excluding 3) COMMUNIST.

WORKSHEET

NAME:

COURSE:

DATE:

Workbook exercises and software are copyrighted. Copying is prohibited by law.

EXERCISE
5

REVIEW QUESTIONS

Based on the first part of this exercise, answer True or False to the following items:

The milieu of international relations consists of both the tangible and intangible characteristics of states that create the environment within which international events occur.	T	F
Comparative foreign policy refers to the process of comparing how different U.S. presidents pursue their interests in foreign affairs.	T	F
Rationality in international relations refers to the sanity of decision makers like presidents and foreign ministers.	T	F
When measured by the level of conflictive events, the European states were in the least conflictive region during the period from 1948 to 1978.	T	F
Isolated states with few neighbors on their border tend to engage in fewer conflictive events in international relations than do states with many other states on their borders..	T	F
It is estimated that Saudi Arabia has more than twice as much crude oil reserve as Iraq.	T	F
Larger states are more likely to have higher levels of conflictive events than are smaller states.	T	F
Democracies have engaged in fewer wars since 1945 than have either one-party/ military governments or communist governments.	T	F
During the UNCTAD meeting in 1964, the less developed Group of 77 nation-states tended to support the U.S. position in the debates.	T	F
In the initial meetings of UNCTAD in 1964, more democratic states tended to support the U.S. positions regardless of their level of economic development.	T	F

EXPLORIT QUESTIONS

1. What patterns can we find in cooperative events? Remember that the variables we used to measure level of conflict measured the percentage of conflictive events in the nation-state's total volume of events. That means that if 29% of a nation-state's events were conflictive (as was the case with the United States), no more than 71% of the state's events could be cooperative (100% − 29% = 71%). Thus, by definition, states with a high percentage of conflict must have a low percentage of cooperation.

Create a comparison ranking that shows both the percentage of conflictive events (CONFLICT %) and the percentage of cooperative events (COOP %).

> ➤ *Data File:* **NATIONS**
> ➤ *Task:* **Mapping**
> ➤ *Variable 1:* **27) CONFLICT %**
> ➤ *Variable 2:* **29) COOP %**
> ➤ *Views:* **List: Rank**

a.   List the 5 nation-states with the highest percentage of **conflictive** events and note their percentage of conflictive events.

NATION-STATE	PERCENT
_____	_____
_____	_____
_____	_____
_____	_____
_____	_____

List the 5 nation-states with the lowest percentage of **cooperative** events and note their percentage of cooperative events.

NATION-STATE	PERCENT
_____	_____
_____	_____
_____	_____
_____	_____
_____	_____

Does this evidence support the hypothesis?   Yes   No

Scroll down the lists and you will note that only four states have a majority (greater than 50%) of their events as conflictive events and only six nation-states have less than a majority of cooperative events. This supports the assertion we made in Exercise 1 that most of the events in the international system are cooperative rather than conflictive. We can explore this assertion by looking at the univariate distribution of the percentages of conflictive and cooperative events.

> *Data File:* **NATIONS**
> ➤ *Task:* **Univariate**
> ➤ *Primary Variable:* **27) CONFLICT %**
> ➤ *View:* **Statistics (Summary)**

b.   What is the average (mean) percentage of conflictive events?   _____

> *Data File:* **NATIONS**
> *Task:* **Univariate**
> ➤ *Primary Variable:* **29) COOP %**
>   ➤ *View:* **Statistics (Summary)**

c.   What is the average (mean) of events initiated that are cooperative?   _____

       Does this support our assertion?   Yes   No

2.   If we look at total number of cooperative and conflictive events, instead of percentages, we see a different picture. Make a map that compares the variables CONF EVNTS and COOP EVNTS.

> *Data File:* **NATIONS**
> ➤ *Task:* **Mapping**
> ➤ *Variable 1:* **25) CONF EVNTS**
> ➤ *Variable 2:* **28) COOP EVNTS**
> ➤ *Views:* **List: Rank**

a.   List the 10 nation-states with the highest number of **conflictive** events and note their number of conflictive events.

                    NATION-STATE   NUMBER

                  _____   _____

                  _____   _____

                  _____   _____

                  _____   _____

                  _____   _____

                  _____   _____

                  _____   _____

                  _____   _____

                  _____   _____

                  _____   _____

b. List the 10 nation-states with the highest number of **cooperative** events and note their number of cooperative events.

NATION-STATE   NUMBER

_____   _____

_____   _____

_____   _____

_____   _____

_____   _____

_____   _____

_____   _____

_____   _____

_____   _____

_____   _____

c. How many nation-states appear in both lists? That is, note below the names of the nation-states that are in both the top-ten number of conflictive events and the top-ten number of cooperative events.

_____   _____

_____   _____

_____   _____

_____   _____

d. It appears that nation-states that initiated high numbers of conflictive events also initiated high numbers of cooperative events. We can use a scatterplot to test this hypothesis.

          Data File: **NATIONS**
          ➤ Task: **Scatterplot**
  ➤ Dependent Variable: **25) CONF EVNTS**
  ➤ Independent Variable: **28) COOP EVNTS**
          ➤ View: **Reg. Line**

What is the correlation coefficient?   r = _____

Is the correlation coefficient statistically significant?   Yes   No

What does this imply? Write a short paragraph providing a possible explanation for this relationship.

3. In the preliminary section of Exercise 5, we found that larger states had higher levels of conflictive events than smaller states. Did these higher levels of conflict translate into more wars?

    a. Create a cross-tabulation that compares size measured by physical area with whether or not the nation-state entered into a war during the period 1945–1992.

              Data File: **NATIONS**
          ➤ Task: **Cross-tabulation**
    ➤ Row Variable: **116) WARS 45–92**
  ➤ Column Variable: **13) AREA2**
          ➤ View: **Tables**
       ➤ Display: **Column %**

Hint: You can temporarily collapse rows One and Two into a single row to obtain the results for the questions below. To collapse the rows together, click on the two rows to highlight them. Then click the [Collapse] button on the left of your screen. You will then be prompted to enter a new row name. Enter One, and leave the Action set to Create New Collapsed Category. Then click [OK]. These rows are now collapsed for this analysis only. If you reselect your variables and rerun the analysis, you will see your original table with three rows.

What percentage of the **low** area nation-states fought a war during the period 1945–1992? _____

What percentage of the **high** area nation-states fought a war during the period 1945–1992? _____

    ➤ View: **Summary Statistics**

What is the probability of chi-square? _____

What is Cramer's V? _____

    b. Create a cross-tabulation that compares 1977 population with whether or not the nation-state entered into a war during the period 1945–1992.

WORKSHEET

> Data File: **NATIONS**
> Task: **Cross-tabulation**
> Row Variable: **116) WARS 45–92**
> ➤ Column Variable: **80) POP77B**
> ➤ View: **Tables**
> ➤ Display: **Column %**

Hint: Once again, you should collapse rows One and Two into a single row to answer the following questions

What percentage of the **low** population nation-states fought a war during the period 1945–1992? _____

What percentage of the **high** population nation-states fought a war during the period 1945–1992? _____

> ➤ View: **Summary Statistics**

What is the probability of chi-square? _____

What is Cramer's V? _____

c.   Create a cross-tabulation that compares the 1977 gross national product whether or not the nation-state entered into a war during the period 1945–1992.

> Data File: **NATIONS**
> Task: **Cross-tabulation**
> Row Variable: **116) WARS 45–92**
> ➤ Column Variable: **48) GNP 77B**
> ➤ View: **Tables**
> ➤ Display: **Column %**

What percentage of the **low** GNP nation-states fought a war during the period 1945–1992? _____

What percentage of the **high** GNP nation-states fought a war during the period 1945–1992? _____

> ➤ View: **Summary Statistics**

What is the probability of chi-square? _____

What is Cramer's V? _____

d.   Looking at these three cross-tabulations that compare area, population, and GNP with war, what can you say about the effect of size on whether or not a nation-state fought a war in the period 1945–1992?

THE INDIVIDUAL AND INTERNATIONAL RELATIONS

Tasks: Univariate, Cross-tabulation
Data Files: FPSURVEY, FPELITES

We began the discussion of frameworks for analyzing international relations in Exercise 4 with the system level of analysis where we claimed that patterns in international events can, in part, be explained by understanding the nature of the international system as a whole. In Exercise 5 we attributed some of those patterns to the nature of the nation-state. With this exercise, we come full circle from the largest, most abstract concept—the system—to the smallest most concrete concept—individuals like you. The **individual level of analysis** provides explanations of international events that are drawn from psychology, group dynamics, human nature (if such a thing exists), and individual characteristics such as history, culture, religion, gender, experience, education, and health. The individual level of analysis does not contradict the system level or the state level. It does, however, recognize that all decisions and actions in international relations are taken by individuals—whether those people act alone or in the context of larger institutions. The individual level also recognizes that the larger institutions of state and system are constructed from the desires and actions of individual actors.

People differ along many different dimensions. Some important individual characteristics include differences in knowledge and experience, cultural and racial background, and in class (income, wealth, and status). For key policy makers, individual characteristics are important variables that help explain their actions in domestic and international affairs. Mikhail Gorbachev, who became the General Secretary of the Communist Party of the Soviet Union in 1985, was a very different person from Leonid Brezhnev, who ruled from 1964 to 1982. Brezhnev was an old-line communist who had seen the Soviet losses of the two world wars. He was a close associate of both Stalin and Khruschev and had witnessed Stalin's purges in which millions of Soviet dissidents and political rivals were imprisoned or killed (Garraty and Gay, 1981:1002). He rose through the political and military ranks within the party. Gorbachev was a young boy during World War II and did not directly experience its devastation. He rose through the ranks of the party mostly in functional posts in the Ministry of Agriculture. It is no surprise that Gorbachev, who spent his political life trying to improve productive efficiency, was willing to reform the economy and politics of the Soviet Union that Brezhnev had worked so hard to preserve.

INDIVIDUALS AND THE NATIONAL INTEREST

In Exercise 5 we mentioned that one approach to the state level of analysis is the national interest approach. Using this method, we try to understand what the vital national interest of a state is and infer from this what actions it is likely to take. Since all nation-states are constructed from the desires and actions of individuals, the national interest is in some way an aggregate of the interests of these individuals. Clearly, the interests of some individuals, like the President of the United States or the Prime Minister of India, have more influence on international relations than do the interests of others. Nonetheless, if the national interest is national, it must reflect the complex web of interests of the citizens of the nation-state. This raises a number of questions: Who forms the national interest, what is the national interest, and do the elites who make decisions for the society have the same interests as the general population? We will address each of these questions by using a survey of elites and the general population in the United States in 1994.

Even in a democratic society, only those who take an interest will have their interests heard. Not everyone pays attention to news about foreign policy or international relations. The variables NEWSFP and NEWSINTL measure the degree to which the respondents to the survey are interested in news about U.S. foreign policy and general international affairs respectively.

➤ *Data File:* **FPSURVEY**
    ➤ *Task:* **Univariate**
➤ *Primary Variable:* **23) NEWSFP**
      ➤ *View:* **Pie**

NEWSFP -- HOW INTERESTED ARE YOU IN NEWS ABOUT THE RELATIONS OF THE UNITED STATES WITH OTHER COUNTRIES? (FPS)

		Freq.	%
■	1) Very Int.	1840	46.1
▦	2) Somewhat	1563	39.2
■	3) Hardly Int	551	13.8
▦	4) No Int.	37	0.9
	TOTAL (N)	3991	100.0
	Missing	83	

[Weight]

Only 46.1% of the respondents to the survey said they were "very interested" in news about U.S. foreign policy.

Data File: **FPSURVEY**
    Task: **Univariate**
➤ *Primary Variable:* **24) NEWSINTL**
      ➤ *View:* **Pie**

NEWSINTL -- HOW INTERESTED ARE YOU IN NEWS ABOUT OTHER COUNTRIES? (FPS)

		Freq.	%
■	1) Very Int.	1196	29.9
▦	2) Somewhat	1858	46.4
■	3) Hardly Int	913	22.8
▦	4) No Int.	40	1.0
	TOTAL (N)	4008	100.0
	Missing	66	

[Weight]

Only 29.9% of the respondents said they were "very interested" in general news about international affairs. Who follows news about international affairs the most? We can answer this question with some simple cross-tabulations.

Data File: **FPSURVEY**
➤ Task: **Cross-tabulation**
➤ Row Variable: **24) NEWSINTL**
➤ Column Variable: **1) AGE**
➤ Views: **Table**
➤ Display: **Column %**

NEWSINTL by AGE
Weight Variable: WEIGHT
Cramer's V: 0.145 **

		AGE				
		Under 30	30-64	65+	Missing	TOTAL
NEWSINTL	Very Int.	245	708	238	5	1192
		27.7%	29.8%	33.2%		29.9%
	Somewhat	300	1215	324	19	1839
		33.8%	51.2%	45.1%		46.2%
	Hardly Int	337	424	148	4	909
		38.1%	17.8%	20.6%		22.8%
	No Int.	4	28	8	0	40
		0.5%	1.2%	1.1%		1.0%
	Missing	16	43	7	0	66
	TOTAL	886	2375	719	28	3980
		100.0%	100.0%	100.0%		

The table above shows that only 27.7% of the respondents who were under 30 years old said they were very interested in news about international affairs compared with 29.8% of those between 30 and 64 years old and 33.2% of those 65 and over. This relationship is statistically significant (chi-square Prob. = .0000). Interest in international affairs seems to increase with age.

Does a person's level of education influence his or her interest in news about international affairs? We can test this with the variable EDUC which measures the survey respondent's years of education.

Data File: **FPSURVEY**
Task: **Cross-tabulation**
Row Variable: **24) NEWSINTL**
➤ Column Variable: **4) EDUC**
➤ Views: **Table**
➤ Display: **Column %**

NEWSINTL by EDUC
Weight Variable: WEIGHT
Cramer's V: 0.113 **

		EDUC					
		< High Sch	H.S. Grad	Some Coll.	Coll Grad	Missing	TOTAL
NEWSINTL	Very Int.	176	333	372	314	1	1195
		25.7%	29.0%	29.0%	36.1%		30.0%
	Somewhat	247	531	645	422	13	1845
		36.0%	46.2%	50.2%	48.5%		46.2%
	Hardly Int	247	277	266	120	4	910
		35.9%	24.1%	20.7%	13.8%		22.8%
	No Int.	16	8	1	14	0	40
		2.4%	0.7%	0.1%	1.7%		1.0%
	Missing	9	24	24	9	0	66
	TOTAL	686	1150	1284	870	18	3990
		100.0%	100.0%	100.0%	100.0%		

This cross-tabulation illustrates that people with more education are more interested in international affairs. The statistically significant relationship (chi-square prob. = .0000) shows that 36.1% of the respondents with college degrees said they were very interested in international news compared to only 25.7% of the respondents with only a high school education. Education does seem to stimulate interest in foreign affairs.

If interest in foreign affairs is not distributed uniformly throughout the society, is it likely that the national interest represents the interests of all groups? This raises a fundamental question about national interest that has vexed analysts of international relations for years: What is the national interest? Followers of the realist school of thought have a simple answer for this—survival. Survival encompasses "the integrity of the nation's territory, of its political institutions, and of its culture" (Morgenthau, 1952:961). Realists believe that survival is guaranteed only through sufficient power. Thus "the signpost that helps political realism to find its way through the landscape of international politics is the concept of interest defined as power" (Morgenthau and Thompson, 1985:5). Critics of realism point out that survival can take many forms. Ann Tickner (1988), a professor of international relations at the University of Southern California, asserts that national interest is not unidimensional. There are many forms of survival. We can think of survival as maintaining the sovereign integrity, material integrity, and moral integrity of a society. A society's sovereign integrity is based (as we saw in Exercise 3) upon its territory and population. Material integrity is maintained through the survival of a society's system of economic well-being. Moral integrity is the survival of a society's moral ideals (such as democracy).

One problem with understanding the national interest is the problem of scale and public support. If the national interest is identified with grand claims that have universal support (like survival), it provides little guidance for specific policy. That is, if we can all accept that survival is our national interest, we will probably disagree about how best to ensure that survival. We can explore this problem by applying a basic model to our data on American views about foreign policy. The model has three stages: (1) there is a perceived threat to a national interest; (2) this threat generates a goal for foreign policy; and (3) specific actions or policies are pursued to achieve this goal. If our problem of scale and support is evident, we should find that where there is general agreement about the threat, there will be progressively less support for goals derived from that threat and for specific policies that implement those goals. We will examine this model in relation to the three types of survival mentioned above: sovereign integrity, material integrity, and moral integrity.

The most common threats to sovereign integrity are military threats. These are the threats that most interest realists and neo-realists. According to realism, the world is a place of competing interests where each state must fend for itself against the desires for power of the other states. The United States' chief opponent from the end of World War II through the early 1990s was the Soviet Union. By 1998, when the data we are using were collected, the Soviet Union had disbanded, but Russia still had a powerful military. We can see if the individuals in the United States agreed on a perceived threat from the Russian military.

Data File: FPSURVEY
➤ <i>Task:</i> Univariate
➤ <i>Primary Variable:</i> 31) THRRUSS
➤ <i>View:</i> Pie

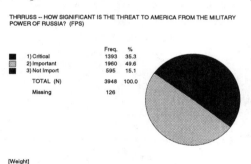

THRRUSS -- HOW SIGNIFICANT IS THE THREAT TO AMERICA FROM THE MILITARY POWER OF RUSSIA? (FPS)

		Freq.	%
■	1) Critical	1393	35.3
▨	2) Important	1960	49.6
■	3) Not Import	595	15.1
	TOTAL (N)	3948	100.0
	Missing	126	

[Weight]

We see here that by 1998, only 35.3% of the respondents in the survey believed that the Russian military posed a critical threat to the United States. There were, however, other nation-states that were seen as a threat.

Data File: FPSURVEY
Task: Univariate
➤ <i>Primary Variable:</i> 29) THRCHN
➤ <i>View:</i> Pie

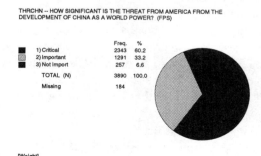

THRCHN -- HOW SIGNIFICANT IS THE THREAT FROM AMERICA FROM THE DEVELOPMENT OF CHINA AS A WORLD POWER? (FPS)

		Freq.	%
■	1) Critical	2343	60.2
▨	2) Important	1291	33.2
■	3) Not Import	257	6.6
	TOTAL (N)	3890	100.0
	Missing	184	

[Weight]

We see that 60.2% of the respondents viewed China's becoming a world power a critical threat to the United States. One might expect that those who are concerned about the power of other states will see maintaining U.S. military power as a very important goal of U.S. foreign policy. Let's check this with a cross-tabulation.

Data File: **FPSURVEY**
➤ Task: **Cross-tabulation**
➤ Row Variable: **14) GOALPOWR**
➤ Column Variable: **31) THRRUSS**
➤ Views: **Table**
➤ Display: **Column %**

GOALPOWR by THRRUSS
Weight Variable: WEIGHT
Cramer's V: 0.119 **

| | | THRRUSS | | | | |
		Critical	Important	Not Import	Missing	TOTAL
GOALPOWR	Very	932	1154	281	50	2368
		69.0%	59.8%	49.9%		61.6%
	Somewhat	363	669	204	28	1236
		26.9%	34.7%	36.2%		32.2%
	Not at All	55	107	78	8	240
		4.1%	5.5%	13.9%		6.3%
	Missing	43	30	31	40	143
	TOTAL	1350	1930	564	126	3845
		100.0%	100.0%	100.0%		

There are two rather remarkable things about this table. First, it shows that the relationship is significant (chi-square probability = .0000) but that it is fairly weak (V = 0.119). Second, among those who feel that the threat from the Russian military is critical, only 69.0% agree about power being a very important goal of U.S. foreign policy.

How does the goal of maintaining U.S. power translate into a specific policy recommendation such as increasing the U.S. defense budget? Again, one would expect that those who think that maintaining power is an important goal would want more money spent on defense.

Data File: **FPSURVEY**
Task: **Cross-tabulation**
➤ Row Variable: **2) DEFENSE**
➤ Column Variable: **14) GOALPOWR**
➤ Views: **Table**
➤ Display: **Column %**

DEFENSE by GOALPOWR
Weight Variable: WEIGHT
Cramer's V: 0.186 **

| | | GOALPOWR | | | | |
		Very	Somewhat	Not at All	Missing	TOTAL
DEFENSE	Expand	937	227	33	28	1197
		40.4%	18.4%	14.1%		31.6%
	Keep Same	864	573	78	42	1515
		37.2%	46.4%	33.3%		40.0%
	Cut Back	521	434	123	47	1077
		22.4%	35.1%	52.6%		28.4%
	Missing	96	31	15	26	168
	TOTAL	2322	1234	234	143	3789
		100.0%	100.0%	100.0%		

There is a moderate, statistically significant relationship between the respondent's view of defense spending (DEFENSE) and their view of the importance of maintaining U.S. power (chi-square probability = .0000, V = 0.186). The numbers in the first column of the table are interesting. The respondents who believe maintaining U.S. power is a very important foreign policy goal are split on the specific policy regarding the defense budget. Forty percent of the respondents who thought U.S. power was a very important foreign policy goal believed that U.S. military spending should be expanded, 37.2% believed it should be kept the same, and 22.4% believed it should be cut back.

Except in times of war, threats against the material integrity of the nation-state strike closer to home for most of the population than do military threats. These threats come from foreign competition in an increasingly global marketplace.

Data File: **FPSURVEY**
➤ *Task:* **Univariate**
➤ *Primary Variable:* **30) THRJPN**
➤ *View:* **Pie**

THRJPN -- HOW SIGNIFICANT IS THE THREAT TO AMERICA FROM ECONOMIC
COMPETITION FROM JAPAN? (FPS)

	Freq.	%
1) Critical	1831	46.6
2) Important	1849	47.1
3) Not Import	249	6.3
TOTAL (N)	3929	100.0
Missing	145	

[Weight]

The pie chart and percentages above show that 46.6% of the respondents to the survey felt that threats from the Japanese economy were critical threats to the United States. These threats come mostly in the form of fears of reduced employment in the United States because of foreign competition. Thus, one would expect that people who feel the threat from the Japanese economy is critical will see protecting U.S. jobs as a very important goal of U.S. foreign policy and that is what we find in our data.

Data File: **FPSURVEY**
➤ *Task:* **Cross-tabulation**
➤ *Row Variable:* **12) GOALJOBS**
➤ *Column Variable:* **30) THRJPN**
➤ *Views:* **Table**
➤ *Display:* **Column %**

GOALJOBS by THRJPN
Weight Variable: WEIGHT
Cramer's V: 0.129 **

		THRJPN				
		Critical	Important	Not Import	Missing	TOTAL
GOALJOBS	Very	1608	1426	164	80	3199
		89.2%	78.9%	67.6%		83.0%
	Somewhat	161	360	71	24	591
		8.9%	19.9%	29.1%		15.3%
	Not at All	34	22	8	9	64
		1.9%	1.2%	3.2%		1.7%
	Missing	28	41	6	31	107
	TOTAL	1803	1808	243	145	3854
		100.0%	100.0%	100.0%		

Among those who saw threats from the Japanese economy to be a critical threat in this figure, 89.2% believed that protecting U.S. jobs was a very important U.S. foreign policy goal. Does this overwhelming support for a policy goal translate into similar support for the policies that implement the goal? One of the key ways to protect an economy from the effects of foreign competition is to place tariffs on products imported from abroad. Tariffs are taxes that raise the price of foreign-produced goods thereby making it easier for domestic goods to compete with them. One would expect that with such a large majority believing that protecting jobs is a very important foreign policy goal, there would be similar support for placing tariffs on imported goods.

Data File: **FPSURVEY**
Task: **Cross-tabulation**
➤ *Row Variable:* **28) TARIFFS**
➤ *Column Variable:* **12) GOALJOBS**
➤ *Views:* **Table**
➤ *Display:* **Column %**

TARIFFS by GOALJOBS
Weight Variable: WEIGHT
Cramer's V: 0.140 **

		GOALJOBS				
		Very	Somewhat	Not at All	Missing	TOTAL
TARIFFS	Eliminate	978	271	35	28	1284
		36.6%	53.3%	64.2%		39.7%
	Keep	1693	238	19	27	1950
		63.4%	46.7%	35.8%		60.3%
	Missing	607	106	20	52	784
	TOTAL	2671	509	54	107	3235
		100.0%	100.0%	100.0%		

International Relations

The table shows that among those who felt that protecting U.S. jobs was a very important goal, 63.4% believed that tariffs should be kept.

In international affairs, the United States publicly stands up for its ideal of promoting democracy and protecting human rights. Are these moral imperatives seen as very important goals for U.S. foreign policy? Two univariate pie charts reveal what proportion of the American public support these goals.

Data File: **FPSURVEY**
➤ Task: **Univariate**
➤ Primary Variable: **8) GOALDEMO**
➤ View: **Pie**

GOALDEMO -- HOW IMPORTANT IS HELPING TO BRING A DEMOCRATIC FORM OF GOVERNMENT TO OTHER NATIONS AS A U.S. FOREIGN POLICY GOAL? (FPS)

	Freq.	%
1) Very	1181	30.5
2) Somewhat	2031	52.4
3) Not at All	664	17.1
TOTAL (N)	3876	100.0
Missing	198	

[Weight]

Only 30.5% of the respondents to the survey thought that supporting democratic governments is a very important foreign policy goal.

Data File: **FPSURVEY**
➤ Task: **Univariate**
➤ Primary Variable: **15) GOALRHTS**
➤ View: **Pie**

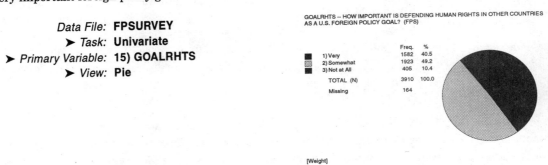

GOALRHTS -- HOW IMPORTANT IS DEFENDING HUMAN RIGHTS IN OTHER COUNTRIES AS A U.S. FOREIGN POLICY GOAL? (FPS)

	Freq.	%
1) Very	1582	40.5
2) Somewhat	1923	49.2
3) Not at All	405	10.4
TOTAL (N)	3910	100.0
Missing	164	

[Weight]

A slightly larger percentage (40.5%) believe that promoting human rights is a very important goal. These are important findings, because, as we will see in Exercise 9 on international law and organization, many of the U.S. foreign policy initiatives in the post-cold war era are intended to support democracy and protect human rights. One would expect that people who believe that such issues should guide foreign policy would support an activist foreign policy. That is, it is unlikely that such people would be isolationist. Instead, they would support active intervention—diplomatic or military—in order to promote their moral values. The variable USACTIVE asked if the respondent believed that it would be best for the future of the country if the United States takes an active part in world affairs.

Data File: **FPSURVEY**
➤ Task: **Cross-tabulation**
➤ Row Variable: **34) USACTIVE**
➤ Column Variable: **15) GOALRHTS**
➤ View: **Graph**
➤ Display: **Bar - Stack**

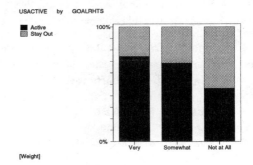

The BAR STACK graph clearly shows that those who believe that human rights is an important goal also support an active foreign policy while those who do not see human rights as a valid goal believe the United States should stay out of foreign affairs.

FORMATION OF THE NATIONAL INTEREST—ELITE VS. POPULATION ATTITUDES

One more set of questions must be addressed in this examination of the individual and national interest. In democratic states, we hope and believe that the national interest reflects the collective interests of the citizens. We understand, nevertheless, that in most representative democracies, the framing of the national interest is in the hands of a small group of people made up of government officials and leaders of business and other organizations within the society. The American Public Opinion and U.S. Foreign Policy Survey interviewed members of the general public and members of elite opinion leader groups[1] that influence the national interest. This allows us to determine whether or not the interests of the foreign policy elites are in concert with those of the general population.

Issues related to jobs are pocket-book issues that enjoy a fair amount of agreement among the populace. One threat to these issues is the threat of immigration. Immigration, especially illegal immigration, is seen by some as a serious threat to jobs and economic well-being. Our previous analysis showed that there was overwhelming belief among the populace that protecting U.S. jobs is a very important foreign policy goal. Do the opinion leader elites share this concern? Two simple cross-tabulations will examine these questions. Note that we are using a different file for these analyses.

➤ Data File: **FPELITES**
➤ Task: **Cross-tabulation**
➤ Row Variable: **11) THRIMMIG**
➤ Column Variable: **10) SAMPLE2**
➤ Views: **Table**
➤ Display: **Column %**

THRIMMIG   by   SAMPLE2
Weight Variable: WEIGHT
Cramer's V: 0.274 **

		SAMPLE2		
		Gen. Pop	Elites	TOTAL
THRIMMIG	Critical	2235	67	2302
		56.5%	17.7%	53.2%
	Important	1431	195	1626
		36.2%	51.6%	37.6%
	Not Import	286	116	402
		7.2%	30.7%	9.3%
	Missing	123	1	124
	TOTAL	3952	378	4330
		100.0%	100.0%	

---

[1] As you may remember from Exercise 1, the elite opinion leader group in the survey is itself a diverse group. It consists of religious, business, and labor leaders, members of the news media, educators, members of special interest groups, members of the House of Representatives and Senate, and members of the executive branch of the federal government.

The table provides some rather stunning results. Whereas 56.5% of the general population believe that immigration is a critical threat to U.S. foreign policy, only 17.7% of the elites believe that these threats are critical. Is there similar disagreement about the importance of protecting jobs?

Data File: **FPELITES**
Task: **Cross-tabulation**
➤ Row Variable: **5) GOALJOBS**
➤ Column Variable: **10) SAMPLE2**
➤ Views: **Table**
➤ Display: **Column %**

GOALJOBS   by   SAMPLE2
Weight Variable: WEIGHT
Cramer's V: 0.268 **

		SAMPLE2		
		Gen. Pop	Elites	TOTAL
GOALJOBS	Very	3278	169	3447
		82.6%	44.8%	79.4%
	Somewhat	615	174	789
		15.5%	46.2%	18.2%
	Not at All	74	34	108
		1.9%	9.0%	2.5%
	Missing	107	2	109
	TOTAL	3968	377	4345
		100.0%	100.0%	

Again, there is significant difference between the views of the general population and the views of this elite group. Whereas 82.6% of the general population believe that protecting jobs is a very important foreign policy goal, only 44.8% of the elite group believe that the goal is very important. There are many other differences between the views of the elites and the views of the general population. We will, however, leave these questions to the worksheets that follow and to your own explorations.

WORKSHEET

EXERCISE

6

NAME:

COURSE:

DATE:

REVIEW QUESTIONS

Based on the first part of this exercise, answer True or False to the following items:

The individual level of analysis looks only at the international relations of individual nation-states.   T   F

The individual level of analysis does not contradict the assumptions of the state level of analysis that nation-states are the primary actors in international relations.   T   F

The national interest always represents the interests of the majority of the population of a nation-state.   T   F

According to survey results, most Americans are very interested in news about U.S. foreign policy.   T   F

According to survey results, less than half of the American population is very interested in news about international affairs.   T   F

Older people generally are less interested in international affairs than are younger people.   T   F

Education stimulates interest in international affairs.   T   F

The problem of scale and public support refers to the fact that the public does not generally support grand claims that survival is the primary national interest.   T   F

While people may agree on threats to survival, there is less agreement on what policies should be followed to deal with those threats.   T   F

Both the general public and the foreign policy elites believe that protecting U.S. jobs is a very important policy goal.   T   F

EXPLORIT QUESTIONS

1.   In the preliminary section of Exercise 6, we saw that there was some disagreement about the appropriate goals of U.S. foreign policy. Now we will explore this issue in more depth. For each of the six goals for U.S. foreign policy shown in section b. below, do the following:

   a.   Rank the goals from the most important to the least important in your own mind, (1 is most important and 6 is least important).

GOALS

Most Imp   1._____

                2._____

                3._____

                4._____

                5._____

Least Imp   6._____

b.   Using Student ExplorIt, go to the data and find the percentage of respondents in the general population survey that rated each of the goals "very important" and note the percentage in the space provided below. To obtain these percentages, substitute the variable for each goal in the following Student ExplorIt guide:

> ➤ *Data File:* **FPSURVEY**
> ➤ *Task:* **Univariate**
> ➤ *Primary Variable:* _____ **(place the variable here)**
> ➤ *View:* **Pie**

Rank each goal according to your list above. Then rank each goal according to the percentage found in the survey.

Foreign Policy Goal	Variable	Your Rank	Percent	Rank
Protecting weaker nations against foreign aggression	17) GOALWEAK	_____	_____	____
Strengthening the United Nations	16) GOALUN	_____	_____	____
Defending our allies' security	7) GOALALLY	_____	_____	____
Improving the global environment	10) GOALENVI	_____	_____	____
Preventing the spread of nuclear weapons	13) GOALNUC	_____	_____	____
Stopping the flow of illegal drugs into the United States	9) GOALDRUG	_____	_____	____

c.   Write a few sentences discussing how your rankings compare with the survey rankings.

2.   As we stated in Exercises 2 and 6, realism is based on a view that nation-states have national interests and act to benefit those interests in international affairs. The main national interest is sovereign
survival. According to realism, to survive in an anarchical world one must have power, and thus, the
most important national goal is maintaining power. Look at the interests of the general public and the
elites in the foreign policy survey to see if they conform to this realist logic. Create each of the following three cross-tabulations as indicated and fill in column percentages from the first row of each table
as shown. Use the SUMMARY view to find the values for Cramer's V and the probability of the chi-
square statistic.

Maintaining power as a foreign policy goal

> *Data File:* **FPELITES**
> *Task:* **Cross-tabulation**
> *Row Variable:* **7) GOALPOWR**
> *Column Variable:* **10) SAMPLE2**
> *View:* **Tables**
> *Display:* **Column %**

a.   GOALPOWR - How important is maintaining American power as a U.S. foreign policy goal?

	General Population	Elites	Cramer's V	Prob. of Chi-Square
% Very Important	_____	_____	_____	_____

Combatting world hunger as a foreign policy goal

> *Data File:* **FPELITES**
> *Task:* **Cross-tabulation**
> *Row Variable:* **4) GOALHUNG**
> *Column Variable:* **10) SAMPLE2**
> *View:* **Tables**
> *Display:* **Column %**

b.   GOALHUNG - How important is combatting world hunger as a U.S. foreign policy goal?

	General Population	Elites	Cramer's V	Prob. of Chi-Square
% Very Important	_____	_____	_____	_____

Protecting the interests of American jobs as a foreign policy goal

                Data File: **FPELITES**
                    Task: **Cross-tabulation**
  ➤ Row Variable: **5) GOALJOBS**
➤ Column Variable: **10) SAMPLE2**
        ➤ View: **Tables**
    ➤ Display: **Column %**

c.   GOALJOBS - How important is protecting American jobs as a U.S. foreign policy goal?

	General Population	Elites	Cramer's V	Prob. of Chi-Square
% Very Important	_____	_____	_____	_____

d.   Write a paragraph that discusses your findings.

POWER IN INTERNATIONAL RELATIONS

Tasks: Mapping, Scatterplot, Cross-tabulation
Data Files: NATIONS, FPSURVEY

Power is a central concept in international relations. Power is not the same as the use of force, which we will discuss in the next exercise, but power is a key element of the use of force. What is power? This question is not easy to answer. We certainly know power when we see it. France is a powerful nation-state and Comoros is not. Yet expressing an analytical basis for this comparison can be tricky. Certainly in the 1960s and 70s the United States was one of the most powerful nation-states in the world. Yet, the small, seemingly less powerful North Vietnam was able to hold off American might, and North and South Vietnam unified under communist rule in 1975. How could it be that North Vietnam succeeded in this struggle against such a powerful opponent? Vietnam is by no means the only example of a smaller state imposing its will on an apparently powerful nation-state. The former Soviet Union met its match in Afghanistan where Soviet power was unable to succeed in the civil war from 1979 to 1985.

This phenomenon has been called the *paradox of unrealized power* (Baldwin, 1979). The paradox occurs when we put too much emphasis on the things associated with power, such as tanks or planes or even abstract things like technology and strength of will, and not enough emphasis on the elements of the relationship between the two actors. From this distinction, there are two different approaches to the definition and measurement of power. The *resources approach* (also called the means approach) defines power in terms of the resources that are used to achieve desired outcomes (capabilities of the actor). More tanks and guns means more power. The *outcomes approach* (also called the relational approach) defines power by the ability of the actor to achieve its goals. The former approach is decidedly adversarial, pitting my resources against yours. While the outcomes approach does not preclude adversarial relationships, it emphasizes success in achieving goals that can often be obtained through cooperation easier than through conflict.

MEASURING POWER—RESOURCES APPROACH

Power resources can be classified as *potential resources* or *actual resources*. Actual resources are those national capabilities that can be used directly to influence the behavior of other actors. These include military resources, such as weapons that back up threats or bring force to bear, and economic resources that can be used to encourage a target to do the actor's bidding. This is an important distinction because actual power resources can be used to create either positive or negative sanctions. *Negative sanctions* threaten or harm a target in order to gain compliance whereas *positive sanctions* reward a target for compliance. *Potential power* resources are the capabilities needed to build or deploy actual power resources.

Potential power resources include industrial capacity, economic well-being, and levels of technology and education.

Potential power is measured by a nation-state's geographic features, industrial capacity, levels of technology and education, physical infrastructure, and the will and availability of its population. One aspect of potential power is the ability to generate food supplies to sustain its population in a conflict or to use as an incentive in interactions with other nation-states. Nation-states with more arable acreage per person should have more potential power.[1]

> *Data File:* **NATIONS**
> *Task:* **Mapping**
> *Variable 1:* **11) ARABLE**
> *View:* **List: Rank**

RANK	CASE NAME	VALUE
1	Australia	6.19
2	Kazakhstan	6.09
3	Paraguay	4.22
4	Canada	3.95
5	Lithuania	2.15
6	Guyana	2.05
7	Libya	2.00
8	Botswana	1.96
9	Argentina	1.76
10	Mongolia	1.75

Using this measure, large, sparsely populated nation-states, like Australia and Kazakhstan, are seen as having high degrees of potential power. This indicates the problem with measuring power. Power is multidimensional; that is, it consists of many factors.

Traditionally, heavy industry like steel production, railroads, and automobile production were the best indicators of potential power because these were the strategic industries needed to produce ships, tanks, and airplanes. One way to measure industrial capacity is to look at the total production of steel.

> *Data File:* **NATIONS**
> *Task:* **Mapping**
> *Variable 1:* **93) STEEL**
> *View:* **List: Rank**

RANK	CASE NAME	VALUE
1	Japan	99632
2	China	89556
3	United States	88793
4	Russia	58346
5	Germany	37705
6	Ukraine	33709
7	North Korea	33141
8	Italy	25967
9	Brazil	25201
10	India	18616

While, as expected, major industrial powers like Japan, China, the United States, and Russia rank the highest in steel production, a number of seemingly unlikely states, such as North Korea and Ukraine, score high as well. In today's high technology world, the importance of the traditional "smokestack"

---

[1] An arable acre of land is one that is suitable for agriculture because it has an adequate water supply and because its terrain can be tilled. There are 640 acres in a square mile.

industries has diminished while the importance of technology and education have skyrocketed. One measure of the level of a nation-state's technology is the number of scientists and engineers it has.

<table>
<tr><td>Data File:</td><td>NATIONS</td></tr>
<tr><td>Task:</td><td>Mapping</td></tr>
<tr><td>➤ Variable 1:</td><td>90) SCIENTISTS</td></tr>
<tr><td>➤ View:</td><td>List: Rank</td></tr>
</table>

RANK	CASE NAME	VALUE
1	China	1335336.00
2	Russia	878500.00
3	Japan	705346.00
4	France	129215.00
5	India	128036.00
6	South Korea	86953.00
7	Italy	77867.00
8	Canada	65350.00
9	Australia	41837.00
10	Poland	41440.00

China reported the largest number of scientists and engineers in 1989–1995 within the sparsely recorded data. This is not surprising since China also had the largest population. Note that there were no data for the United States on this variable. The nation-states with the most scientists and engineers are the industrial countries of Europe, Asia, and the former Soviet Union.

Another measure of technological capability is the number of personal computers. Computers contribute to both potential power and actual power. Computers help industrial processes that are necessary for building military hardware. They also are increasingly becoming an essential battlefield tool. Computers are used to guide missiles and bombs, determine the location of troops, and maintain communications in the theater of war. The variable COMPUTERS in the NATIONS file estimated the number of computers per 1,000 population for a variety of nation-states in 1993.

<table>
<tr><td>Data File:</td><td>NATIONS</td></tr>
<tr><td>Task:</td><td>Mapping</td></tr>
<tr><td>➤ Variable 1:</td><td>24) COMPUTERS</td></tr>
<tr><td>➤ View:</td><td>List: Rank</td></tr>
</table>

RANK	CASE NAME	VALUE
1	United States	287
2	Australia	192
3	Canada	188
4	Norway	173
5	Denmark	168
6	Finland	167
7	United Kingdom	162
8	Sweden	150
9	New Zealand	147
10	Switzerland	140

In 1993 the United States, with 287 computers per 1,000 population, was the clear leader in personal computers. It had 95 more computers per 1,000 population than its nearest competitor (Australia at 192 per 1,000). As technology becomes more important in determining the potential power of a nation-state, education also becomes important both for creating and for using that technology. In the 18th century, the armies of the European great powers were primarily made up of uneducated peasants and mercenaries. Artillery required higher levels of mathematical and engineering skills and as this weapon became more sophisticated, the armies required higher levels of education, especially among the officer corps. The first computers that were designed and created during World War II were used to plot artillery and missile trajectories. We can explore the different education levels of today's nation-states with the EDUCATION variable in the NATIONS file.

Data File: **NATIONS**
Task: **Mapping**
➤ Variable 1: **44) EDUCATION**
➤ View: **List: Rank**

RANK	CASE NAME	VALUE
1	United States	12.3
2	Canada	12.1
3	Norway	11.6
3	France	11.6
5	Australia	11.5
5	United Kingdom	11.5
7	Sweden	11.1
7	Germany	11.1
7	Austria	11.1
7	Switzerland	11.1

The variable EDUCATION measures the average years of education for people aged 25 and older. Looking at the ranking of education again, it is clear that this measure of a state's potential power is highest among the industrial states in Europe and Asia. Education level emphasizes the importance of a nation-state's population characteristics in determining its power.

During a conflict, a nation-state's population must be willing to sacrifice life and well-being to be an effective element of power. The World Values Survey in 1993 asked questions in various countries related to the willingness of individuals to fight. The variable WILL FIGHT shows the percentage of respondents in each country who would be willing to fight to defend their nation-states.

Data File: **NATIONS**
Task: **Mapping**
➤ Variable 1: **119) WILL FIGHT**
➤ View: **List: Rank**

RANK	CASE NAME	VALUE
1	China	97
1	Latvia	97
3	Slovenia	95
4	Turkey	93
5	Belarus	92
5	Romania	92
5	India	92
5	Estonia	92
5	Poland	92
10	Norway	91

It is difficult to determine what influences a person's willingness to defend his or her state. Certainly, nationalism and willingness to fight should be high among those states such as South Korea that are currently facing external threats. One might expect that new nation-states, especially those that have recently gained their independence such as Latvia or Slovenia, would have a high proportion of people willing to fight to defend the nation-state. Neither of these factors explain why states like China or Norway are among the top ten in the ranking. Neither China nor Norway face a serious external threat and they are hardly newly emerging states. We must conclude that there are also cultural and political factors that affect a population's willingness to defend its state. If you scroll down the table, you will find that the United States ranks only 20th among the 41 nation-states for which we have data. A lack of will has often been cited as a major contributor to the paradox of unrealized power when the United States was unable to achieve its goals in Vietnam.

MILITARY POWER RESOURCES

Actual power resources are usually measured by how much military equipment and personnel a nation-state has. One such measure is the number of active duty military personnel.

Data File: **NATIONS**
Task: **Mapping**
➤ Variable 1: **65) MIL FORCES**
➤ View: **List: Rank**

RANK	CASE NAME	VALUE
1	China	2840.0
2	United States	1448.0
3	Russia	1240.0
4	North Korea	1055.0
5	India	980.0
6	South Korea	560.0
7	Pakistan	520.0
8	Iran	518.0
9	Vietnam	492.0
10	Indonesia	461.0

The nation-states with large numbers of military personnel tend to be either states with large populations, such as China, Russia, or the United States, or states with a high degree of conflict with a neighbor such as North and South Korea or Pakistan and India. The military equipment needed to establish state power is determined by many factors including geography, terrain, and potential threat. Landlocked states, such as Austria, would not normally have large navies. Tanks are more useful to a nation-state with flat terrain such as Iran than to a mountainous nation-state, such as Switzerland. Such equipment can, however, help determine the power of a nation-state.

Data File: **NATIONS**
Task: **Mapping**
➤ Variable 1: **118) WARTANKS**
➤ View: **List: Rank**

RANK	CASE NAME	VALUE
1	Russia	17100
2	United States	16813
3	China	9700
4	Syria	4600
5	Israel	4300
6	Turkey	4205
7	Ukraine	4063
8	North Korea	3500
9	India	3404
10	Germany	3248

The rank listing of the number of combat tanks illustrates that power resources are situational. The United States and Russia both have in excess of 16,000 tanks, over 7,000 more than the next highest country (China with 9,700). This force structure reflects remnants of the cold-war strategic belief that the most likely major theater of conflict was Europe, where tank warfare has a long history. Israel and Syria, both relatively small states, have exceptionally large tank forces due in part to their mutual animosity and to the open terrain in which they are likely to fight.

In the 19th and early 20th centuries, a nation-state's actual power was often directly equated with the size of its navy. It was through the navy that a state's power could be extended beyond its borders. Navies were built around huge battleships that could hurl shells weighing more than 2,000 pounds at targets many miles away.

Data File: **NATIONS**
Task: **Mapping**
➤ *Variable 1:* **117) WARSHIPS**
➤ *View:* **List: Rank**

RANK	CASE NAME	VALUE
1	United States	143
2	Russia	60
3	Japan	58
4	China	54
5	France	42
6	South Korea	40
7	United Kingdom	38
8	Taiwan	36
9	Italy	32
10	India	25

In 1900, Great Britain had 255 major warships. Today, only the United States has more than 100 combat vessels. While ships still provide the platform from which national power can be expressed, their importance has been eclipsed by the versatility and firepower of combat aircraft. In the spring of 1999, NATO states tried to force the Yugoslavian military out of the Serbian region of Kosovo. Intense diplomatic pressure was accompanied by a military campaign of aerial bombardment using only missiles and aircraft. Yugoslavia agreed to withdraw its troops after 78 days of bombardment, without any significant participation by ground forces. Clearly, the combat aircraft is a significant instrument of actual state power.

Data File: **NATIONS**
Task: **Mapping**
➤ *Variable 1:* **114) WARPLANES**
➤ *View:* **List: Rank**

RANK	CASE NAME	VALUE
1	United States	5814
2	China	4275
3	Russia	1855
4	Ukraine	905
5	India	845
6	North Korea	607
7	Syria	589
8	France	574
9	Egypt	572
10	Germany	508

The ultimate instrument of national power in modern warfare has been used only twice on the battlefield. Nuclear weapons were first developed during World War II. Both the United States and Germany had programs for developing these weapons. On August 6, 1945, the atomic bomb was first dropped on Hiroshima, Japan, by the Enola Gay, a B-29 Stratofortress. Three days later a similar bomb was dropped on the Japanese city of Nagasaki. The two bombs killed more than 200,000 people and totally destroyed two cities in an instant. The variable NUCLEAR in the NATIONS file shows the current "nuclear family" of nation-states.

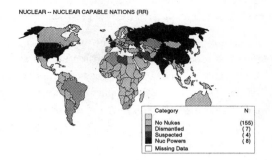

NUCLEAR -- NUCLEAR CAPABLE NATIONS (RR)

Category	N
No Nukes	(155)
Dismantled	(7)
Suspected	(4)
Nuc Powers	(8)
Missing Data	

Only the United States had nuclear weapons after World War II, but the Soviet Union immediately began a crash program to develop the new bombs. Much to the dismay of the United States, the Soviet Union tested its first nuclear device in 1949. The two largest powers surviving World War II now faced each other across a gulf of ideological difference and political competition, each holding the ultimate weapon. This was the genesis of the cold-war bipolar system that would dominate world politics from 1949 to 1991. The United Kingdom and France tested their first nuclear weapons in 1952 and 1961 respectively. China first developed nuclear weapons in 1964. The Nuclear Nonproliferation Treaty was negotiated in 1968 and has been signed by 178 states. This treaty forbids signatory states from developing nuclear weapons programs if they do not already have the weapons and prohibits nuclear powers from distributing either the weapons or the technology needed to develop the weapons to non-nuclear states. Since that time Algeria, Argentina, Brazil, and South Africa have abandoned nuclear weapons programs in response to the treaty, but both India and Pakistan publicly tested nuclear devices in 1997. This is particularly troubling because India and Pakistan have been fighting a war over disputed territory in Kashmir for many years. Although it has never publicly admitted it, Israel has a well-documented nuclear weapons program (see Hersh, 1991). Iran, Iraq, Libya, and North Korea are all suspected of having nuclear weapons programs. The break-up of the former Soviet Union left Belarus, Kazakhstan, and Ukraine holding part of the Soviet Union's nuclear arsenal. Each of these states have agreed to supervised dismantling of the weapons they hold. Thus, eight nation-states hold nuclear weapons and at least another four are suspected of developing the weapons while seven states have discontinued development programs or have dismantled existing weapons.

Nuclear weapons do not provide the ultimate instrument of power that one might think. Because of the devastating nature of the weapons, few states would consider using them unless they themselves were attacked with nuclear forces. Thus, under the perverse logic of nuclear strategy, nuclear weapons really only serve the purpose of preventing the use of nuclear weapons.

MULTIDIMENSIONAL SCALES OF POWER

If we use the power resources approach, which nation-state has the most power? Looking back over the the last few pages, we have seen so far, we see certain nation-states consistently near the top of many of the rankings. The United States, for example, ranks first on education, number of major surface warships, and number of armed combat aircraft. The U.S. ranks high on steel production, number of active duty military personnel, and combat tanks. Although it ranks only 20th overall on the willingness of its citizens to fight to defend the state, it is clear from the data, and from our expectations, that the United States is a very powerful nation-state. Russia's power, especially since the fall of the Soviet Union, is not as clear. Russia is highly ranked on variables related to actual power resources (active duty military, tanks, warships, and combat aircraft), but it ranks much lower in the variables that measure potential power (steel production, education, and computers).

The complexity of the resource approach to power prompted some analysts to create multidimensional scales to measure power. A nation-state's score on a multidimensional scale is a single number that attempts to represent the values of many variables through sometimes complex mathematical weighting formulas. The weights permit the researchers to place different importance on the various power measures used to create the scale. Ray Cline (1980) developed one of the best-known scales that attempted to capture both the tangible and intangible aspects of potential power. His formula is

$$P_p = (C + E + M)\,(S + W)$$

where Pp is potential power, C is critical mass (population and territory), E is economic capability, M is military strength, S is strategic purpose, and W is will to pursue national strategy. Some of these variables can be measured through observation (critical mass, economic capability, and military strength) but others (strategy and will) are assigned subjectively by the researcher.

J. David Singer developed another measure of power based on proportions of world resources (Singer, et al. 1972):

$$X = (P + U + S + F + M + D)\,/\,6$$

where X is the value of the Singer power index, P is the proportion of total world population, U is the proportion of world urban population, S is the proportion of world total steel production, F is the proportion of world fuel consumption, M is the proportion of total world military personnel, and D is the proportion of world total defense expenditures. We can explore these two scales with variables in the NATIONS file. The variables represent measures of power in 1980.

Data File:	**NATIONS**
Task:	**Mapping**
➤ Variable 1:	**21) CLINE80**
➤ Variable 2:	**91) SINGER80**
➤ Views:	**List: Rank**

RANK	CASE NAME	VALUE
1	Russia	1509
2	United States	1000
3	Brazil	452
4	Germany	380
5	Japan	355

RANK	CASE NAME	VALUE
1	Russia	1127
2	United States	1000
3	China	782
4	India	366
5	Japan	356

As one might expect, these two scales provide very similar views of the power of nation-states. Eight out of the top ten states in each listing are the same. The relationship between the two indices can be vividly illustrated with a SCATTERPLOT.

Data File: **NATIONS**
➤ Task: **Scatterplot**
➤ Dependent Variable: **21) CLINE80**
➤ Independent Variable: **91) SINGER80**
➤ View: **Reg. Line**

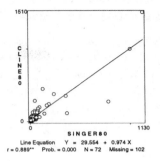

Line Equation   Y = 29.554 + 0.974 X
r = 0.889**   Prob. = 0.000   N = 72   Missing = 102

The plot shows that the two variables are closely correlated. The correlation coefficient is +0.889, which indicates a very strong, statistically significant relationship. The plot also illustrates some of the differences between the two indices. The Cline index places higher weight on military and strategic variables, while the Singer index places higher weight on potential power resources such as population and steel production. Looking back on the earlier ranking of the two indices, you can see that while both the Cline and Singer indices rank Russia and the United States first and second, there are differences in lower ranks. China and India rank high on the Singer index, due mostly to their high populations, whereas Brazil and Germany rank high on the Cline index due to physical area and strength of economy respectively.

MEASURING POWER—OUTCOMES APPROACH

One reason for the paradox of unrealized power is that power resources are often infungible. That is, they cannot be transferred easily from one use to another. The United States learned this well in Vietnam. In the 1960s, much of the actual military resource of the United States was designed to meet another major power, such as the Soviet Union, in an open field of battle. Armored tank divisions were of limited use in the jungle warfare in Southeast Asia. Strategic nuclear weapons are other infungible resources. The billions of dollars of nuclear missiles that formed the basis of the military deterrence during the cold war cannot easily be switched to another use in the post-cold war era. Infungible resources like these contribute to the paradox of unrealized power because apparently powerful states may not be able to transfer their power resources to new situations.

Robert Dahl (1957), an American political scientist, addressed this problem by noting that the resources approach is misleading. Power is known only by the outcome of the relationship between the actor and the target. Dahl's now famous definition of power was "A has power over B to the extent that he can get B to do something that B would not otherwise do." Dahl identified five key components of power. The basis of power is something that B values that A can affect by threat, attack, or reward. The basis might be a nation-state's economic well-being, as in the case of economic sanctions, or its physical survival, as in the case of war. The means of power are the actual and potential power resources that A can bring to bear in the power event. The scope of power is the range of B's actions over which A might have some influence. The range of power is the set of actors that A might be able to affect. Finally, the amount of power is the increased likelihood that B will perform the desired action after the power event.

As we mentioned at the beginning of this exercise, the outcomes approach defines power in terms of what happens in a relationship between two nation-states, not in terms of the resources that each state can bring to bear on the situation. Measuring the outcomes approach is difficult—if not impossible.

Measuring outcomes requires knowing the desired result of each interaction for each nation-state and noting which states were successful in obtaining their desired results.

There are many more questions to be answered about power in the international system. Some of these will be addressed in Exercise 8 where we will discuss the use of force. Some of the questions you can now answer yourself using Student ExplorIt.

REVIEW QUESTIONS

Based on the first part of this exercise, answer True or False to the following items:

The paradox of unrealized power occurs whenever a nation cannot get what it wants.	T	F
The resources approach to power defines power only in terms of the natural resources a nation-state has.	T	F
The outcomes approach defines power in terms of whether or not a nation-state is able to get what it wants in its relations with other nation-states.	T	F
Potential power resources include natural resources, such as coal, that have not yet been mined.	T	F
One reason for the paradox of unrealized power is that power resources are often infungible.	T	F
The basis of power refers to the number of guns, tanks, and other military hardware that can be used to influence the actions of other international actors.	T	F
The range of power is the set of other actors that an actor might be able to affect.	T	F
North Korea produces more steel than the United Kingdom and Canada combined.	T	F
Nation-states with high industrial output tend to have high percentages of people who say they are willing to fight to defend their country.	T	F
Only 8 nation-states are known to be nuclear powers, although others are suspected to have weapons or programs in progress.	T	F

EXPLORIT QUESTIONS

1. In the preliminary section of Exercise 7, we noted that the resources approach to power can be divided into potential resources and actual resources. Since potential resources are those that are used to create actual resources, one might expect that there are high correlations between these two sets of variables. Let's explore our data to see if this is true. Below, you will find two lists. List A contains the variables we examined in Exercise 7 to measure potential power resources. List B contains the variables that we used to measure actual power resources.

List A: Potential Power Resources

11) ARABLE - acreage of arable land

93) STEEL - output of steel

24) COMPUTERS - number of PC's

44) EDUCATION - average years of education

119) WILL FIGHT - percentage who will fight

List B: Actual Power Resources

65) MIL FORCES - number of military personnel

118) WARTANKS - number of combat tanks

114) WARPLANES - number of armed combat aircraft

117) WARSHIPS - number of major surface naval ships

a.   Think about the relationship between these potential power resources and these actual power resources. Select a potential power resource from list A that you think will be a good predictor for an actual power resource in list B. Use Student ExplorIt to create a scatterplot using your selected variable from list A as your independent variable and your selected variable from list B as your dependent variable.

> ➤ *Data File:* **NATIONS**
> ➤ *Task:* **Scatterplot**
> ➤ *Dependent Variable:* **Your variable from list B**
> ➤ *Independent Variable:* **Your variable from list A**
> ➤ *View:* **Reg. Line**

What is the correlation between the two variables?   r = _____

Is the correlation significant (i.e., does it have an asterisk)?   Yes   No

Does the correlation for the graph show that high levels of your selected potential power resource are associated with high levels of your selected actual power resource? (Circle one)   Yes   No

b.   Choose another potential power resource and actual power resource that you think are related. Use Student ExplorIt to create another scatterplot using the variable from list A as your independent variable and the variable from list B as your dependent variable.

> *Data File:* **NATIONS**
> *Task:* **Scatterplot**
> *Dependent Variable:* **Your variable from list B**
> *Independent Variable:* **Your variable from list A**
> ➤ *View:* **Reg. Line**

What is the correlation between the two variables? r = _____

Is the correlation significant (i.e., does it have an asterisk)? Yes No

Does the correlation for the graph show that higher levels of your
selected potential power resource are associated with high
levels of your selected actual power resource? (Circle one) Yes No

2. Exercise 7 showed that measuring power is sometimes difficult. There are many variables that provide sometimes conflicting views of power. It is easy to see that nation-states like China, the United
States, or Russia are powerful. It is harder to determine the relative power of smaller nation-states.
Let's explore this question with our data. Below is a table showing four nation-states and four power
resource variables. Use the rank listing view of the MAPPING function for each variable to fill in the
table with the rank of the states for each of the variables. The four variables are

93) STEEL Crude steel production in millions of metric tons

119) WILL FIGHT Percentage of population who say they are willing to fight to defend their country

76) OIL3 Percentage of total world oil reserves

65) MIL FORCES Number of active duty military forces in thousands

To get the rankings for each variable, do the following in Student ExplorIt:

Data File: **NATIONS**
➤ Task: **Mapping**
➤ Variable 1: _____
➤ View: **List: Rank**

a. Enter the nation-state's ranking for each variable in the following table.

	STEEL	WILL FIGHT	OIL3	MIL FORCE
Argentina	_____	_____	_____	_____
Mexico	_____	_____	_____	_____
Nigeria	_____	_____	_____	_____
Turkey	_____	_____	_____	_____

b.   One way to rank the power of these countries is to add each country's ranking for each of the four variables and consider lower total scores to mean a nation is more powerful. Use this method of ranking to rank the four nation-states in the table above from most powerful to least powerful, indicating in parentheses the score for each nation.

MOST POWERFUL   _____   (_____)

                                 _____   (_____)

                                   _____   (_____)

LEAST POWERFUL   _____   (_____)

c.   Comment on the ease or difficulty of completing this problem.

3.   As we saw in Exercise 6, individuals often have different views about foreign policy. Do all demographic groups feel that acquiring and maintaining national power is a vital national goal? We saw in Exercise 3 that women in the United States were less likely to think that maintaining military power was a very important foreign policy goal than were men. What other demographic differences exist in views on power? You can explore these differences using the data from the 1994 American Public Opinion and U.S. Foreign Policy Study. Demographic variables in the FPSURVEY file include

        4) EDUC - education level,

        26) RACE - ethnic and racial identification, and

        21) INCOME - family income.

Also look at one political variable:

        22) LIBCONS - political ideology

Run the following cross-tabulation in Student ExplorIt using 14) GOALPOWR as the dependent variable (row variable) and each of the variables above as the independent variable (column variable). Fill in the tables below from the output.

➤ *Data File:* **FPSURVEY**
➤ *Task:* **Cross-tabulation**
➤ *Row Variable:* **14) GOALPOWR**
➤ *Column Variable:* _____
➤ *View:* **Table**
➤ *Display:* **Column %**

Copy the column percentages into the appropriate cells of the tables below then look at the

➤ *View:* **Statistics (Summary)**

and enter the Cramer's V statistic in the table and note whether or not the relationship is statistically significant.

In the table below, enter the column percentage responding "very important" for each category of each variable. Also note the Cramer's V and note if the relationship is significant. Remember that a statistical relationship is statistically significant if the probability of the chi-square statistic is less than .05.

	LT H.S.	H.S. Grad.	Some Coll.	Coll. Grad	Cramer's V	Prob. of Chi Sq.
EDUC	_____	_____	_____	_____	_____	_____

	Caucasian	Other	Cramer's V	Prob. of Chi Sq.
RACE	_____	_____	_____	_____

	LT $30K	$30–49K	$50K +	Cramer's V	Prob. of Chi Sq.
INCOME	_____	_____	_____	_____	_____

	Conserv.	Neutral	Liberal	Cramer's V	Prob. of Chi Sq.
LIBCONS	_____	_____	_____	_____	_____

a. Which of these independent variables is most strongly related to the dependent variable, GOALPOWR? _____

b. Which of these independent variables is least strongly related to the dependent variable, GOALPOWR? _____

c. Briefly comment on the results in this cross-tabulation. Remember that if the probability of the chi-square is more than .05 (i.e., not significant), we cannot rule out the possibility that the observed relationship is due to random chance. Also remember that the Cramer's V value ranges from 0 to 1 where values close to zero mean little or no relationship and values close to 1 mean a strong relationship between the two variables.

THE USE OF FORCE

To some, it is a plague which ought to be eliminated; to others, a crime which ought to be punished; to still others, it is an anachronism which no longer serves any purpose. On the other hand, there are some who take a more receptive attitude toward war, and regard it as an adventure which may be interesting, an instrument which may be legitimate and appropriate, or a condition of existence for which one must be prepared.

QUINCY WRIGHT (1942:3)

Tasks: Historical Trends, Cross-tabulation, Univariate, Mapping
Data Files: WARHIST, WARS, WARACTOR, NATIONS, FPSURVEY, FPELITES

What is war? Like power in the previous exercise, we know warfare when we see it, but defining war in an analytical way may be more difficult than it seems at first. William Tecumseh Sherman once said, "War is hell." While this may be glib, it is important to understand that he was speaking to the 1879 graduating class at the Michigan Military Academy. This grizzled old warrior was trying to impress upon these future officers that war is not about glory, it is about death and destruction. John Rourke (1989:281) defined war in his international relations textbook as "the organized killing of human beings." While war is surely this, the definition also applies to criminal activities. Crime control often uses war as a metaphor, as in the "war on drugs." This is meant to invoke the image of an organized campaign against a social problem.

Perhaps one of the best-known definitions of war was given by Baron Carl von Clausewitz. Clausewitz was a retired Prussian general who knew war well when he wrote his book, *On War*. "War is not merely a political act but also a political instrument, a continuation of political relations, a carrying out of the same by other means" (Clausewitz, 1962:23). There are two interpretations of this definition. According to the first interpretation, war is at root a political act. Neither is it separate from politics, nor should it be. Politics is the process by which authoritative decisions are made and implemented. War is the ultimate result of this process. According to the second interpretation, war is a political instrument that can be used to obtain other ends. War provides an implied threat that sets the stage for diplomatic negotiations. When the United States and its NATO allies negotiated with Yugoslavia in December 1998 over the status of the Kosovo province, it did so with the implied threat that failure to come to an agreement would result in war. After the negotiations failed, war was used as a tool to obtain compliance by the Yugoslav government. The intent was not to defeat Yugoslavia's armed forces but, rather, to use war to obtain a diplomatic goal.

While Baron von Clausewitz's definition is useful for understanding the use and purpose of warfare, it does little to help us define and identify wars per se. When does an international conflict rise to the level of war? A border dispute between North and South Korea in which two squads of soldiers exchange fire and two people are killed may not constitute war while the invasion of Kuwait by thousands of Iraqi troops does constitute war. We can apply arbitrary standards to resolve these definitional questions, but such standards will, by nature, be open to criticism because they may be set too high or too low. J. David Singer and Melvin Small addressed these questions in their seminal study of war known as the Correlates of War project (Small and Singer, 1982). The project attempted to gather data about all civil and international wars from 1816 through 1991. The first steps in the project were to define what constitutes war and to classify wars as civil or international. Our concern in this book is only with international wars. The Correlates of War project began its definition of international war with an examination of the international system over the period of the study. As we discussed in Exercise 3, the international system is defined by its actors. The problem is that these actors and the international system itself are constantly changing. In 1816, the modern nation-state was still primarily a European phenomenon. Many colonies were held by European states in Latin America, but Africa and Asia were largely independent of European influence. Most of the Latin American colonies gained their independence by the end of the 1820s. During the rest of the 19th century, European imperialism spread into the Middle East, Africa, and parts of Asia. By 1991, most of the colonies had gained their independence to become recognized nation-states. Thus, it is difficult to construct a definition of "system member" that is consistent across the 176 years of the study.

Singer and Small defined a member of the interstate system as a political entity with at least 500,000 population and with either diplomatic recognition by two major powers or membership in the United Nations or the League of Nations. International wars were defined as deadly conflicts that involved at least one interstate system member and in which there were at least 1,000 battle-related deaths. Using this definition, the project identified 209 international wars. These wars were further classified as interstate wars, imperial wars, and colonial wars. Interstate wars involved two or more members of the interstate system. Imperial wars included one member of the interstate system, but the adversary was an independent political entity that did not qualify as a member of the interstate system because of population size, limitations on independence, or failure to achieve the necessary recognition. Colonial wars involved one interstate system member with an adversary that was a colony, dependency, or protectorate of some interstate system member. The WARHIST file contains information on wars for each of the years from 1816 through 1991. The variable WARS in the WARHIST file shows the number of interstate wars that meet the Correlates of War definition that were initiated per year for the years 1816–1991.

> *Data File:* **WARHIST**
> > *Task:* **Historical Trends**
> *Variable:* **10) WARS**

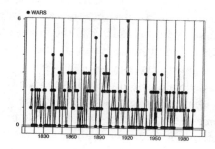

Number of wars started per year

Although war is common in the international system, the graph shows that there were few years in which more than one or two wars were started. One notable exception was 1919 when six wars started in the aftermath of World War I as European power was realigned. You can see the names of the wars by clicking on 1919 on the time-line at the bottom of the graph. The broad fluctuations in numbers of wars initiated per year make the above graph difficult to interpret. Some trends may emerge if we look at the number of wars initiated in five-year intervals, shown in the graph below.

Data File: **WARHIST**
Task: **Historical Trends**
➤ Variable: **11) WARS5**

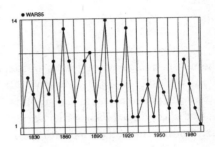

Number of wars in five year intervals

The graph shows that wars seemed to rise and fall. The 19th century generally had more wars initiated, but as we shall see later, the wars of the 20th century tended to be more intense in terms of creating casualties.

Another way to explore the number of international wars is to examine the cumulative total number of wars from 1816 to 1991.

Data File: **WARHIST**
Task: **Historical Trends**
➤ Variable: **9) WAR TOTAL**

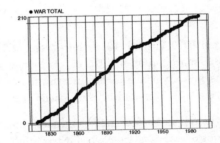

Cumulative number of wars from 1816 to 1991

The graph shows that the total number of international wars since 1816 rises at a relatively constant rate through 1991. The data are still misleading because some of these wars were very short such as when India annexed the autonomous region of Hyderabad in 1948. The Hyderabad War lasted only 5 days. Other wars were much longer, such as the Eritrean War of independence against Ethiopia that started in 1974 and was still ongoing 17 years later when the Correlates of War projected ended its data collection. One way to compensate for these differences is to count nation-months of warfare rather than wars. Nation-months are measured as the number of months that one participant is at war. For example, if two nation-states fight a war that lasts one year, the war itself has 24 nation-months (2 participants times 12 months of warfare). Thus a short war with many participants may have more nation-months than a longer war with only two participants.

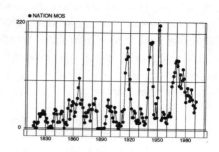

Nation-months of war per year

The nation-months vary greatly but tend to increase throughout the 20th century with peaks during World War I (1914–1918), World War II (1939–1945), and the Korean War (1950–1953). A particularly interesting phenomenon in the graph is the high number of nation-months of warfare from 1960 through the end of the data. Much of this warfare was surrogate fighting for alignment during the cold war. This is particularly evident if we look at the cumulative total number of nation-months of war from 1900 to 1991.

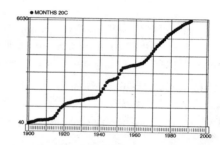

Cumulative total of nation-months of war from 1900–1992

From 1900 through 1949, there were 2,678 nation-months of war. From 1950 through 1991, there were 3,346 more nation-months of war bringing the total for 1900–1991 to 6,024 (2,678 + 3,346). Thus there was more warfare in the international system from 1950 through 1991 than there was from 1900 through 1949, including the periods of the two world wars.

Although interstate war dominates most international relations study and practice, the other two forms of extrasystemic war far outnumbered interstate war during the period from 1816 through 1991. The WARS file contains data on all the wars in the Correlates of War project. That is, it contains information on each war from 1816 through 1991 that met the project's definition of international war.

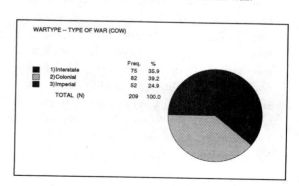

The pie chart shows that during this period, interstate war, as defined by the Correlates of War project, constituted only 35.9% of the total number of wars. Colonial wars made up 39.2% of the total while imperial wars accounted for only 24.9% of the international wars since 1816. Yet, as we mentioned before, the international system was not constant through this time.

> *Data File:* **WARHIST**
> > *Task:* **Historical Trends**
> *Variable:* **6) INTERSTATE**
> > **2) COLONIAL**
> > **5) IMPERIAL**

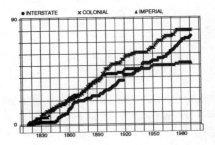

The graph shows the cumulative total number of wars from 1816 to 1991 for interstate, colonial, and imperial wars. The cumulative number of imperial wars rose to around 50 and leveled off in about 1920. The total number of colonial wars rose dramatically from 1816 but leveled off at a total of about 80 in 1976. There were no new colonial wars between that time and the end of the data collection in 1991. The total number of interstate wars increased steadily from around 1843 to 1991. Colonial wars leveled off primarily because by 1976 there were few colonies left in the international system. Imperial wars tapered off after 1920 because from the end of World War I, most of the world's territory either was claimed as some state's colony or was an independent nation-state.

Since 1816, wars have been fought in all corners of the globe. Nevertheless, certain regions of the world seem to have a higher incidence of war than others.

> *Data File:* **WARS**
> > *Task:* **Univariate**
> *Primary Variable:* **8) REGION**
> > *View:* **Pie**

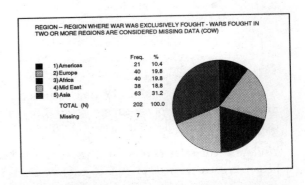

The pie chart reveals that Asia had the most wars and Latin American had the least. Geographic region also affected the type of war that was fought. One hypothesis that seems logical is that Europe had more interstate wars compared with other regions while Africa had more colonial wars from 1816 through 1991. This fits our understanding of the history of the nation-state system whereby the modern nation-state was born of a European model and exported to the other regions during colonial expansion. We can explore this hypothesis with the Correlates of War data.

Exercise 8: The Use of Force

Data File:	**WARS**
➤ Task:	**Cross-tabulation**
➤ Row Variable:	**3) WARTYPE**
➤ Column Variable:	**8) REGION**
➤ Views:	**Table**
➤ Display:	**Column %**

WARTYPE   by   REGION
Cramer's V: 0.310 **

		REGION						
		Americas	Europe	Africa	Mid East	Asia	Missing	TOTAL
WARTYPE	Interstate	14	19	3	14	19	6	69
		66.7%	47.5%	7.5%	36.8%	30.2%		34.2%
	Colonial	5	16	25	18	18	0	82
		23.8%	40.0%	62.5%	47.4%	28.6%		40.6%
	Imperial	2	5	12	6	26	1	51
		9.5%	12.5%	30.0%	15.8%	41.3%		25.2%
	TOTAL	21	40	40	38	63	7	202
		100.0%	100.0%	100.0%	100.0%	100.0%		

Comparing the column percentages across the top row (interstate wars), it is clear that the majority of the wars in the Americas were interstate wars (66.7%). On reflection, this makes sense because by the 1830s nearly all the European colonies in the Western Hemisphere had gained independence. Also, nearly all the land in the Western Hemisphere was claimed by one of the American nation-states leaving little room for imperial expansion and few of the American nation-states held colonies. Continuing across the top row, we can see that 47.5% of the European wars were interstate wars compared to only 7.5% of the African wars. As expected, most of the African wars were colonial wars (look in the second row where the cell for Africa is 62.5%). These differences can be dramatically illustrated if you look at the BAR STACK view of the relationship between WARTYPE and REGION.

Data File:	**WARS**
Task:	**Cross-tabulation**
Row Variable:	**3) WARTYPE**
Column Variable:	**8) REGION**
➤ Views:	**Graph**
➤ Display:	**Bar - Stack**

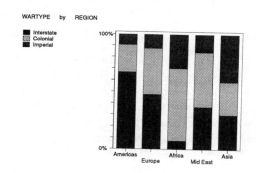

A quick look at the SUMMARY view of the same table shows that the relationship is statistically significant (probability of chi-square < .05). The Cramer's V statistic shows a moderately strong association between the two variables (V = 0.310).

William Tecumseh Sherman was right. War is hell. It is about death and destruction, not glory and honor. As such, we need to explore just how much death war has caused since 1816.

➤ Data File:	**WARHIST**
➤ Task:	**Historical Trends**
➤ Variable:	**3) DEATHS**

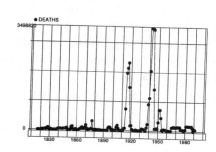

Total number of battle connected deaths per year–1816 to 1992

132

The graph shows two very prominent spikes. While all war involves death, history had not seen wars like World Wars I and II. The DEATHS variable in the graph shows only the deaths of members of the armed forces of the combatant actors, so even these estimates do not represent the actual human loss. Nevertheless, the graph vividly depicts that World War I accounted for over 8.5 million battle-related deaths and World War II accounted for over 15 million battle-related deaths. Another way to examine the number of deaths is to add the cumulative total number of deaths over time. The variable DEATHS TOT shows this cumulative death toll since 1815.

Data File: **WARHIST**
Task: **Historical Trends**
➤ Variable: **12) DEATHS TOT**

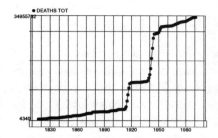

Cumulative total of battle connected deaths to 1991

The graph shows that the cumulative number of battle-related deaths rose slowly throughout the period 1816–1991 with the two dramatic exceptions of the two world wars. It also shows that during the 176 years of the Correlates of War project, nearly 35 million people were killed in direct combat.

WHY WAR?

Why is there so much war? As Clausewitz pointed out, wars are the outcome of an intentional political process. People choose to go to war. Wars do not merely "break out." People who make this choice may feel that they are forced into war due to the circumstances of either the needs of their nation-state or the conditions they face in the international system. Like any phenomenon in international relations, we can seek explanations for this behavior using the individual, state, and system levels of analysis.

INDIVIDUAL-LEVEL EXPLANATIONS OF WAR

In what situation would you decide to go to war? At the individual level, we need to examine the interests of the population as well as the interests of policy-makers. We will leave the policy-makers for the worksheets. We can explore what the American public has said about its willingness to go to war using the data from the American Public Opinion and U.S. Foreign Policy study conducted by the Chicago Council on Foreign Affairs in 1998. The survey described a series of hypothetical international situations and asked the respondents if they would be willing to send U.S. troops to resolve the situation.

In 1991 the United States led a military action against Iraq after Iraq invaded Kuwait and threatened Saudi Arabia. Would U.S. residents be willing, once again, to defend Saudi Arabia from an Iraqi attack?

> *Data File:* **FPSURVEY**
> *Task:* **Univariate**
> *Primary Variable:* **35) WARIRAQ**
> *View:* **Pie**

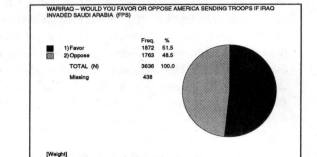

A slim majority of the respondents (51.5%) favored defending Saudi Arabia, but the difference between those who favored U.S. involvement and those opposed to it was within the survey's margin of error. Another nation-state that has been an ally in the Middle East is Israel. The United States was the first nation-state to recognize Israel's declaration of sovereignty in 1948 after a United Nations General Assembly resolution partitioned the former British mandate of Palestine in 1947 into Jewish and Arab sectors. From that time forward, Israel and the United States have had a particularly close military and economic relationship. Were the respondents to the survey willing to defend Israel against an Arab attack?

Data File: **FPSURVEY**
Task: **Univariate**
> *Primary Variable:* **36) WARISR**
> *View:* **Pie**

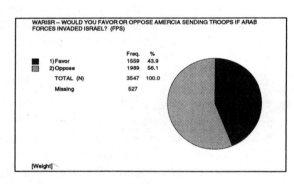

No, only 43.9% of the respondents favored sending U.S. troops to defend Israel.

One of the variables (WARPOL) asked respondents if they thought that the United States should send troops to aid Poland if Russia invaded.

Data File: **FPSURVEY**
Task: **Univariate**
> *Primary Variable:* **37) WARPOL**
> *View:* **Pie**

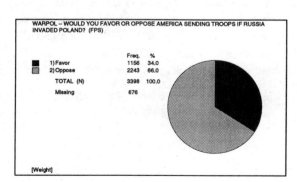

In this situation, only 34.0% of the respondents favored committing U.S. military resources to defend Poland against Russia.

International Relations

Why are Americans willing to commit troops to some areas but not to others? The state-level analysis tells us that these differences are because of different perceptions of national interest. Saudi Arabia holds the world's largest reserves of crude oil, so it could be that people responded to defending this oil rather than the more abstract concept of defending the state of Saudi Arabia. The individual-level analysis tells us to look for explanations that are embedded in the characteristics of the individual respondents. One of these differences is religion. While Israel holds a geopolitically important position in the Middle East, it also enjoys major support from the Jewish population of the United States. We can see how religious differences affect individual views on the use of force.

Data File: **FPSURVEY**
➤ Task: **Cross-tabulation**
➤ Row Variable: **36) WARISR**
➤ Column Variable: **27) RELIG**
➤ Views: **Graph**
➤ Display: **Bar - Stack**

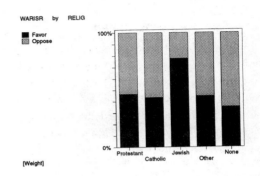

The bar stack graph dramatically shows that support for defending Israel against Arab attack is highest among Jewish respondents. The SUMMARY view of the cross-tabulation shows a weak association between religion and willingness to defend Israel that is statistically significant (chi-square probability < .0005 and Cramer's V = 0.117).

Support for defending Israel also varies according to demographic variables such as education. This should not be surprising, because individuals' perceptions of the importance of Israel to U.S. interests also vary depending on these variables.

Data File: **FPSURVEY**
Task: **Cross-tabulation**
Row Variable: **36) WARISR**
➤ Column Variable: **4) EDUC**
➤ Views: **Graph**
➤ Display: **Bar - Stack**

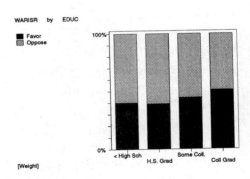

People with higher education are more likely to have business and professional connections in Israel. They are also more likely to understand the geopolitical strategic importance of Israel in U.S. foreign policy. This is demonstrated in the bar stack graph. Support for defending Israel increased as the respondents' education level increased. For example, only 40.1% of the respondents with less than a high school education favored sending U.S. troops to defend Israel compared to 50.9% of the respondents with college degrees.

Operation Desert Storm in 1991 was a joint military campaign of units from 31 nation-states to defend Saudi Arabia against Iraq and to liberate Kuwait from Iraqi occupation. Operation Allied Force in 1999 was carried out by the member states of the North Atlantic Treaty Organization to stop Yugoslavia from violence against the ethnic Albanian people in Kosovo, a province of Yugoslavia. Both of these major military campaigns emphasized the importance of coalition warfare in the post-cold war era. Increasingly, the United States will be faced with situations where it must commit its troops to multilateral peacekeeping and peacemaking campaigns. How did the American public feel about U.S. troops participating in multilateral peacekeeping efforts?

Data File: **FPSURVEY**
➤ Task: **Univariate**
➤ Primary Variable: **25) PKEEP**
➤ View: **Pie**

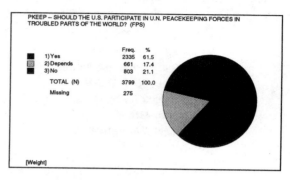

The pie chart shows that the majority of respondents (61.5%) favored U.S. participation in peacekeeping missions.

STATE-LEVEL EXPLANATIONS OF WAR

State-level explanations in international relations are derived from the behavior and characteristics of nation-states and other significant collective actors (such as major ethnic groups or nationalist organizations). One of the first things we must discover in order to use state-level explanations is how common war is among the nation-states.

➤ Data File: **NATIONS**
➤ Task: **Univariate**
➤ Primary Variable: **115) WARS**
➤ View: **Statistics (Summary)**

WARS -- NUMBER OF WARS ENTERED INTO FROM 1815-1991 (COW)

| Mean: | 2.720 | Std Dev.: | 6.651 | N: | 150 |
| Median: | 1.000 | Variance: | 44.230 | Missing: | 24 |

99% confidence interval +/- mean: 1.317 to 4.123
95% confidence interval +/- mean: 1.652 to 3.788

Value	Freq.	%	Cum.%	Z-Score
0	74	49.3	49.3	-0.409
1	22	14.7	64.0	-0.259
2	13	8.7	72.7	-0.108
3	12	8.0	80.7	0.042
4	5	3.3	84.0	0.192
5	6	4.0	88.0	0.343
6	3	2.0	90.0	0.493
7	4	2.7	92.7	0.644
8	1	0.7	93.3	0.794
9	3	2.0	95.3	0.944
13	1	0.7	96.0	1.546
15	1	0.7	96.7	1.846
17	1	0.7	97.3	2.147
25	1	0.7	98.0	3.350
27	1	0.7	98.7	3.651
44	1	0.7	99.3	6.207
52	1	0.7	100.0	7.410

Although our image of international relations often revolves around the centrality of warfare, nearly half of the current nation-states (49.3%) did not participate in an international war between 1816 and 1991. A clear majority of nation-states (64%) were in no more than one war during that period (look at the cumulative percentage column). There were some states, however, that engaged in many wars. We can see which states had the most wars by ranking the WARS variable.

Data File:	**NATIONS**
Task:	**Mapping**
➤ Variable 1:	**115) WARS**
➤ View:	**List: Rank**

RANK	CASE NAME	VALUE
1	United Kingdom	52
2	France	44
3	Turkey	27
4	Russia	25
5	China	17
6	Italy	15
7	Spain	13
8	Japan	9
8	Austria	9
8	United States	9

From 1816 to 1991, the United Kingdom had 52 wars that met the Correlates of War project's definition of international war. Many of these were colonial and imperial wars, since the research period spans the height of the British empire. France was second in the ranking with 44 international wars. What characteristics link the top ten nation-states? All of the top ten states, with the possible exceptions of Italy and the United States, were major imperial or colonial powers during the period 1816–1991. Some, like Austria, Spain, and Turkey, were losing their empires. Japan was building its empire during this period. Most of the top ten, with the exception of China and Japan, were members of the core European system. Yet other core European states, like Germany, did not have as many wars. Germany, ranked 11th with eight wars, went through dramatic changes from 1816 to 1991. In fact, prior to 1870, the data shown for Germany actually apply to the state of Prussia. It was not until 1870 that a number of northern European states unified to form Germany. The data for Germany also do not include the period 1945–1989 when Germany was split into the German Democratic Republic (East Germany) and the Federal Republic of Germany (West Germany). During this period, however, neither East nor West Germany engaged in an international war that fits the definition.

All of the nation-states at the top of the WARS ranking were relatively large nation-states. Are large nation-states more likely to go to war than small nation-states? To answer this question, we can focus on a subset of the entire Correlates of War research period. The variable WAR45–91 simply notes whether or not a nation-state entered a war between 1945 and 1991. The variable POP77B categorizes 1977 population at the median, giving us a measure of low population and high population nation-states.

Data File:	**NATIONS**
➤ Task:	**Cross-tabulation**
➤ Row Variable:	**113) WAR45–91**
➤ Column Variable:	**80) POP77B**
➤ Views:	**Graph**
➤ Display:	**Bar - Stack**

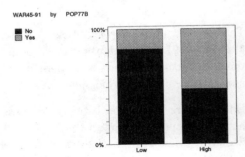

The graph shows that large states are much more likely than small states to have entered a war. There can be many reasons for this. Large nation-states have more complex interests. Large nation-states may have more enemies. They have longer borders, which may stimulate dispute. Large nation-states also have more resources for pursuing their goals with warfare. Regarding this last issue, we might expect that rich nation-states have more war than poor nation-states. We can test this with a measure of the gross national product per capita in 1977.

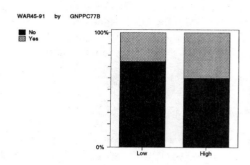

Data File: **NATIONS**
Task: **Cross-tabulation**
Row Variable: **113) WAR45–91**
➤ Column Variable: **51) GNPPC77B**
➤ Views: **Graph**
➤ Display: **Bar - Stack**

While there appears to be a difference in the number of wars between high GNP per capita and low GNP per capita nation-states, this difference is not statistically significant (probability of chi-square = 0.098; Cramer's V = 0.154). This means that we cannot say with certainty that our findings are not due to random chance.

National resources can both facilitate war and be the target of war. It seems unlikely that a nation-state will be attacked because of its gross national product, but vital natural resources such as oil can cause an attack. When Iraq attacked Kuwait in August 1990 one of the issues was Iraq's claims that Kuwait had "slant drilled" oil wells from its side of the border to tap the rich Rumaila oil field in southern Iraq. Do nation-states with high oil reserves enter more wars than those with less oil?

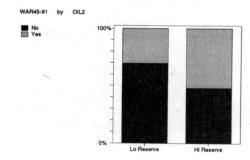

Data File: **NATIONS**
Task: **Cross-tabulation**
Row Variable: **113) WAR45–91**
➤ Column Variable: **75) OIL2**
➤ Views: **Graph**
➤ Display: **Bar - Stack**

The bar stack graph shows that 52.2% of the nation-states with high oil reserves entered a war between 1945 and 1991 compared to only 30.4% of the nation-states with low oil reserves. The SUMMARY view of the cross-tabulation shows that there is a weak association between oil reserves and war, but that this association is statistically significant (probability of chi-square = 0.034, Cramer's V = 0.221).

One theory regarding war is that democracies do not fight with other democracies. Unfortunately, we do not have enough data to test this hypothesis because we do not have data on which nation-states go to war with which other nation-states. In Exercise 5 we found that there was no apparent relationship between the type of government and the number of wars fought between 1945 and 1991. Is there, however, a relationship between the level of democratic freedoms and whether or not the nation-state initiated a war between 1945 and 1991?

Data File: **NATIONS**

Task: **Cross-tabulation**

➤ Row Variable: **112) WAR START**

➤ Column Variable: **36) DEMOCRACY2**

➤ Views: **Graph**

➤ Display: **Bar - Stack**

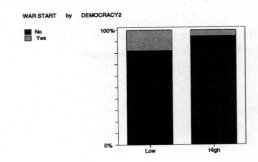

The graph shows that although few nation-states have initiated war since 1945, it appears that nation-states with a high degree of democratic freedoms initiated fewer wars than non-democratic states. This difference, though small, is statistically significant (chi-square probability = 0.012, Cramer's V = 0.191). It appears that our limited data support the theory that democratic nation-states are less likely to go to war, in general.

SYSTEM-LEVEL EXPLANATIONS OF WAR

The characteristics of the international system may contribute to the causes of war. Superpowers in the bipolar system pursue competition with their opponent through surrogate conflict in non-aligned states. This should mean that there is little warfare within a superpower's pole but that there should be increased levels of war among the non-aligned states. In Exercise 4, we used the variable ALIGN CW to indicate alignment with either the United States or the Soviet Union during the cold war. We can use a cross-tabulation to see if this measure of alignment is associated with the number of wars entered between 1945 and 1991.

Data File: **NATIONS**

Task: **Cross-tabulation**

Row Variable: **112) WAR START**

➤ Column Variable: **10) ALIGN CW**

➤ Views: **Table**

➤ Display: **Column %**

WAR START   by   ALIGN CW
Cramer's V: 0.216 *

| | | ALIGN CW | | | | |
		Aligned W	Neutral	Aligned E	Missing	TOTAL
WAR START	No	73	7	31	39	111
		90.1%	63.6%	81.6%		85.4%
	Yes	8	4	7	2	19
		9.9%	36.4%	18.4%		14.6%
	Missing	0	0	0	3	3
	TOTAL	81	11	38	44	130
		100.0%	100.0%	100.0%		

A larger percentage of non-aligned states initiated wars from 1945 to 1991 (36.4%) than either those nation-states aligned with the West (9.9%) or those aligned with the East (18.4%). The Cramer's V (0.216*) shows that the relationship between alignment and starting a war is a moderate association that is statistically significant. These results generally support our views about how the bipolar system worked. In Exercise 4 we discussed that in a bipolar system, conflict is more likely to involve the non-aligned states because the superpowers do not want to fight each other and because the polarity is maintained by competing for alignment among the non-aligned. We also discussed that stability is maintained within a pole by its superpower. That is, it is less likely that aligned nation-states will fight because conflict is managed by the superpower.

Why nation-states go to war is obviously a difficult and complex question. We have examined war in this exercise by first examining its definition and occurrence and then by looking at a few of the relationships about war at the individual, state, and system levels of analysis. While this may have been enlightening, it has left many more questions unanswered. You can now answer some of these questions in the worksheets.

NAME:

COURSE:

DATE:

REVIEW QUESTIONS

Based on the first part of this exercise, answer True or False to the following items:

The Correlates of War project defined interstate war as any deadly conflict involving two or more nation-states with at least 1,000 battle-related deaths.	T	F
The retired Prussian general, Baron von Clausewitz, believed that politics should not be part of warfare.	T	F
In the Correlates of War data, interstate wars far outnumbered the other types of international wars.	T	F
When measured as nation-months, there was more international warfare in the second half of the 20th century than in the first half.	T	F
Europe had the most wars in the Correlates of War data.	T	F
Even though the Western Hemisphere was entirely colonized by Europe, the majority of wars in the Americas between 1816 and 1991 were interstate wars.	T	F
A majority of respondents to the American Public Opinion and U.S. Foreign Policy study conducted by the Chicago Council on Foreign Affairs in 1998 who had less than a high school education, opposed sending U.S. troops to defend Israel.	T	F
The American public opposes U.S. participation in multilateral peacekeeping missions.	T	F
There is no apparent relationship between a nation-state's gross national product and whether or not the state has gone to war since 1945.	T	F
During the cold war, nation-states aligned with the Soviet Union were more likely to go to war than were states aligned with the United States.	T	F

EXPLORIT QUESTIONS

1. It is always interesting to compare how the people who make decisions for society compare with the people in the society. The American Public Opinion and U.S. Foreign Policy study conducted by the Chicago Council on Foreign Affairs collected data from the general population and from a sample of foreign policy elites, including members of Congress, members of the executive branch of the federal government (Department of State, etc.), and opinion leaders from the news media, business, labor unions, religious organizations, education, and interest groups. See how the general population's views on war compare with those of the foreign policy elites on the following variables in the FPELITES file.

Exercise 8: The Use of Force

12) WARCUBA	Send U.S. troops if Cuban people attempt to overthrow Castro
13) WARIRAQ	Send U.S. troops if Iraq invades Saudi Arabia
14) WARISR	Send U.S. troops if Arabs invade Israel
15) WARPOL	Send U.S. troops if Russia invades Poland
16) WARSKOR	Send U.S. troops if North Korea invades South Korea

Insert each of the above variables in the following Student ExplorIt guide as the dependent variable in the cross-tabulation using 10) SAMPLE2 as the independent variable.

➤ Data File: **FPELITES**
➤ Task: **Cross-tabulation**
➤ Row Variable: _____
➤ Column Variable: **10) SAMPLE2**
➤ View: **Table**
➤ Display: **Column %**

a.   Look at the Column % view of the cross-tabulation to fill out the table below.

Percent Favoring U.S. Troops

	Gen. Pop.	Elites	Cramer's V	Significant?
12) WARCUBA	_____	_____	_____	Yes No
13) WARIRAQ	_____	_____	_____	Yes No
14) WARISR	_____	_____	_____	Yes No
15) WARPOL	_____	_____	_____	Yes No
16) WARSKOR	_____	_____	_____	Yes No

b.   Review the results of your cross-tabulations above and answer the following questions.

Using U.S. troops for which situation listed above is the general population
more willing to support than the elites?   _____

Which use of U.S. troops has the strongest support among elites?   _____

2. We have examined what war is and why nation-states go to war, but we have not discussed the question that is on the minds of all those who have ever fought in a war: Who wins and why? The answer to this question must be largely situational. That is, wars are often won or lost based on the highly specific situations on the field—not due to some grand statistical scheme. Nevertheless, there may be some patterns we can find in who wins and who loses a war. The WARACTOR file contains records of each actor's experience in each war between 1816 and 1991. One variable on the file, OUTCOME, simply indicates if the actor was the winner, the loser, or tied in the outcome of the war. A tie is a war that ends with neither side prevailing. The variables in the file that could help explain who wins and who loses are

4)	DEATHS2	Number of battle-related deaths among the actor's military forces.
6)	FORCES2	Size of armed forces at the beginning of the war (collapsed at the median to high/low categories).
8)	MAJPOWER	Whether or not the nation-state was a major power.
11)	POP2	Size of population at beginning of war (collapsed at the median to high/low categories).

a. Which of the above variables do you believe is the most important in determining the outcome of a war? Explain your answer.

Run a cross-tabulation for each of the above variables using OUTCOME as the row variable, fill out the associated tables using the column percentages in the first row of each cross-tabulation, and answer the questions given.

b. Number of Battle Connected Fatalities (DEATHS2)

> ➤ *Data File:* **WARACTOR**
> ➤ *Task:* **Cross-tabulation**
> ➤ *Row Variable:* **9) OUTCOME**
> ➤ *Column Variable:* **4) DEATHS2**
> ➤ *View:* **Table**
> ➤ *Display:* **Column %**

	Low	High	Cramer's V	Significant?
% WINNER	_____	_____	_____	Yes No

c.   Size of Military Forces (FORCES2)

             Data File: **WARACTOR**
                  Task: **Cross-tabulation**
    Row Variable: **9) OUTCOME**
 ➤ *Column Variable:*   **6) FORCES2**
          ➤ *View:*   **Table**
      ➤ *Display:*   **Column %**

	Low	High	Cramer's V	Significant?
% WINNER	_____	_____	_____	Yes No

d.   Was Actor a Major Power at the Time of the War? (MAJPOWER)

             Data File: **WARACTOR**
                  Task: **Cross-tabulation**
    Row Variable: **9) OUTCOME**
 ➤ *Column Variable:*   **8) MAJPOWER**
          ➤ *View:*   **Table**
      ➤ *Display:*   **Column %**

	No	Yes	Cramer's V	Significant?
% WINNER	_____	_____	_____	Yes No

e.   Population Size at the Time of the War (POP2)

             Data File: **WARACTOR**
                  Task: **Cross-tabulation**
    Row Variable: **9) OUTCOME**
 ➤ *Column Variable:*   **11) POP2**
          ➤ *View:*   **Table**
      ➤ *Display:*   **Column %**

	Low	High	Cramer's V	Significant?
% WINNER	_____	_____	_____	Yes No

f.   Review your results for questions b–e above and write a short summary of your findings.

INTERNATIONAL LAW AND ORGANIZATION

*In order to promote international cooperation and to
achieve international peace and security,*

by the acceptance of obligations not to resort to war,
*by the prescription of open, just and honorable
    relations between nations,*
*by the firm establishment of the understandings of
    international law as the actual rule of
    conduct among governments,*
*and by the maintenance of justice and a scrupulous
    respect for all treaty obligations in the
    dealings of organized peoples with one
    another,*
Agree to this Covenant of the League of Nations

PREAMBLE TO THE COVENANT OF
THE LEAGUE OF NATIONS (1919)

Tasks: Cross-tabulation, Historical Trends, Mapping, Univariate
Data Files: NATIONS, HISTORY, FPSURVEY

INTERNATIONAL ORGANIZATION—DEFINITION AND SCOPE

By signing the Covenant of the League of Nations in 1919, the nation-states of the world established the first global intergovernmental organization and affirmed the rule of international law. While the effectiveness of the League and its successor, the United Nations, can be criticized, these two organizations significantly reshaped international relations and the meaning of the sovereign nation-state. The devastation of World War I led to calls for world government and organizational solutions to international strife. In Exercise 2 we referred to this period as the roots of the idealist, or neo-liberal, approach to the study of international relations. Other analysts have captured the atmosphere of this time by calling it the organizational phase of international relations (Olson and Onuf, 1985). They call it the organizational phase because many formal and informal international organizations were created with the express purpose of outlawing war, or at least understanding and preventing it.

As we mentioned in Exercise 2, the first department of international relations at a university was created at the University of Aberystwyth in Wales in 1919. Many non-governmental, semi-academic organizations dedicated to studying and preventing war were also created during the early 1920s. These included the Council on Foreign Affairs and the Carnegie Endowment for International Peace in

New York, the Royal Institute of International Affairs in London, and the International Institute for Intellectual Cooperation in Paris. Scholars and statesmen alike believed that the intellectual power centered in these organizations along with the commitment to the rule of law and the pacific settlement of disputes embodied in the League of Nations would create a well-ordered and peaceful world. These hopes were dashed as fascism arose in Italy and Germany in the early 1920s and as the world fell into the economic pit of the Great Depression in the 1930s. The organizational procedures for peacefully settling disputes had no effective enforcement and were discredited by the Japanese invasion of Manchuria in 1931 and the Italian invasion of Ethiopia in 1935. The League of Nations responded with economic sanctions against Japan and Italy. It is arguable that the sanctions against Japan contributed to its entry into World War II and Ethiopia felt betrayed as the sanctions against Italy had little effect.

This failure of international organizations to achieve peaceful order was called the "twenty years' crisis" in the title of a book by E. H. Carr (1939). Carr's book became a leading text in the realist movement that followed World War II. He claimed that the conflict of the interwar period and World War II itself was due largely to the misplaced trust in international organizations and an unrealistic expectation that conflict could be studied or legislated away. Nevertheless, the reliance on both intergovernmental and nongovernmental international organizations continued after World War II, albeit with a somewhat more realistic understanding of their limits.

The simplest definition of an international organization is any organization with members in more than one nation-state. Unfortunately, this definition does not tell us much about the nature of the organizations. International organizations can be classified using three variables.[1] The first is *membership*. Intergovernmental organizations (IGOs) only have governments as members. The United Nations and the World Health Organization are intergovernmental organizations. Nongovernmental organizations (NGOs) have a much more open membership. Members can include individuals, governments, or groups. The second classification variable is *scope*. Some organizations, such as the Food and Agricultural Organization (FAO), have a global scope. That is, they have members from all over the world and they address problems around the globe. Others, such as the Organization for African Unity (OAU), are regional organizations that deal only with issues relevant to specific areas of the world. The final classification variable is *purpose*. General purpose organizations such as the Organization of American States (OAS) or the United Nations will address any issue—from art and culture to international security. Specialized organizations, such as the International Civil Aeronautics Organization (ICAO), work only in very narrowly defined areas. The table below shows how these three variables can be used to classify a small sampling of international organizations.

	INTERGOVERNMENTAL		NONGOVERNMENTAL	
	GLOBAL	*REGIONAL*	*GLOBAL*	*REGIONAL*
General Purpose	United Nations	Organization of American States	Union of International Associations	European Radical Alliance
Specialized	World Health Organization	Pan American Health Organization	World Wildlife Fund	Atlantic Salmon Federation

[1] The following classification scheme is attributed to John Rourke (1999: 217–218).

We can explore the growth of international organizations in the 20th century with the variables IGO and NGO in the HISTORY file. These variables record the number of intergovernmental and non-governmental organizations per year respectively.

➤ *Data File:* **HISTORY**
　➤ *Task:* **Historical Trends**
➤ *Variable:* **26) IGO**

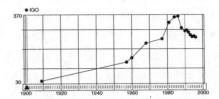

Total number of inter-governmental organizations

The number of intergovernmental organizations grew rapidly from 1910 through the middle 1980s but has declined since 1986. Perhaps this decline is a result of the end of the cold war and the breakup of the Soviet Union. The number of nongovernmental organizations continues to grow. This number should expand as globalized marketplaces require more specialized associations to operate effectively.

Data File: **HISTORY**
　Task: **Historical Trends**
➤ *Variable:* **33) NGO**

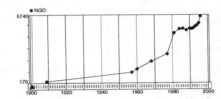

Total number of non-governmental organizations

Most nation-states belong to a general purpose regional intergovernmental organization. The first of these in the era of the modern nation-state was possibly the Council of Europe that was created in 1815 to deal with the political and social consequences of the Napoleonic Wars. We can map some of the more prominent regional intergovernmental organizations.

➤ *Data File:* **NATIONS**
　➤ *Task:* **Mapping**
➤ *Variable 1:* **85) REGION IGO**
　➤ *View:* **Map**
　➤ *Display:* **Legend**

The map above shows that the entire Western Hemisphere belongs to the Organization of American States (OAS), the oldest of the current regional organizations. Although Cuba is officially a member of the OAS, the other states in the organization voted in 1962 to prohibit participation by the current government under Fidel Castro. Most African states are members of the Organization of African Unity.[2] The Association of South East Asian States consists of the nation-states on the South East Asian Peninsula as well as the Philippines and Indonesia. The European Union represents a radical experiment in regional integration. Under the terms of the Maastricht Treaty signed in 1992, Western European nation-states agreed to develop unified trade and economic policies, eliminate border checks for travel within the European Union, and even convert to a common currency known as the Euro.

When a nation-state joins an international organization, such as the European Union, it agrees to abide by its rules and often agrees to surrender some of its sovereignty to permit the organization to make decisions that the nation-state would otherwise make. These decisions can range from something as important as the right to control entry of individuals across its borders to something as mundane as standardizing how postal charges will be paid to facilitate international mail. Why would an autonomous nation-state be willing to submit to the decisions of an international organization? In the early 19th century, nation-states relinquished little or no sovereign power to the organization. The Concert of Europe operated instead by the principle of joint consultation (Claude, 1971:27) whereby the organization provided little more than a forum where interested states could meet to coordinate policies. The League of Nations in the early 20th century represented a radical departure from this principle, at least in theory. Member states agreed to submit disputes to bodies of the League, such as the Permanent International Court of Justice, rather than pursue violent alternatives. As we mentioned before, this process was flawed but it opened both a theoretical and practical discussion about how and why a state should surrender sovereignty to an organization. This discussion explored the functional benefits of international organization over the legal benefits by embracing the increasing complexity of international life. It is to a nation-state's advantage to join organizations such as the World Meteorological Organization for two reasons. First, sharing weather data and standardizing forecasts has a real functional benefit for all involved and, second, it is believed that nation-states that cooperate in functional areas are less likely to come into conflict in other areas. This so-called functionalism became the rationale for the United Nations system after World War II.

THE UNITED NATIONS SYSTEM

The United Nations was created when 51 nation-states signed the United Nations Charter in San Francisco on June 26, 1945. The Charter lists the following four main purposes for the organization: to prevent war, to promote human rights and equality, to establish the rule of international law and enforce treaty obligations, and to promote social and economic development. From the original 51 member states, the United Nations had grown to 189 members in 2001.

---

[2] Many states belong to more than one regional organization. For example, the map shows that the nation-states of northern Africa are members of the Arab League, yet Algeria, Djibouti, Egypt, Libya, Sudan, and Tunisia are also members of the Organization for African Unity.

> *Data File:* **HISTORY**
>   > *Task:* **Historical Trends**
> > *Variable:* **51) UN MEMBERS**

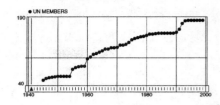

Number of United Nations member states

We can see above that the membership grew steadily from 1945 to 1999 with three spurts of growth. It may be interesting to see when specific nation-states joined the United Nations. We can do this with the variable UNDATE in the NATIONS file.

> *Data File:* **NATIONS**
>   > *Task:* **Mapping**
> *Variable 1:* **102) UNDATE**
>   > *View:* **List: Rank**

RANK	CASE NAME	VALUE
1	Macedonia	1993
1	Slovak Republic	1993
1	Eritrea	1993
1	Czech Republic	1993
5	Kyrgyzstan	1992
5	Moldova	1992
5	Bosnia	1992
5	Kazakhstan	1992
5	Georgia	1992
5	Croatia	1992

If you begin at the bottom of the ranking, you can see the states in our file that were the original signatories of the Charter. Moving up the ranking, there were a number of nation-states that joined the United Nations in 1955. Many of these states, such as Albania, Austria, and Bulgaria, were rebuilding after the devastation of World War II. Others, like Cambodia and Laos, were former colonies that gained their independence. The next surge of memberships came in 1960. Most of these were African states that gained independence from European colonialism. Finally, a large group of states became members in the early 1990s. These states, like Croatia, Kyrgyzstan, and Moldova, emerged from the breakup of the Soviet Union and the political changes in Eastern Europe at the end of the cold war.

The challenge of the United Nations has always been to represent the diverse interests of the whole of the system of nation-states while maintaining enough consensus, especially among the most powerful states, to provide an effective and active organization. The solution to this problem was to divide the major decision-making between a General Assembly, in which every member has equal vote and representation, and a Security Council with a rotating membership whereby the most powerful nation-states can protect their interests. They can do this because the five most powerful states at the end of World War II—China, France, the United Kingdom, the United States, and the Soviet Union (now Russia)—were given permanent membership and the power of the veto. The veto means that if any one of these five states disagrees with a resolution before the Council, the resolution will fail.

The General Assembly sets general policy for the United Nations, directs most of its annual activities, establishes the budget, and provides a forum for international discussion of any issue that members wish to bring forward. Its resolutions do not carry the weight of law, but they do serve to establish the general will of the system of nation-states. The General Assembly begins its annual meeting on the third Tuesday of September with the "General Debate," in which any nation-state can bring any issue to the table. The General Debate usually starts with speeches by many of the world's heads of state.

The Security Council is empowered by Chapter 7, Article 39 of the Charter to "determine the existence of any threat to the peace, breach of the peace, or act of aggression and shall make recommendations, or decide what measures shall be taken in accordance with Articles 41 and 42, to maintain or restore international peace and security." Article 41 empowers the Security Council to use non-violent means, such as economic sanctions, to maintain or restore peace while Article 42 empowers the Council to use force, often referred to as peacekeeping forces.

The U.N. has many other specialized administrative bodies in addition to the General Assembly and the Security Council. The Economic and Social Council has 54 member states elected for three-year terms. It is empowered to examine issues related to economic and social development and establish U.N. policies in these areas. The Trusteeship Council was created by the Charter to oversee the trust system by which oversight of territories and colonies was granted to various nation-states. The operation of the Trusteeship Council was suspended in 1994 when the last trust territory, Palau, achieved independence. The International Court of Justice in the Hague (Netherlands) provides a forum where nation-states can present disputes for neutral third-party adjudication based on the principles of international law. We will discuss the operations of the Court later in this exercise. The Secretariat of the United Nations provides the bureaucratic structure and personnel to carry out the desires of the General Assembly, Security Council, and the Economic and Social Council.

The United Nations System also consists of independent international organizations called the Specialized Agencies of the United Nations. These agencies include the World Bank, the Food and Agricultural Organization, the World Intellectual Property Organization, and the International Postal Union. It is in these organizations that many of the functions of functionalism are performed. Critics complain that the United Nations fails at its task of being fully representative of the whole of the nation-states merely by the location of the offices and headquarters of these many U.N. organizations. We can explore this critique with the variable UNHQ in the NATIONS file.

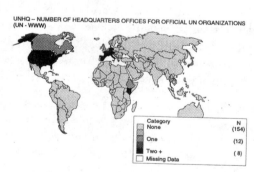

Data File: **NATIONS**
Task: **Mapping**
➤ Variable 1: **104) UNHQ**
➤ View: **Map**
➤ Display: **Legend**

The map seems to support the criticism. Only 9 of the 87 major U.N. headquarters offices are located outside of North America or Western Europe. The United Nations is a large, complex organization. It has a large budget that in recent years has been attacked as wasteful, especially by members of the U.S. Congress.

152

➤ *Data File:* **HISTORY**
  ➤ *Task:* **Historical Trends**
➤ *Variable:* **49) UNBUDGET**

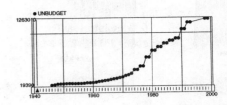

Annual budget of the United Nations excluding peacekeeping operations–
thousands of current U.S. dollars

The graph above shows that the U.N. budget has risen steadily. Note, however, that these data are in "current" U.S. dollars. This means that the data have not been adjusted for inflation. Thus, some increase in spending is justified merely by trying to keep up with prices. Since 1973, the United Nations has used a two-year budget cycle. This is represented above by dividing the budget by two every other year. While the biennieal U.N. budget exceeds 2.5 billion U.S. dollars, this is less than 1% of the U.S. defense budget. This number is also somewhat misleading. As the world's population grows, the number of problems and issues addressed by the United Nations also grows. We can explore the U.N. budget per capita—that is, the budget adjusted by the size of the world's population.

Data File: **HISTORY**
  Task: **Historical Trends**
➤ *Variable:* **52) UN$PERCAP**

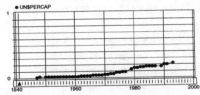

United Nations budget per capita–U.S. dollars

While the budget per capita has increased, its rate of increase has been slow. At the highest, the U.N. budget represented only 22 cents per person, worldwide.

The budget reported in this historical trend does not include United Nations peacekeeping operations. Peacekeeping is funded separately on a mission-by-mission basis. Although peacekeeping represents a small proportion of overall U.N. spending and staff time, it is certainly the most visible of the U.N.'s activities and possibly the most controversial. The first peacekeeping mission began soon after the U.N. was founded. In 1948, the nation-states of Pakistan and India were created by a resolution in the United Nations that ended the British colonial rule in South Asia. At the time, there were factions within India that did not want to partition the territory into two nation-states and there were others that wanted to push for more cultural autonomy. Into this tense setting U.N. troops were first inserted, and they have been there ever since. Since that time 49 peacekeeping missions, varying from combat troops to administrative observers, have been deployed by the Security Council around the world. The variable PEACE KEEP in the HISTORY file shows the number of U.N. peacekeeping missions active per year.

Data File: **HISTORY**
Task: **Historical Trends**
➤ Variable: **34) PEACE KEEP**

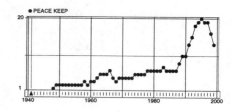

Number of active U.N. peacekeeping missions per year

The graph shows that the number of peacekeeping missions dramatically increased beginning in 1989. Can you think of a reason for this based on what you have learned so far about international relations? The year 1989 was a dramatic year in international relations. It was the year that the nation-states of Eastern Europe broke away from the Soviet bloc. It marked the end of the bipolar system. In Exercise 4 we stated that one of the propositions of the system level of analysis is that periods of system change tend to be inherently unstable because constraints that held ethnic and political conflict in check are reduced or removed. The systemic institutions for responding to conflict are disrupted, and other institutions must step in to take their place to maintain order. Such was the case in the early 1990s. The nation-states looked to the United Nations to quell local conflict instead of looking to more entrenched superpower controls that had waned. So, where were these peacekeeping missions? Mapping the variable PKEEP in the NATIONS file can answer this question.

➤ Data File: **NATIONS**
➤ Task: **Mapping**
➤ Variable 1: **77) PKEEP**
➤ View: **Map**
➤ Display: **Legend**

Peacekeeping missions have not been uniformly distributed throughout the world. Over the history of the United Nations, which coincides with the years of the cold war, peacekeeping has been concentrated in the Middle East, Africa, South Asia, Southeast Asia, and Central America. It is no mere coincidence that these are also the regions where cold-war competition was the greatest.

POLITICS AND THE UNITED NATIONS

Although the United Nations was founded on high-sounding ideals, it is not immune from politics and controversy. We can explore these conflicts at individual, state, and system levels of analysis. Respondents to the 1998 American Public Opinion and U.S. Foreign Policy Survey were asked "How important is strengthening the United Nations as a U.S. foreign policy goal?" We can see the responses using the GOALUN variable in the FPSURVEY file.

154

International Relations

➤ *Data File:* **FPSURVEY**
➤ *Task:* **Univariate**
➤ *Primary Variable:* **16) GOALUN**
➤ *View:* **Pie**

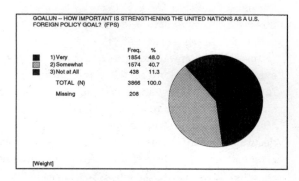

GOALUN -- HOW IMPORTANT IS STRENGTHENING THE UNITED NATIONS AS A U.S. FOREIGN POLICY GOAL? (FPS)

	Freq.	%
1) Very	1854	48.0
2) Somewhat	1574	40.7
3) Not at All	438	11.3
TOTAL (N)	3866	100.0
Missing	208	

[Weight]

Less than half (48.0%) of the respondents believed that strengthening the United Nations was a "very important" foreign policy goal for the United States. While this shows some support for the United Nations, not all sectors of the public have the same opinion.

Data File: **FPSURVEY**
➤ *Task:* **Cross-tabulation**
➤ *Row Variable:* **16) GOALUN**
➤ *Column Variable:* **4) EDUC**
➤ *Views:* **Table**
➤ *Display:* **Column %**

GOALUN by EDUC
Weight Variable: WEIGHT
Cramer's V: 0.067 **

GOALUN	EDUC					
	< High Sch	H.S. Grad	Some Coll.	Coll Grad	Missing	TOTAL
Very	340	563	591	347	13	1841
	53.1%	50.0%	48.3%	40.4%		47.8%
Somewhat	221	458	491	401	4	1570
	34.5%	40.7%	40.1%	46.7%		40.8%
Not at All	79	105	142	111	1	437
	12.4%	9.3%	11.6%	12.9%		11.4%
Missing	55	48	84	21	0	208
TOTAL	641	1126	1224	858	18	3848
	100.0%	100.0%	100.0%	100.0%		

Support for the United Nations seems to decrease among more educated respondents. Fifty-three percent of those with less than high school education believe that supporting the U.N. is a very important foreign policy goal compared with only 40.4% of those who have graduated from college. The Cramer's V = 0.067 shows that the relationship between support for the U.N. and educational level is weak but statistically significant. In American politics, the U.N. has always had more support among liberals than conservatives. We can see if that relationship holds with our data.

Data File: **FPSURVEY**
Task: **Cross-tabulation**
Row Variable: **16) GOALUN**
➤ *Column Variable:* **22) LIBCONS**
➤ *Views:* **Table**
➤ *Display:* **Column %**

GOALUN by LIBCONS
Weight Variable: WEIGHT
Cramer's V: 0.109 **

GOALUN	LIBCONS				
	Conserv.	Neutral	Liberal	Missing	TOTAL
Very	624	821	360	49	1805
	41.0%	53.2%	52.7%		48.2%
Somewhat	650	611	264	49	1525
	42.8%	39.5%	38.7%		40.7%
Not at All	247	113	59	20	419
	16.2%	7.3%	8.6%		11.2%
Missing	34	91	32	51	208
TOTAL	1521	1545	683	168	3749
	100.0%	100.0%	100.0%		

Among respondents who identified themselves as political liberals, 52.7% believed that supporting the U.N. was an important goal, compared to only 41.0% of the conservative respondents (Cramer's V = 0.109**). It seems that our data do support the conventional hypothesis that liberals are more likely to support the United Nations than are conservatives.

Because of the veto, the U.N. Security Council is a forum where the five permanent members can assert their will. They cannot do so without impunity, for even though the veto is absolute, it does have consequences. A nation-state that vetoes a resolution important to another permanent member can expect a reciprocal veto on a resolution that it feels is important. Nonetheless, the veto is an effective vehicle for expressing national interest. It is interesting to see how members have used the veto through the years. In the early years of the Council, the United States had support of many of the members and the Soviet Union used the veto to stand in opposition to American interests. This opposition began in earnest in 1950 with a resolution supported by the Soviet Union to remove the Nationalist Chinese from the Security Council, claiming that China should be represented by a representative of the communist government that had successfully defeated the nationalists and had driven them from the mainland to the island of Taiwan. The Soviet proposal was defeated and in anger they boycotted the Security Council. Shortly after that, South Korea came to the Council to seek protection from the North Korean invasion. In the absence of Soviet vetoes, the United States sponsored a series of resolutions that established the United Nations forces to protect South Korea in the Korean War and to place the forces under unified command led by the United States. Thus, in the Korean War, North Korea, supported by the Soviet Union, fought forces legitimately under the flag of the United Nations, of which the Soviet Union was a member. The Soviet Union returned to the Council in August of 1950 and used the veto for many years to limit the powers of U.N. peacekeeping. We can explore the veto with our data by looking at the number of vetoes by the United States and the Soviet Union over time.

> *Data File:* **HISTORY**
>> ➤ *Task:* **Historical Trends**
> ➤ *Variable:* **53) VETO USA**
>>>> **54) VETO USSR**

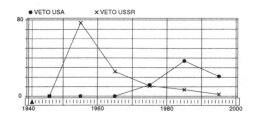

This trend graph shows the Security Council vetoes in ten-year periods. In the first ten years of the Council, the Soviet Union used its veto 77 times. The United States did not use a single veto until the mid-1960s. However, as the cold war wore on, support for the United States in both the Security Council and the General Assembly declined. In the 1970s and 1980s the United States found itself more isolated and it had to use its veto to protect its interests. This shift of support from the United States to the Soviet Union was particularly clear in voting in the General Assembly.

> *Data File:* **HISTORY**
>> *Task:* **Historical Trends**
> ➤ *Variable:* **2) AGREEUS**
>>>> **3) AGREEUSSR**

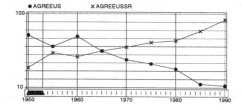

The variables in the trend graph above show the percentage of times per year that the United States and the Soviet Union voted with the majority of the general assembly over five-year periods. Through the mid-1960s the United States voted with the majority of the other members more than the Soviet Union did. After the mid-1960s, the majority of the nation-states tended to vote more with the Soviet Union than the United States. What changed in the early 1960s to bring this shift about? Two things probably account for most of the change. First, in 1960 many less developed countries became members of the United Nations as the colonies of the British and French empires gained independence. These states were courted by the Soviet Union and tended to see their economic interests more in line with the policies of the USSR than with those of the USA. Second, as we mentioned in Exercise 5, many of these new nation-states joined together to form the Group of 77, a group of non-aligned states explicitly constituted to represent the interests of the less developed states, especially when those interests diverged from the interests of the United States and the other industrialized nation-states. You can explore other aspects of the politics of the United Nations, especially those related to peacekeeping, in the worksheets for this exercise

INTERNATIONAL LAW

The preamble to both the Covenant of the League of Nations and the United Nations Charter affirm that the relations between nation-states must be ruled by international law. But what is international law? Is it real law? Not only does international law exist, it is the most followed body of law in the world. What criteria must be fulfilled for a body of law to exist and be effective? First, there must be agreement, or at least understanding, about what the laws are. Second, there must be an institutional means for creating the laws. Third, there must be a means for adjudicating disputes under the law. Finally, there must be a mechanism for enforcing the laws. We will address each of these questions in turn, but first let us also understand what criteria do not have to be achieved for a body of law to exist. It is not required that the laws always be followed. There is little doubt that a body of law exists that controls how one drives on the highway. Within that body of law are specific laws that determine maximum speed limits. That people exceed the speed limits does not mean that traffic laws do not exist—they merely are broken.

If sovereigns are truly autonomous, no higher authority exists to obligate the state to recognize the law. Yet sovereigns can bind themselves to the law. They do so by treaty, by explicit membership in organizations like the Organization of American States, or by years of practices that conform with the law. No other body of law requires explicit recognition. The International Court of Justice in The Hague is the main organ, constituted through the United Nations, for adjudicating disputes between nation-states under international law. We will explore the workings of the Court later. For now, however, we need to address the question of how the International Court of Justice gains jurisdiction over a dispute. There are a number of ways this can happen. First, states can bind themselves to the power of the Court through treaties they sign that explicitly refer disputes to the Court. Second, states can, on a case-by-case basis, agree to submit to the ruling of the Court. Finally, many nation-states have explicitly made statements recognizing compulsory jurisdiction of the International Court of Justice. We can see how many nation-states chose to make these statements with the ICJ JURIS variable in the NATIONS file.[3]

---

[3] We need to distinguish between submitting a statement of compulsory jurisdiction and having one in force. A state can conditionally submit a statement or it can do so with a time limit.

➤ *Data File:* **NATIONS**
➤ *Task:* **Univariate**
➤ *Primary Variable:* **61) ICJ JURIS**
➤ *View:* **Pie**

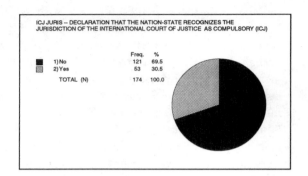

ICJ JURIS -- DECLARATION THAT THE NATION-STATE RECOGNIZES THE
JURISDICTION OF THE INTERNATIONAL COURT OF JUSTICE AS COMPULSORY (ICJ)

		Freq.	%
■	1) No	121	69.5
▨	2) Yes	53	30.5
	TOTAL (N)	174	100.0

Most of the nation-states (69.5%) have not made statements explicitly acknowledging the Court's jurisdiction. It is also interesting to see which nation-states currently have statements of compulsory jurisdiction in force.

Data File: **NATIONS**
Task: **Mapping**
Variable 1: **61) ICJ JURIS**
➤ *View:* **List: Rank**

RANK	CASE NAME	VALUE
1	Senegal	Yes
1	Gambia	Yes
1	Finland	Yes
1	Estonia	Yes
1	Philippines	Yes
1	Portugal	Yes
1	Guinea-Bissau	Yes
1	Poland	Yes
1	Haiti	Yes
1	Sudan	Yes

Scrolling up and down the ranking, you will see that the United Kingdom has a statement of jurisdiction to the Court in force while the United States does not. Other notable states that do not have statements in force are Russia, China, France, and Germany. Does this mean that they are not bound by international law or by the decisions of the Court? No, they can still bring cases to the Court and they are bound by the treaties they sign that refer to the Court.

There are many sources of international law. Since nation-states bind themselves to the law, these sources are, for the most part, derived from the explicit behavior of the states. One source is treaty law. When a treaty is properly signed and ratified, it has the force of law. Another source of law is custom. Practices followed over many years or centuries become the customary law of the international system. One example of this is the rules of right-of-way at sea. When two ships approach each other on the high seas, there is a complex set of rules that determine which has the right-of-way. These rules emerged out of customary practice over 5,000 years of marine transport. Although they carried the weight of law from customary practice alone, it was not until 1883 that the rules were codified in an international treaty.

The primary mechanism for adjudicating disputes under international law is the International Court of Justice at The Hague. Any nation-state can bring a case to the Court, although that case will not be heard unless both parties agree. We can see how many cases have been heard by the International Court of Justice per year since it was created in 1946.

➤ Data File: **HISTORY**
   ➤ Task: **Historical Trends**
➤ Variable: **25) ICJ CASES**

Number of active cases before the international court of justice

The historical trends graph above shows open cases per year before the International Court of Justice. A case is open if it has been presented to the court but the court has not yet issued a final ruling. While the number of open cases has fluctuated widely, it has been growing steadily since the mid-1970s. Which nation-states have been parties to cases, as either plaintiff or defendant?

➤ Data File: **NATIONS**
   ➤ Task: **Mapping**
➤ Variable 1: **60) ICJ CASES**
    ➤ View: **List: Rank**

RANK	CASE NAME	VALUE
1	United States	18
2	United Kingdom	12
3	Serbia	11
3	France	11
5	Libya	6
6	Belgium	4
6	Spain	4
6	Germany	4
6	Congo, Dem. Republic	4
6	Iran	4

The ranking shows that the United States had the most cases before the Court followed by the United Kingdom. It is expected that large states with many international events are likely to generate more opposition to these events and may end up before the Court as either defendant or plaintiff.

How is international law enforced? Perhaps the best way to answer this question is to look at how laws are enforced within a nation-state. Clearly, the major difference between national laws and international law is the presence of a supreme authority that can mete out punishment. Yet, even within the nation-state, the government is unable to prevent law-breaking. It can only make the consequences of law-breaking undesirable. Enforcement requires that the law-breaker believe that he or she will get caught and that once caught, he or she will receive a punishment that places a high cost on law-breaking. In the absence of a world government, international law must also be enforced by first catching the offender and then placing a high cost on law-breaking. Catching an offender is easy. Since all sovereign states are legally equal, any aggrieved party can legitimately make a claim against another state. We identified Nauru in Exercise 3 as the world's smallest nation-state. On May 19, 1989, Nauru filed an application at the International Court of Justice against Australia over a claim that Australia had violated a treaty that required it to restore mined land in Nauru. The case proceeded with various filings and decisions in the Court, but was, in the end, settled by agreement between the two parties. The cost of law-breaking can be imposed in two ways. First, there is direct punishment of the offender by military force. Iraq was challenged and finally defeated by a coalition of nation-states in 1990–1991 when it invaded Kuwait in violation of accepted standards of international law. This ultimate punishment is rare, but it can be effective. Second, there is direct punishment of the offender

Exercise 9: International Law and Organization

through economic sanctions and diplomatic isolation. In 1988, Pan Am Flight 103 was destroyed by a bomb as it flew over Scotland. Two Libyans were accused of the bombing. When Libya refused to extradite the accused for trial, the United Nations Security Council placed economic sanctions on Libya. In 1999, Libya agreed to a complicated plan to try the accused in Netherlands under Scottish law. In response, the United States and other nation-states agreed to remove some of the sanctions.

WORKSHEET

NAME:

COURSE:

DATE:

EXERCISE
9

REVIEW QUESTIONS

Based on the first part of this exercise, answer True or False to the following items:

The League of Nations was created after World War I in the hopes that international organization could eliminate war.　　T　F

The period from 1920 to 1940 is called by some the "organizational phase" of international relations.　　T　F

The League of Nations' mechanisms for settling disputes between nation-states were discredited when Italy invaded Ethiopia and Japan invaded Manchuria.　　T　F

United Nations peacekeeping missions has increased dramatically since 1989.　　T　F

The United Nations is a nongovernmental organization (NGO) because it does not try to fulfill the role of a world government.　　T　F

The number of intergovernmental organizations (IGOs) has increased since the end of the cold war.　　T　F

Because of their majority voting power in the United Nations General Assembly, most headquarters offices of U.N. organizations are located in the less-developed, non-aligned nation-states.　　T　F

In the United States, liberals are more likely than conservatives to believe that strengthening the United Nations is a vital U.S. foreign policy goal.　　T　F

As part of its fight against communism during the 1950s, the United States used more vetoes in the U.N. Security Council than did the Soviet Union.　　T　F

Most of the nation-states have deposited statements with the International Court of Justice recognizing the compulsory jurisdiction of the Court in disputes between two nation-states.　　T　F

EXPLORIT QUESTIONS

1. Peacekeeping operations are a controversial activity of the United Nations. Support for peacekeeping is affected by politics at the local and international level. We saw in the preliminary section of Exercise 9 that support for the United Nations was related to the political ideology of the respondent in the 1998 American Public Opinion and U.S. Foreign Policy Survey (FPSURVEY). We can now explore if the same holds true for United States participation in U.N. peacekeeping operations. The variable PKEEP asked whether or not the United States should contribute troops to U.N. peacekeeping operations.

Exercise 9: International Law and Organization

161

a.   What do you expect to find in the data? That is, answer the following questions, before you turn to our data files, by circling one answer per question.

Most respondents believe that the United States

     a. **should** participate in U.N. peacekeeping.

     b. **should not** participate in U.N. peacekeeping.

Liberals are more likely to

     a. **support U.S.** participation in U.N. peacekeeping.

     b. **not support** U.S. participation in U.N. peacekeeping than are conservatives.

b.   Follow the instructions below and fill in the blanks.

     ➤ *Data File:* **FPSURVEY**
     ➤ *Task:* **Univariate**
     ➤ *Primary Variable:* **25) PKEEP**

What percentage of the respondents to the survey answered "yes" to the question about whether or not the United States should participate in U.N. peacekeeping?   _____%

c.   Fill in the table below with the results of the following cross-tabulation.

     Data File: **FPSURVEY**
     ➤ *Task:* **Cross-tabulation**
     ➤ *Row Variable:* **25) PKEEP**
     ➤ *Column Variable:* **22) LIBCONS**
     ➤ *View:* **Table**
     ➤ *Display:* **Column %**

Enter the % YES in the blanks below.

	Conservative	**Neutral**	**Liberal**	**Cramer's V**	**Significant?**
U.S. should participate in peacekeeping	_____%	_____%	_____%	_____	Yes No

2.   Politics affected voting in the General Assembly during the cold war. As we saw in Exercise 9, the United States found itself more and more in opposition to the majority position throughout the 1960s and 70s. This raises two questions: Did General Assembly voting follow cold-war alignment, and was voting affected by U.S. efforts to gain support? We will address the second question first. To measure support for the United States in the General Assembly, we will use a variable (AGREEUSA2) that records the percentage of times each member nation-state voted in agreement with the United

States in General Assembly voting in 1970. We will measure U.S. efforts to gain support with a variable (USAID65B) that measures the amount of U.S. foreign aid given to each state between 1965 and 1970. Finally, we will measure cold-war alignment with the variable ALIGN CW that we used in Exercise 4. Remember that ALIGN CW measures alignment through the proportion of arms bought from either the East or the West. In Exercise 4 we found that this variable indicates whether the nation-state was part of the Western bloc or Eastern bloc during the bipolar system.

a.   Fill in the blanks below regarding agreement with the United States in U.N. General Assembly voting in 1970.

> ➤ *Data File:* **NATIONS**
> ➤ *Task:* **Univariate**
> ➤ *Primary Variable:* **7) AGREEUSA2**

Percentage of states that voted in agreement with the U.S. **less than 50%** of the time in 1970.   _____%

Percentage of states that voted in agreement with the U.S. **50% or more** of the time in 1970.   _____%

b.   Create a map of the variable USAID65–75 to see which nation-states received the most U.S. foreign aid.

> *Data File:* **NATIONS**
> ➤ *Task:* **Mapping**
> ➤ *Variable 1:* **107) USAID65–75**
> ➤ *View:* **Map**
> ➤ *Display:* **Legend**

Which regions of the world received high U.S. foreign aid in 1965? (circle all that apply)

1. Latin America   3. South Asia

2. Sub-Saharan Africa   4. Southeast Asia

c.   Create a map of the variable ALIGN CW to see which nation-states were aligned with the Eastern or Western blocs during the cold war.

> *Data File:* **NATIONS**
> *Task:* **Mapping**
> ➤ *Variable 1:* **10) ALIGN CW**
> ➤ *View:* **Map**
> ➤ *Display:* **Legend**

With which block were most countries in South America aligned?

a. East

b. West

c. Neutral

With which block were most countries in Southeast Asia aligned?

a. East

b. West

c. Neutral

d. Create cross-tabulations that compare agreement with the United States in General Assembly voting (AGREEUSA2) with foreign aid (USAID65B) and cold-war alignment (ALIGN CW) and fill out the tables below.

> Data File: **NATIONS**
> ➤ Task: **Cross-tabulation**
> ➤ Row Variable: **7) AGREEUSA2**
> ➤ Column Variable: **108) USAID65B**
> ➤ View: **Tables**
> ➤ Display: **Column %**

Column Percents: USAID65B

	Low US Aid	High US Aid	Cramer's V	Significant?
States with 50%+ agreement with the USA	_____ %	_____ %	_____	Yes No

> Data File: **NATIONS**
> Task: **Cross-tabulation**
> Row Variable: **7) AGREEUSA2**
> ➤ Column Variable: **10) ALIGN CW**
> ➤ View: **Tables**
> ➤ Display: **Column %**

Column Percents: ALIGN CW

	Aligned West	Neutral	Aligned East	Cramer's V	Significant?
States with 50%+ agreement with USA	_____ %	_____ %	_____ %	_____	Yes No

Examine the results of the two cross-tabulations. Which independent variable is a better predictor for how a nation votes in the United Nations?

a.   USAID65B

b.   ALIGN CW

Write a short paragraph that discusses your findings.

EXERCISE 10

THE POLITICS OF THE WORLD ECONOMY

Tasks: Cross-tabulation, Historical Trends, Mapping, Univariate, Scatterplot
Data Files: NATIONS, HISTORY

THE GROWTH AND SCALE OF INTERNATIONAL POLITICAL ECONOMY

We introduced international relations in Exercise 1 as a science of events. Remember that an international event is an action taken by an actor directed at a target where the actor and target are in different nation-states. That is, an international event crosses a border by definition. Too often, students and practitioners of international relations think only of military events when they think of international relations. While military events such as wars, threats, or treaties are very important in international relations, other events, such as economic events, have increased both in number and in importance.

Remember from Exercise 2 that the Conflict and Peace Data Bank (COPDAB) was a study that attempted to catalog every international event from 1948 through 1978. The COPDAB data permit us to compare the number of military and economic events over time.

➤ *Data File:* **HISTORY**
  ➤ *Task:* **Historical Trends**
➤ *Variable:* **15) ECON EVNTS**
       31) MIL EVNTS

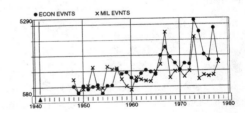

The figure shows that although the number of military and economic events in the COPDAB dataset are close, economic events exceeded military events each year from 1968 to the end of the data in 1978.[1] Now, more than 20 years after the COPDAB data, economics is even more important in world affairs. This is evident by examining the growth of international economic activities. Trade is perhaps the most visible form of international economic relations.

---

[1] You have seen these figures before in a slightly different form. The third figure in Exercise 2 displayed the number of economic and military events per year along with the political events per year. That graph also showed that political events were the most numerous of the three. This is not surprising because the coding schemes that were used to create the COPDAB files mostly identified events where nation-states were the actors or targets. If we use our expanded definition of an event that includes non-state actors (such as corporations, groups, or individuals), surely the number of economic events would exceed all other types.

167

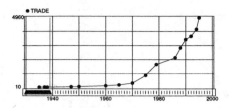

Total value of world exports in billions of current U.S. dollars

The graph shows the growth of trade from 1935 to 1995. This measure of trade as the total value of world exports in current U.S. dollars is not adjusted for inflation, so it is biased in favor of showing too much trade. Nevertheless, the graph shows a dramatic increase in the volume of world trade over the 60 years of data.

We will discuss the concepts, theories, and politics of international economic relations in this exercise and in Exercise 11. Here, we will introduce you to the basic concepts and terms of international political economy and explore how economics affects domestic and international politics. We will also explore major issues that affect the politics of the world economy. In Exercise 11, we will explore the special issues related to economic development. We reserve a separate exercise for economic development for two reasons. First, it is warranted because the majority of the world's population and land mass are in less developed countries. Second, the problems of persistent underdevelopment are specialized enough to require their own investigation and they have long-term implications for stability in world politics.

One of the key concepts of international political economy is the gross national product (GNP) which is a measure of the value of all the goods and services produced and consumed in a nation-state in a given year. The gross national product differs from the gross domestic product because the GNP includes goods and services imported and exported. One calculation of the GNP is the following identity:

$$\text{GNP} \equiv C + I + G + (X - M)$$

where C is the value of goods consumed by individuals and companies, I is the value of all investment, G is the value of government spending, X is the value of exports and M is the value of imports. It is easy to see from the GNP identity that if the value of exports (X) is greater than the value of imports (M), the GNP goes up. Alternatively, if imports exceed exports, GNP decreases. Thus, it is better to sell more than you buy. This difference is called the merchandise trade balance, and we explored it in Exercise 2. Gross national product can be a very large number. It is usually reported in the local currency (i.e., the GNP of United Kingdom is reported in pounds and the GNP of Guatemala is reported in quetzals). Therefore it needs to be converted to a common currency, such as dollars, using an exchange rate to be useful as a comparison. It is compared from nation-state to nation-state to illustrate differences in the overall scale of the economies.

RANK	CASE NAME	VALUE
1	United States	6737.4
2	Japan	4321.1
3	Germany	2075.5
4	France	1355.0
5	Italy	1101.3
6	United Kingdom	1069.5
7	China	630.2
8	Canada	569.9
9	Brazil	536.3
10	Spain	525.3

This ranking shows the GNP in billions of U.S. dollars. One million dollars in twenty-dollar bills will form a stack of money about 1½ feet long by 1 foot wide by 1¼ feet high. That is a lot of money. One billion dollars would make a stack just about as high as the Empire State Building in New York City.[2] In 1994, the GNP of the United States was 6.7 trillion dollars, that is, 6.7 thousand billion. Or, using our stacking system, it would be a stack of twenty-dollar bills 6,700 Empire State Buildings high! GNP increases with population. This does not mean that larger nation-states have healthier economies; it means that there is more economic activity where there are more people. To adjust for this, the gross national product per capita (GNPPC) is often reported instead of the GNP. GNP per capita is the GNP divided by the size of the population.

Data File: **NATIONS**
Task: **Mapping**
➤ Variable 1: **53) GNPPC94**
➤ View: **List: Rank**

RANK	CASE NAME	VALUE
1	Luxembourg	39600.0
2	Switzerland	37930.0
3	Japan	34630.0
4	Denmark	27970.0
5	Norway	26390.0
6	United States	25880.0
7	Germany	25580.0
8	Iceland	24630.0
8	Austria	24630.0
10	Sweden	23530.0

The United States ranked first in overall GNP in 1994 but ranked only sixth in GNP per capita. Generally, GNP per capita is considered to be a better measure of a nation-state's economic health and productivity than GNP alone.

The difference between the value of exports and the value of imports in a given year is the merchandise trade balance. A positive trade balance means the nation-state is exporting more than it is importing. A negative trade balance means imports exceed exports.

---

[2] A bundle of 100 twenty-dollar bills is about 1/2 inch high by 2½ inches wide by 6 inches long. The Empire State Building is 1,250 feet high (without the radio tower). Thus, 1/1000 of the Empire State Building is 1¼ feet. That would be a stack of 30 bundles of twenties. At $60,000 per stack we need about 16⅔ bundles to make a million dollars, or 15 stacks with a little left over. Fifteen stacks would be about 1½ feet long by 1 foot wide by 1¼ feet high.

RANK	CASE NAME	VALUE
1	Japan	106.750
2	Germany	75.000
3	Italy	22.100
4	Saudi Arabia	20.400
5	Russia	19.900
6	Canada	18.300
7	Netherlands	13.000
8	Sweden	9.400
9	Mexico	8.000
10	Indonesia	7.900

Scrolling down the ranking of trade balance, you will find that industrialized countries like Japan and Germany and oil-exporting countries like Saudi Arabia and Venezuela have strong positive trade balances. Most of the less developed countries like Senegal or Uruguay have negative trade balances. Why is the United States at the bottom of the ranking? It certainly is not because it has a weak economy. We just saw that the U.S. had the largest GNP and ranked sixth overall in GNP per capita. The U.S. has a large trade deficit because it is the strongest market in the world with consumers who are willing to buy overseas products. Thus, while exports from the United States are very high, imports are higher. How does the trade balance affect the domestic economy? Before we answer this, we need to examine another aspect of international political economy.

Most nation-states have their own currency. These currencies, like the U.S. dollar, are used to value transactions between buyers and sellers in the domestic economy. Problems arise, however, when buyers and sellers are in different nation-states. Imagine that a Japanese electronic company would like to sell CD players to buyers in Ecuador. The company is probably unwilling to take Ecuadorean sucres in payment. The company may be willing to take U.S. dollars or Swiss francs, even though their costs and wages are paid in Japanese yen. Currencies that can be easily traded in the world market and for which there is a high demand in the international economy are considered to be "hard currencies." Soft currencies like the sucre have little international value. Many students find foreign exchange a difficult concept. The best thing to do is forget that we are talking about money and think of the transaction as if you were buying apples instead of currencies. If the price of apples goes up, you have to pay more dollars for them. Thus the value of each dollar is lower because you have to pay more dollars to get an apple. The value of the Ecuadorean sucre fell dramatically against the U.S. dollar from 1995 to 2000. In 1995 the exchange rate was 2,564.5 sucres per dollar. In 2000 the exchange rate was 24,860.7 sucres per dollar. We can explore these ideas by comparing three currencies against the dollar.

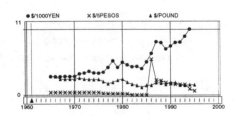

The graph shows the cost of the one British pound, 1000 Japanese yen, and five Mexican pesos in U.S. dollars over the years 1965 to 1995. The value (cost) of the yen increased throughout this period. The value of the British pound fell somewhat. The value of the Mexican peso was very low until 1986 when the Mexican government officially revalued the peso. Even so, the value of the peso fell steadily from 1986 to 1995. The rise in the value of the Japanese yen meant there was a corresponding fall in the value of the dollar. In 1965 it cost about $2.77 to buy 1000 yen. By 1994, the cost of 1000 yen rose to over 10 dollars. Thus the yen was worth more and the dollar was worth less.

In order to buy imports, one needs to have the currency of the exporting country. If the cost of that currency rises, imports will fall and exports will rise. This is beneficial for the balance of trade. This is, however, a complicated relationship that is affected by many other factors including the types of goods being traded and the quality of goods being traded. The relationship between foreign exchange and the balance of trade is best illustrated by looking at the U.S. trade balance against the value of the British pound.

Data File: **HISTORY**
➤ Task: **Scatterplot**
➤ Dependent Variable: **4) BAL TRADE**
➤ Independent Variable: **61) $/POUND**
➤ View: **Reg. Line**

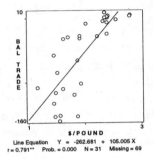

Line Equation   Y = -262.681 + 105.005 X
r = 0.791**   Prob. = 0.000   N = 31   Missing = 69

The plot shows that years when the cost of the pound was low (strong dollar), the United States ran a significant trade deficit. In years when the cost of the pound was high (weak dollar), the U.S. trade balance was improved. The relationship between these two variables is statistically significant with a correlation coefficient of +0.791.

While the volume of imports and exports measures the scale of the international activity of an economy, it does not tell us enough about the effects of these transactions. Another measure of a nation-state's international economic position is the terms of trade. Terms of trade measures the differences over time between the price of imports and the price of exports. If the price of exports rises relative to the price of imports, the nation-state has improving terms of trade. This is good because the price of what the country sells is rising compared to the price of what the country buys. If the price of exports falls relative to the price of imports, then the country has deteriorating terms of trade. Constant terms of trade occur when the prices of exports and imports are relatively constant.

➤ Data File: **NATIONS**
➤ Task: **Mapping**
➤ Variable 1: **96) TERMTRADE**
➤ View: **List: Rank**

RANK	CASE NAME	VALUE
1	Venezuela	157
2	Spain	122
3	Mexico	120
4	Myanmar	119
5	Chile	118
6	Jordan	116
7	Guinea-Bissau	115
8	Dominican Republic	113
9	Israel	112
10	Turkey	111

The variable in this ranking is indexed so that 1987 equals 100. That is, it measures changes in the terms of trade relative to 1987. If, since 1987, the terms of trade have improved, the value will be greater than 100. If the terms of trade have deteriorated since 1987, the variable will be less than 100. Values around 100 show constant terms of trade. Countries with improving terms of trade include oil exporters like Mexico and Venezuela. Many of the industrialized countries like Germany and the United States had fairly constant terms of trade while many of the less developed countries like Honduras and Uganda had deteriorating terms of trade. Deteriorating terms of trade can be very harmful to economic growth. This means that what the *country buys* is rising in price relative to *what it sells*. Thus, the economy must produce more and more exports just to stay even. If a country cannot produce more exports, it faces significant strains on its economy. We will discuss this problem more in Exercise 11.

ISSUES IN THE POLITICS OF THE INTERNATIONAL POLITICAL ECONOMY

The term *international political economy* is a popular description of the connection between politics and economics in international relations. It can refer to something as mundane as the politics of the World Trade Organization or to something more abstract like whether or not actors create economic and political structures or whether those structures create the legal and empirical conditions that create actors. There are many issues that connect politics and economics, however defined. We will briefly examine the politics of trade and the concerns that the growth of multinational corporations and global investment cause for national sovereignty.

There are many arguments for and against free trade. Proponents of free trade claim that the increased competition in the domestic economy by foreign suppliers will give the consumer more choices, provide a better product, and reduce prices. There is little doubt that the American-manufactured automobile has improved in quality and customer service since the 1970s due to competitive pressures from Japan, Europe, and Korea. Free-trade economists point out that the increased efficiency of the competitive market will benefit the whole economy. Free-trade political scientists claim that, like the functionalism of international organization discussed in Exercise 9, free trade reduces the likelihood of conflict because economically dependent trading partners do not fight each other. All of these arguments fall on deaf ears of the workers who are laid off due to foreign competition. Opponents of free trade claim that trade restrictions protect jobs. They are quick to claim that even in free-trade regimes, opposing nation-states will cheat. On a macro-economic scale, opponents assert that the benefits from free trade are outweighed by the need to protect infant industries that can stimulate economic growth. Finally, free-trade opponents fear the consequences of foreign competition in strategic industries, such as steel production, electronics, or agriculture, that are vital to producing national power and protecting national interests.

The concept of free trade itself is a misnomer. Free trade exists when the producers in two different countries have exactly the same position in the market in the other country; that is, there are no restrictions on imports of any type. Trade is rarely, if ever, completely free of restrictions. We should, instead, speak of trade that is more or less restricted. There are many types of trade restrictions. Tariffs are the most common restriction. A tariff is simply a tax placed on an import. Thus, if there is a 10% tariff on imports, a car that normally costs $20,000 will cost $22,000. By raising the sales price, the government hopes to reduce the volume of imports and it gains some revenue as well.

Data File: **NATIONS**
Task: **Mapping**
➤ Variable 1: **95) TARIFFS**
➤ View: **List: Rank**

RANK	CASE NAME	VALUE
1	India	30.0
1	Sri Lanka	30.0
3	Mauritius	29.1
4	Malawi	25.3
5	Zimbabwe	24.3
6	China	23.9
7	Tanzania	21.6
7	Philippines	21.6
9	Papua New Guinea	20.7
10	Central African Republic	18.6

The ranking shows the average tariffs for all imported products. Some states impose 100% tariffs on some products, especially high-end consumer goods (cars, stereos, etc.) or technical products like computers. Other forms of trade restrictions include quotas, subsidies, technical restrictions, and embargos. Quotas are limits on the number of units of a product that can be imported. Subsidies are government payments to the producers of a product. This gives an unfair advantage over other producers that are trying to compete in the global marketplace. Technical restrictions are prohibition on imports based on some technical quality of the import. For example, in 1989 the European Union banned imports of beef from cattle raised using growth hormones. The European Union claimed that this was done to protect its consumers against health risks of hormone-treated beef. The United States claimed that its farmers had been unfairly targeted for political and economic reasons, not for health reasons. An embargo is simply a ban on all imports or specific products from a particular country. The United States embargos Cuban products.

Trade restrictions are very political. Industries with political influence can get restrictions placed on their competitors' products. Often, nation-states with high unemployment rates will be pressured by their people to restrict imports.

Data File: **NATIONS**
➤ Task: **Scatterplot**
➤ Dependent Variable: **95) TARIFFS**
➤ Independent Variable: **103) UNEMPLYRT**
➤ View: **Reg. Line**

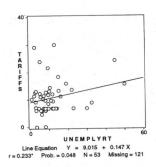

Line Equation $Y = 9.015 + 0.147 X$
$r = 0.233^*$ Prob. $= 0.048$ N $= 53$ Missing $= 121$

The plot seems to confirm our hypothesis. The correlation for this relationship is +0.233, which indicates a weak to moderate relationship between a nation-state's unemployment rate and its tariff rate. This correlation is statistically significant. Therefore, nation-states with high unemployment rates do have higher tariffs. An alternative interpretation of these data is that high tariffs cause high unemployment. Thus, the relationship stands, but the direction of causality is reversed.

One crude indicator of a problem with unfair trade is the balance of trade with specific states. We mentioned earlier that the balance of trade is the difference between the volume of exports and the volume of imports. This indicator is often calculated for all trade for one year, but it can also be calculated on a bilateral basis. That is, the United States can calculate its balance of trade with Japan by subtracting all imports from Japan in a year from the value of all exports to Japan. The news is often filled with complaints about the trade balance with Japan. You can compare the balance of trade between Japan and the United States with Japan's level of tariff.

Data File: **NATIONS**
➤ Task: **Mapping**
➤ Variable 1: **16) BALTRADEUS**
➤ Variable 2: **95) TARIFFS**
➤ Views: **List: Rank**

RANK	CASE NAME	VALUE
1	Netherlands	12533.8
2	Australia	7460.0
3	Brazil	6289.2
4	Belgium	5508.4
5	United Kingdom	3766.0

RANK	CASE NAME	VALUE
1	India	30.0
1	Sri Lanka	30.0
3	Mauritius	29.1
4	Malawi	25.3
5	Zimbabwe	24.3

If you scroll down the rankings, you will find that the U.S. trade deficit with Japan ranks 148th, making it the worst trade balance with the United States of any nation-state. Yet, Japan ranks 55th in overall tariff level, placing it in the same category as the United States. Thus, the trade deficit with Japan does not seem to be due to excessive tariffs alone. But, as we mentioned above, there are other trade barriers besides tariffs.

The U.S. trade deficit with China ranks 147th, making it the second worst trade deficit with the United States of all the nation-states (after Japan). There are other political issues raised in the trading relationship between the U.S. and China. One of the most significant of these issues is human and civil rights. Many politicians in the United States, both liberal and conservative, believe that the U.S. should not open trade relations with China until the Chinese government reduces abuses of human and civil rights. This raises a serious question for international relations. How much should political or economic foreign policy be based on moral imperatives? With over 1.2 billion people, China represents a significant market for foreign goods. Is the national interest served by limiting access to this market in order to make a political statement about human and civil rights? Moreover, how much does U.S. trade follow the moral flag? That is, does the United States trade with other countries with poor human and civil rights?

Data File: **NATIONS**
➤ Task: **Mapping**
➤ Variable 1: **111) USTRADE97**
➤ Variable 2: **19) CIVIL LIBS**
➤ Views: **Map**

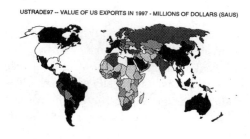

USTRADE97 -- VALUE OF US EXPORTS IN 1997 - MILLIONS OF DOLLARS (SAUS)

r = 0.214**

CIVIL LIBS -- EXTENT OF INDIVIDUAL CIVIL LIBERTIES, 7 = MOST (FITW, 1995)

There is a small, but statistically significant, correlation (r = 0.214**) between the value of U.S. exports and the extent of civil liberties. This implies that countries with greater levels of civil liberties have somewhat higher levels of trade with the United States. We must be careful, however, in interpreting this correlation. Traditionally, the U.S. has its strongest economic ties in North America and Europe. We would expect, therefore, that these regions have the largest value of U.S. exports. These regions are also where democratic ideals and protection of civil liberties are strong. The two variables may show a correlation, but we have no evidence of a causal link. On the contrary, when we look at the two variables case-by-case, we see that there are many nation-states with a high volume of U.S. trade but low values for civil liberties. For example, if you click on China in either map, you will see that it ranks 13th in overall exports and 149th in civil liberties. Similarly, Egypt ranks 30th in exports and 129th in civil liberties. Trade with politically oppressive nation-states is sometimes justified on the basis of "constructive engagement," whereby it is thought that the U.S. can have more influence over ending political oppression by keeping lines of communication and commerce open than it can by cutting off trade. While China's vast population represents a large potential market, it is not at this point a large trading partner, per se. We can see this by taking a closer look at the USTRADE97 variable.

Data File: **NATIONS**
Task: **Mapping**
➤ Variable 1: **111) USTRADE97**
➤ View: **List: Rank**

RANK	CASE NAME	VALUE
1	Canada	151766.7
2	Mexico	71388.4
3	Japan	65548.5
4	United Kingdom	36425.3
5	South Korea	25046.1
6	Germany	24458.3
7	Taiwan	20365.7
8	Netherlands	19826.0
9	Singapore	17696.2
10	France	15964.9

Scrolling down the ranking of the value of U.S. trade with various nation-states in 1997, you will see that, while China ranks 13th overall in U.S. exports, many smaller countries, including Singapore (population = 3.0 million) and Belgium (population = 10.2 million), have a larger volume of the U.S. overseas market. Critics of constructive engagement point out that the relatively small volume of trade between the United States and China is not likely to be enough to gain the influence needed to affect civil liberties, while proponents of U.S.-China trade use the same figures to claim that cutting off this amount of trade will hardly hurt China enough to affect its human rights practices.

Another issue in the international political economy is the effect of large multinational corporations on the domestic economy and on sovereignty. A multinational corporation is any business enterprise with either production facilities or sales facilities in more than one nation-state. There are few reliable counts of the number of multinational corporations because these enterprises can range in size from Exxon Corporation, an oil company with annual revenue in excess of $100 billion, to a small manufacturing company based in the U.S. with an assembly plant in Mexico. The United Nations Conference on Trade and Development Division on Transnational Corporations and Investment attempts to catalog multinational corporations. In 1995, it estimated that there were over 34,000 multinational corporations in the world (UNCTAD, 1995:8). Most multinational corporations are based in the industrialized countries and, contrary to much popular opinion, most of their overseas facilities are also in the industrialized countries. Businesses go where the business is. The variables MNC HQ and MNC HOST in the NATIONS data file show the number of headquarters and overseas facilities in each country respectively.

Data File:	**NATIONS**
Task:	**Mapping**
➤ *Variable 1:*	**67) MNC HQ**
➤ *Variable 2:*	**66) MNC HOST**
➤ *Views:*	**Map**

MNC HQ -- NUMBER OF PARENT MULTINATIONAL CORPORATIONS BASED IN COUNTRY - (UNWIR)

r = 0.151

MNC HOST -- FOREIGN AFFILIATES OF MULTINATIONAL CORPORATIONS LOCATED IN COUNTRY (UNWIR)

The map shows no correlation between the location of the headquarters and the facilities worldwide. We can explore this further with a Scatterplot of the two variables.

Data File: **NATIONS**
➤ Task: **Scatterplot**
➤ Dependent Variable: **67) MNC HQ**
➤ Independent Variable: **66) MNC HOST**
➤ View: **Reg. Line**

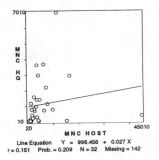

Line Equation   Y = 998.456 + 0.027 X
r = 0.151   Prob. = 0.209   N = 32   Missing = 142

Although the plot seems to show that there is a positive relationship between these two variables, the correlation coefficient is small and not statistically significant (r = 0.151, prob. = 0.209). Note the case in the lower right side of the graph. If you click on this case you will find that it is China. China has an exceptionally large number of MNC facilities (45,000) and an exceptionally low number of MNC headquarters (379). This is not surprising. China's 1.2 billion people and low wages attract many corporations trying to sell and produce their wares. Yet China's Maoist economic policies preclude its being a major location for multinational corporations' headquarters. If you remove China from the graph, the rest of the data show a strong correlation implying that multinational corporation headquarters and multinational corporation facilities tend to congregate in the same countries (r = 0.472 and prob. = 0.004).

Regardless of where they invest, there is concern about the effect of multinational corporations on local economies. In 1994, the total revenue of General Motors was larger than the gross national product of Norway (Kegley and Wittkopf, 1997:194). This type of economic wealth coincides with political power. There are many arguments against and in favor of the operations of multinational corporations. Those in favor cite the investment that multinationals bring to the host country, which can stimulate jobs and provide tax revenue for the government. Critics point out that multinational corporations often turn to local investment markets rather than international direct investment. When this happens, funds that could be used to stimulate domestic industries are drained into the enterprises of the multinational corporation, which ultimately profits shareholders in other countries. Critics also complain that while multinational corporations do create jobs, wages are low and working conditions are poor. Locally trained managers and technicians are often reassigned outside the host country creating a "brain drain" of local talent. Finally, it is often only by giving the multinational corporation tax breaks that it is willing to locate a facility in the host country, so tax revenues are lost.

One way to measure the growth in multinational enterprises is through the level of foreign direct investment (FDI), which is the value of investment in a country's economy by people and organizations abroad. FDI is not the same as foreign aid, which usually takes the form of grants or loans. Like any investment, FDI is purchasing a share of the foreign enterprise and is given with the expectation of a return. The variables FDI DC and FDI LDC in the HISTORY file give the level of foreign direct investment per year in the developed countries and the less developed countries respectively.

> *Data File:* **HISTORY**
> > *Task:* **Historical Trends**
> *Variables:* **19) FDI DC**
> > **20) FDI LDC**

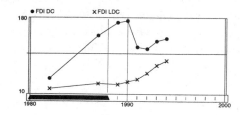

Foreign direct investment in developed and less developed countries

Foreign direct investment in the developed countries increased through 1990 and then took a sharp decline. At that point, however, the level of FDI in the less developed countries expanded rapidly. As the graph shows, foreign direct investment is highest in the developed countries. We can confirm this by comparing the level of foreign direct investment with the gross national product per capita.

> *Data File:* **NATIONS**
> > *Task:* **Mapping**
> *Variable 1:* **45) FDI**
> *Variable 2:* **53) GNPPC94**
> > *Views:* **Map**

FDI -- PRIVATE FOREIGN DIRECT INVESTMENT - MILLIONS OF US$ (WDI98)

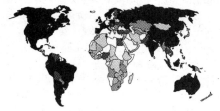

r = 0.393**

GNPPC94 -- GROSS NATIONAL PRODUCT PER CAPITA FOR 1994 IN CURRENT $US
(HDR)

The correlation coefficient (r = 0.393) shows a moderate, statistically significant relationship between the level of foreign direct investment and the gross national product per capita of the nation-state. States with higher GNP per capita also received more foreign direct investment.

THE INSTITUTIONAL AND POLITICAL SETTING OF THE INTERNATIONAL POLITICAL ECONOMY

Prior to World War II there was little effort to control the international economy. To some extent, management of the world economy fell into the laps of the one or two largest nation-states that were interested in a stable world economy because of their size. Some analysts refer to this process as hegemonic leadership whereby the powerful economy leads the rest of the economies by providing investment

178

International Relations

capital and open markets to stimulate a sagging world economy. The United Kingdom supposedly played this role through most of the 19th century. Charles Kindleberger (1973:291), a famous economic historian, claimed that the Great Depression of the 1930s occurred, in part, because "the international economic system was rendered unstable by British inability and United States unwillingness to assume responsibility for stabilizing it. World War II left most of the major economies in shambles. Forty-four nation-states met at Bretton Woods, New Hampshire, in 1944 to discuss how best to reconstruct the world economy. Out of this "Bretton Woods" agreement came a system of economic coordination that centered around two international organizations, the International Bank for Reconstruction and Development (better known as the World Bank) and the International Monetary Fund (IMF). These new organizations were created as specialized agencies of the United Nations (see Exercise 9). The World Bank was charged with giving loans and grants to help rebuild the war-torn economies, while the IMF was charged with maintaining stability in the world markets to foster growth. By 1947, it became clear that the effort needed to reconstruct Europe and Asia was larger than a self-supporting international bank could handle so the United States developed a grant and loan program that became known as the Marshall Plan, in honor of the U.S. Secretary of State at the time, George Marshall.

Through the 1950s and 60s the United States took a leadership role in the world economy, much like the United Kingdom did in the 19th century. By 1973, the United States, facing its own financial problems, stepped away from the leadership role and let the dollar fluctuate against other currencies. From that time on, leaders of the major world economies have met at least once per year to coordinate economic policy. This meeting has become known as the Group of Seven, because of the seven nation-states involved in the meeting (Canada, France, Germany, Italy, Japan, United Kingdom, and United States). Since 1998, Russia has been added to create the Group of Eight, although its participation has been spotty.

Regardless of U.S. leadership, the period since World War II has been marked by increasing economic coordination and increasing integration of economic policies. Nowhere is this more evident than in the major economic integration regimes like the European Union, the Latin American Integration Association (LAIA), the Common Market for Eastern and Southern Africa (COMESA), the Economic Community of West African States (ECOWAS), and the Asia-Pacific Economic Cooperation organization (APEC).

    Data File: **NATIONS**
       Task: **Mapping**
➤ Variable 1: **43) ECONORG**
      ➤ View: **Map**
   ➤ Display: **Legend**

ECONORG -- MAJOR ECONOMIC INTEGRATION AND FREE TRADE ORGANIZATIONS (RR)

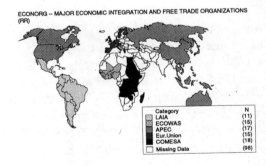

Category	N
LAIA	(11)
ECOWAS	(15)
APEC	(17)
Eur.Union	(15)
COMESA	(18)
Missing Data	(98)

The map shows that much of the globe is now involved with some type of economic integration regime. The degree of coordination and flexibility for the individual nation-state varies considerably among these organizations. The European Union now issues its own passports and prints its own money while APEC is little more than a general plan to coordinate policies. Some of these integration regimes are overlapping. For example, the North American Free Trade Agreement was negotiated to open trade between the United States, Canada, and Mexico. It is not included on the map. You will note, however, that each of these countries also belongs to one of the other integration regimes.

The General Agreement on Tariffs and Trade (GATT) was both an organization and a process by which the countries of the world came together to negotiate general trading principles. There have been eight rounds of these negotiations since 1947. The most recent round, called the Uruguay Round, began in 1986 and ended in 1994 with a treaty that created the World Trade Organization (WTO). Both GATT and the WTO established the rules of the bilateral trading system. Neither GATT nor the WTO managed world trade as a whole. Rather, the member states agreed to follow the rules in their trading with other member states (thus the concept of a bilateral system). Member states agreed to abide by the basic principle of non-discrimination, which means that barriers to foreign goods will ultimately be eliminated so that products produced at home and abroad will be treated in the same way. Disputes will be settled by an arbitration panel. If a member state does not comply with a finding of the panel, the aggrieved member will be given authorization to retaliate by restricting trade with the offending state. As of August 1999, the WTO had been presented with 179 cases for arbitration. Of these, 22 were decided by the panel. Others are pending or were settled by the parties. Not all nation-states are members of the WTO. China's membership is pending as this book is being written. The variable WTO on the NATIONS file shows membership in the WTO as of August 1999.

> Data File: **NATIONS**
> Task: **Mapping**
> ➤ Variable 1: **122) WTO**
> ➤ View: **Map**
> ➤ Display: **Legend**

WTO – MEMBERS OF THE WORLD TRADE ORGANIZATION (RR)

Category	N
Non Member	(46)
Member	(128)
Missing Data	

The United States has opposed Chinese membership due to complaints about unfair trading practices and, as we discussed previously, as part of an ongoing debate over Chinese civil and human rights policies.

Another aspect of the politics of the international political economy is economic sanctions. Sanctions are restrictions of economic activity placed on a nation-state due to political considerations. Sanctions can be placed by the U.N. Security Council under the authority of Article 41 of the United Nations Charter. Sometimes sanctions are placed bilaterally. That is, they are placed by one country against another. Such is the case with U.S. sanctions against Cuba. This type of sanction is sometimes called "economic statecraft" because it involves using the tool of economic relations to affect a political outcome. The variable SANCTIONS on the NATIONS file shows the nation-states where the U.S. had imposed economic sanctions at the end of 1999.

Data File: **NATIONS**
Task: **Mapping**
➤ Variable 1: **88) SANCTIONS**
➤ View: **Map**
➤ Display: **Legend**

SANCTIONS -- NATION-STATES UNDER U.S. ECONOMIC SANCTIONS AS OF AUGUST 1999 (USOFAC)

Category	N
No Sanct.	(164)
Sanctions	(10)
Missing Data	

As you can see, there are not many countries where the United States had imposed economic sanctions.. Are sanctions effective? That depends on the purpose of the sanctions. During the 1980s there were many calls for U.S. economic sanctions against South Africa due to its policy of racial apartheid. Critics responded with the constructive engagement argument discussed previously, and they pointed out that South Africa's economy was strong enough to withstand the sanctions. The only people getting hurt were the blacks and coloured at the lower end of the economic spectrum. Proponents of sanctions claimed that sanctions are effective if only to assuage our own soul by knowing that we are not trading with such a country. In the case of South Africa, sanctions did contribute, along with other diplomatic pressures, to the removal of apartheid.

WORKSHEET

NAME:

COURSE:

DATE:

EXERCISE
10

REVIEW QUESTIONS

Based on the first part of this exercise, answer True or False to the following items:

In most years, there are many more military events in international relations than economic events.	T	F
Unlike gross domestic product, gross national product includes the value of exports and imports in its calculation of economic activity for a nation-state.	T	F
The more goods a nation-state imports, the higher its gross national product will be.	T	F
The gross national product is the best measure of the productivity of a nation-state's economy.	T	F
When the U.S. dollar falls against the British pound, it costs more dollars to buy one pound.	T	F
A falling national currency usually has the effect of raising the country's volume of imports.	T	F
Rising terms of trade result from the cost of a nation-state's exports rising faster than the cost of its imports.	T	F
Free trade benefits consumers by creating competition that can lower prices and provide a better quality good.	T	F
A tariff is the number of goods that can be imported from a particular nation-state.	T	F
The United States, in general, will not engage in trade with nation-states that violate basic human and civil rights.	T	F

EXPLORIT QUESTIONS

1. In the preliminary section of Exercise 10, we noted that one's views on politics of the international economy are affected by such things as one's employment status. A basic axiom of public opinion and foreign policy is that people are generally not interested in foreign policy issues unless they involve direct warfare or the pocketbook. Although many of the issues are complicated, people do tend to follow policies related to international economics because these issues affect their lives directly. We can explore some of the connections between public opinion and international political economy.

a.   We begin by looking at how the respondents to the American Public Opinion and U.S. Foreign Policy Survey viewed some recent major economic policies. Specifically, what did the respondents think about tariffs, trade between the U.S. and the European Union, trade between the U.S. and Japan? Run the analysis listed below using Student ExplorIt and answer the questions.

> ➤ *Data File:* **FPSURVEY**
> ➤ *Task:* **Univariate**
> ➤ *Primary Variable:* **28) TARIFFS**

What percentage of respondents believed that tariffs should be eliminated?   _____%

> *Data File:* **FPSURVEY**
> *Task:* **Univariate**
> ➤ *Primary Variable:* **32) TRADEEU**

What percentage of respondents believed that the European Union is unfair
in its trade with the United States?   _____%

> *Data File:* **FPSURVEY**
> *Task:* **Univariate**
> ➤ *Primary Variable:* **33) TRADEJPN**

What percentage of respondents believed that Japan is unfair
in its trade with the United States?   _____%

b.   The three issues discussed above may be affected by the respondent's political ideology. That is, political liberals and conservatives are unlikely to agree on these issues. Pick one of the issues, write a hypothesis for the relationship between the respondent's political ideology (LIB-CON2) and your dependent variable, then test your hypothesis by following the directions to create a cross-tabulation using Student ExplorIt.

Pick one of the three issues (tariffs, views on the EU's fairness in trade, or views on Japan's fairness in trade) and write a statement that describes how you think political liberals and conservatives will differ (or be the same) in their opinions about the issue.

Run a cross-tabulation that compares the values of the variable you chose against respondent's political ideology (conservative, neutral, liberal) by following the Student ExplorIt Guide below and then fill in the table as needed. The variable names in the FPSURVEY file that correspond to each of the issues are

28) TARIFFS   Should tariffs be eliminated (yes/no)

32) TRADEEU   EU countries practice fair trade (fair/unfair)

33) TRADEJPN   Japan practices fair trade (fair/unfair)

> Data File: **FPSURVEY**
> ➤ Task: **Cross-tabulation**
> ➤ Row Variable: _____ **(variable name for your issue)**
> ➤ Column Variable: **22) LIBCONS**
> ➤ View: **Table**
> ➤ Display: **Column %**

Fill in the table below using the results of your cross-tabulation.

Row Variable: _____

	CONSERVATIVE	NEUTRAL	LIBERAL
% IN FIRST ROW (i.e., % yes or % fair)	_____%	_____%	_____%

What is Cramer's V?   V = _____

Is V statistically significant?   Yes   No

Does this analysis support your hypothesis?   Yes   No

Please explain.

2. Economic performance varies greatly from country to country as we saw when we compared the different values of GNP per capita. We will see in the next exercise that there are other measures besides GNP per capita that indicate the level of economic development. Differences in economic development are sources of political strife as nation-states struggle to gain access to markets and financing. Although we will discuss the causes and effects of international development in the next exercise, let's begin that topic here by exploring differences in economic performance.

Economic performance varies substantially by region. Less developed countries as a whole are sometimes referred to as the "global South," because they are concentrated in the Southern Hemisphere. The variable GNPPC94B in the NATIONS data file divides the GNP per capita of each nation-state into two categories, high and low, at the median. That is, approximately 50% of the cases are in the high category and 50% are in the low category. We can now explore which region has the most high GNP per capita countries. Follow the Student ExplorIt guide below and answer the following questions.

> ➤ *Data File:* **NATIONS**
> ➤ *Task:* **Cross-tabulation**
> ➤ *Row Variable:* **54) GNPPC94B**
> ➤ *Column Variable:* **84) REGION**
> ➤ *View:* **Table**
> ➤ *Display:* **Column %**

	SUB SAHARAN	ARAB	ASIA/ PACIFIC	WEST. HEMIS.	EUROPE
% COUNTRIES WITH HIGH GNP PER CAPITA (second row of table)	_____%	_____%	_____%	_____%	_____%

3. Next, use a series of scatterplots to try to describe the economic characteristics associated with GNP per capita. The characteristics that we will explore are

106) URBAN %	Percent of population living in cities
105) URBAN GRWT	Rate of urban growth
125) % AGRIC $	Percent of GDP generated by agriculture
103) UNEMPLYRT	Unemployment rate
41) ECON GROW	Growth rate of the gross domestic product

a. Do you expect high GNP per capita countries to be more urbanized than low GNP per capita countries?   Yes   No

> *Data File:* **NATIONS**
> ➤ *Task:* **Scatterplot**
> ➤ *Dependent Variable:* **106) URBAN %**
> ➤ *Independent Variable:* **53) GNPPC94**
> ➤ *View:* **Reg. Line**

What is the correlation coefficient?   r = _____

Is the analysis significant?   Yes   No

Does the scatterplot support your answer above?   Yes   No

b. Do you expect the rate of urban growth in the low GNP per capita countries to be
higher than the rate of urbanization in the high GNP per capita countries?   Yes   No

> Data File: **NATIONS**
> Task: **Scatterplot**
> ➤ Dependent Variable: **105) URBAN GRWT**
> ➤ Independent Variable: **53) GNPPC94**
> ➤ View: **Reg. Line**

What is the correlation coefficient?   r = _____

Is the analysis significant?   Yes   No

Does the scatterplot support your answer above?   Yes   No

c. Do you expect low GNP per capita countries to be more agricultural than
high GNP per capita countries?   Yes   No

> Data File: **NATIONS**
> Task: **Scatterplot**
> ➤ Dependent Variable: **125) % AGRIC $**
> ➤ Independent Variable: **53) GNPPC94**
> ➤ View: **Reg. Line**

What is the correlation coefficient?   r = _____

Is the analysis significant?   Yes   No

Does the scatterplot support your answer above?   Yes   No

d. Do you expect the unemployment rate in the low GNP per capita countries to be
higher than the unemployment rate in the high GNP per capita countries?   Yes   No

> Data File: **NATIONS**
> Task: **Scatterplot**
> ➤ Dependent Variable: **103) UNEMPLYRT**
> ➤ Independent Variable: **53) GNPPC94**
> ➤ View: **Reg. Line**

What is the correlation coefficient?   r = _____

Is the analysis significant?   Yes   No

Does the scatterplot support your answer above?   Yes   No

e. GNP per capita is an indicator of the overall productivity of an economy. Is economic growth higher in countries with high GNP per capita than it is in countries with low GNP per capita?   Yes   No

Data File: **NATIONS**
Task: **Scatterplot**
➤ Dependent Variable: **41) ECON GROW**
➤ Independent Variable: **53) GNPPC94**
➤ View: **Reg. Line**

What is the correlation coefficient?   r = _____

Is the analysis significant?   Yes   No

Does the scatterplot support your answer above?   Yes   No

4. Write a brief statement summarizing what characteristics you would find in a nation-state with low GNP per capita and what you would find in a nation-state with high GNP per capita.

EXERCISE **11**

THE DEVELOPMENT DILEMMA

Tasks: Cross-tabulation, Historical Trends, Mapping, Scatterplot
Data Files: NATIONS, HISTORY, DEVELOP

IMAGES AND REALITY OF ECONOMIC DEVELOPMENT

In Exercise 10, we discovered that there are significant differences in economic performance between nation-states. These differences affect many aspects of life such as access to medical care and availability of proper nutrition. We will see later that the results of these differences are reduced life expectancy and substantially diminished quality of life. Why do such substantial economic differences exist between nation-states, and why, as the title of this exercise implies, are they so hard to alleviate?

Economic development implies a process in time. The economies of some nation-states grow rapidly while others flounder. We saw in Exercise 10 that differences in economic performance seem to be regionally concentrated. How has economic performance changed over time in these regions? Four variables in the HISTORY file, GNPPC IND, GNPPC LA, GNPPC AFR, and GNPPC ASIA, measure the average gross national product per capita for the industrialized countries, Latin America, Africa, and Asia respectively. A historical trends graph of these four variables will show how GNP per capita has changed in each group over time.

> *Data File:* **HISTORY**
>   *Task:* **Historical Trends**
>   *Variable:* **21) GNPPC AFR**
>   **22) GNPPC ASIA**
>   **23) GNPPC IND**
>   **24) GNPPC LA**

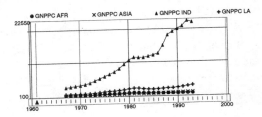

The GNP per capita of the industrialized nation-states is substantially higher than that of the other regions throughout the graph. The old adage that the rich get richer and the poor get poorer seems to hold true. Yet, it would be incorrect to treat all less developed regions and countries alike. If we remove the industrialized countries from the historical trends graph, we see that there are differences within the less developed countries that are masked by the data for the industrialized countries.

Data File: **HISTORY**

Task: **Historical Trends**

➤ Variable: **21) GNPPC AFR**

22) GNPPC ASIA

23) GNPPC LA

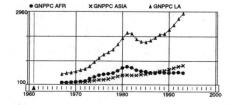

To remove variable 23) GNPPC IND from the analysis, click the [[⟳]] button, highlight the variable by clicking once on it, and <Delete>. Then click <OK> for the new trends graph.

It is clear from the graph without the industrial nations that some of the so-called less developed countries have seen substantial improvement in their economies over the years. The GNP per capita growth rate in Latin American rivals that of the industrialized countries. These findings mean that we must address another question. Not only do we wish to find out why some countries are underdeveloped and others are not, but we also need to find out why some less developed countries seem to develop rapidly while others do not.

There are at least two approaches to addressing these questions. Marshall Wolfe (1974) described these approaches as images of economic development. In one image the nation-states are marching along in a progression toward economic development. Those at the front have achieved sustainable economic growth and are enjoying its benefits. Those in the middle are struggling to enter the promised land and are achieving various levels of success. Those at the rear of the progression are slowing down and may never achieve sustainable growth. At minimum, the gap between them and those at the front is growing wider and wider. The key to success is finding the right formula of resources, skills, government intervention, and will. Nation-states are lined up as they are in the progression because some states have found the right mix and others simply may not have the inputs needed to succeed. Wolfe calls his second image of development the "living pyramid." In this image, the successful states sit atop a pyramid made up of the less developed states. They sit on the backs of those states and owe their position in economic development to their ability to exploit those below them. Some progress can be made moving up the pyramid, but gains are always relative—not absolute. That is, Brazil may become more developed but is unlikely to become as developed as the United States and unlikely to reach the top of the pyramid. Nation-states are not at the bottom of the pyramid because of any failure to perform adequately, but, rather, because of the structure of the international economy itself.

If the progression image is correct, then we should be able to find variables that can be affected by economic or governmental policy that correlate with the GNP per capita. Although we cannot explore this in great depth here, we can look at two policy variables that seem to imply that development requires the right mix of policies. The first is a purely economic variable, the savings rate. Nation-states where the people save more of their income are likely to have higher GNP per capita because savings generates investment whereas consumption does not.

190

International Relations

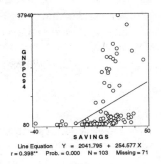

➤ Data File: **NATIONS**
➤ Task: **Scatterplot**
➤ Dependent Variable: **53) GNPPC94**
➤ Independent Variable: **89) SAVINGS**
➤ View: **Reg. Line**

The scatterplot seems to support the progression image. Clearly, nation-states with higher savings rates have higher GNP per capita. There is a fairly strong correlation (r = 0.398**) between savings rate and GNP per capita that is statistically significant. Another policy variable often discussed in the context of the progression image is the level of political stability. Investors are unlikely to invest in nation-states where there is a high degree of social unrest. If the progression image is correct, we would expect that states with low levels of cultural conflict have high levels of GNP per capita.

Data File: **NATIONS**
➤ *Task:* **Cross-tabulation**
➤ *Row Variable:* **54) GNPPC94B**
➤ *Column Variable:* **31) C.CONFLICT**
➤ *Views:* **Graph**
➤ *Display:* **Bar - Stack**

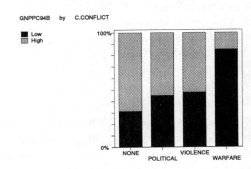

The bar stack graph seems to provide stunning confirmation of the progression image. Eighty-five percent of the nation-states that experienced cultural wars had GNP per capita below the median. Only 31% of the nation-states with no cultural conflict had GNP per capita below the median (Cramer's V = 0.363**). Using only these two variables, it would seem that the path to development requires a population that saves a significant portion of its income and has political and cultural stability.

But there are structural barriers to development that are difficult to overcome. In 1964, Raoul Prebisch, the first Secretary-General of the United Nations Conference on Trade and Development (UNCTAD), identified the relationship between terms of trade and the structure of imports and exports as one of these barriers. Prebisch contended that due to climate, location, and technology, most less-developed countries export primary goods and import secondary goods. A primary good is one that is sold in its original form—that is, a raw material like iron ore or grain. A secondary good is processed or manufactured, such as steel, automobiles, or bread. The price of primary goods tends to rise slower than the price of secondary goods. Thus, most less-developed countries have deteriorating terms of trade. As we discussed in Exercise 10, deteriorating terms of trade raises international debt and slows economic growth.

The development dilemma has two horns. First, economic underdevelopment is persistent. After two special United Nations decades of development and nearly a half century of economic aid, many nation-states are still facing persistent underdevelopment. The second horn is that our approach to economic development policy is affected by our "image" of development, and, as we shall see in our data, neither image can be completely rejected through data analysis.

THE LIVING PYRAMID, TERMS OF TRADE, AND THE STRUCTURE OF WORLD ECONOMY

To test the effect of structures such as the terms of trade on economic development, we must first determine whether or not less-developed countries were primarily exporters of primary goods and developed countries were exporters of secondary goods. The variable PRIM EXP85 in the NATIONS file measures the percentage of a nation-state's exports that are primary goods.[1] Major oil exporters, like Iran, have values close to 100% for PRIM EXP85 because they mostly export crude oil. For Japan, a highly industrialized country with few natural resources, primary goods made up only 2% of its 1985 exports.

<table>
<tr><td align="right">Data File:</td><td>NATIONS</td></tr>
<tr><td align="right">➤ Task:</td><td>Scatterplot</td></tr>
<tr><td align="right">➤ Dependent Variable:</td><td>83) PRIM EXP85</td></tr>
<tr><td align="right">➤ Independent Variable:</td><td>52) GNPPC85</td></tr>
<tr><td align="right">➤ View:</td><td>Reg. Line</td></tr>
</table>

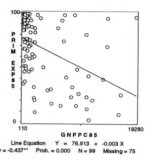

There is a strong negative correlation ($r = -0.437$**) between PRIM EXP85 and GNPPC85. This means that, as we expected, nation-states with higher GNP per capita mostly export secondary goods and those with lower GNP per capita export primary goods.

The variables PRICE PRIM and PRICE SEC in the HISTORY file measure how international prices have changed over time for primary and secondary goods. These variables are indexed to 1980. This means that the price in 1980 is standardized as 100 and subsequent years show the proportion above or below the 1980 price.

<table>
<tr><td align="right">➤ Data File:</td><td>HISTORY</td></tr>
<tr><td align="right">➤ Task:</td><td>Historical Trends</td></tr>
<tr><td align="right">➤ Variable:</td><td>36) PRICE SEC</td></tr>
<tr><td></td><td>37) PRICE PRIM</td></tr>
</table>

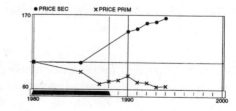

Changes in the international prices of primary and secondary goods

Prices of secondary (manufactured) goods rose over time and prices of primary goods tended to fall. So far, the data follow Prebisch's argument. Less developed countries tend to export primary goods. The

---

[1] We need a case study in time to test the terms of trade theory. That is, we need to look at one time period when we have sufficient data that can address our question. All the data in this section are for the year 1985 or the years surrounding 1985.

price of those primary exports tends to fall relative to the secondary goods that the less developed country must purchase on the international market. Logically, we would expect that less developed countries have deteriorating terms of trade over the same time period.

> ➤ *Data File:* **NATIONS**
> ➤ *Task:* **Scatterplot**
> ➤ *Dependent Variable:* **99) TRMTRD85**
> ➤ *Independent Variable:* **52) GNPPC85**
> ➤ *View:* **Reg. Line**

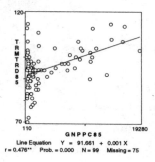

The positive correlation (r = 0.476**) between the terms of trade and the GNP per capita is statistically significant. This implies that less developed countries had deteriorating terms of trade and more developed countries had improving terms of trade. This is due to the structure of imports and exports. Since deteriorating terms of trade inhibits economic growth, the pyramid image seems to be valid here. Less developed countries may be impoverished due to structural aspects of the international economy, not their failure to find the right mix of policies.

THE ECONOMIC PROGRESSION: GHANA, GUATEMALA, AND SOUTH KOREA

One way to understand the process and problems of international development is to look at some specific cases. We will examine the economic development of Ghana, Guatemala, and South Korea since 1960. Table 11.1 illustrates some of the major differences and similarities between these three nation-states.

Ghana is a constitutional democracy in West Africa. The current President, Jerry Rawlins, took control of the government in a military coup in 1979 and again in 1981. He has since been elected President to a succession of four-year terms in 1992 and 1996. Ghana is well endowed with natural resources and has thriving hardwood, cocoa, and latex production. Guatemala is a democratic republic located in Central America. Its government has suffered under a succession of military coups and shaky democratic regimes throughout the 1960s and 70s. Guatemala's economy is built around family and large corporate agriculture. Korea has a recorded history that spans 2,000 years. In 1910, Japan annexed Korea. At the Potsdam conference in 1945, the allied forces fighting against Japan in World War II established the 38th parallel as the dividing line between American and Soviet occupying forces following the war. After the war, attempts to reunite Korea were effectively stopped by the Soviet Union. South Korea declared its independence in 1948. In 1950, North Korean troops invaded the South. The Korean War ended in 1953 with an uneasy and informal peace. South Korea, scarred by war, struggled in its economic development through the 1950s but with large amounts of foreign aid began rapid industrialization in the 1960s. South Korea was ruled by a succession of military governments until 1987 when, after a series of violent public demonstrations, the government agreed to open and free elections.

TABLE 11.1: COMPARISON OF GHANA, GUATEMALA, AND SOUTH KOREA ON MAJOR CHARACTERISTICS

	GHANA	**GUATEMALA**	**SOUTH KOREA**
Region	West Africa	Central America	East Asia
Date of Independence	1957, from UK	1821, from Spain	1948, from partition after World War II
Area (sq. km)	238,540	108,890	98, 480
Population (1996 est.)	17,698,271	11,277,614	45,482,291
Life Expectancy	54.2 years	65.2 years	73.3 years
Unemployment Rate	10% (1993 est.)	4.9% (1994 est.)	2% (1995 est.)
Major Resources	Gold, Timber, Diamonds, Bauxite	Oil, Nickel, Rare Woods, Fish, Chicle	Coal, Tungsten, Lead, Graphite, Molybdenum
Major Industries	Mining, Lumber, Light Manufacturing	Sugar, Furniture, Textiles, Chemicals	Electronics, Autos, Chemicals, Ships, Building, Clothing
Major Exports	$1 Billion (1993) Cocoa, Gold, Timber	$2.3 Billion (1995) Coffee, Sugar, Beef, Bananas, Cardamom	$124 Billion (1995) Electronics, Autos, Machinery, Steel, Ships, Footwear
Major Imports	$1.7 Billion (1993) Oil, Food, Consumer Goods	$2.85 Billion (1995) Oil Products, Grain, Machinery, Autos,	$135 Billion (1995) Machinery, Oil, Steel, Steel, Electronics, Chemicals

Source: The World Factbook, 1996. U.S. Central Intelligence Agency.

In 1967, Ghana, Guatemala, and Korea had similar low values of GNP per capita ($240, $300, and $140 respectively). We can explore what happened to these three economies from this point on.

➤ *Data File:* **DEVELOP**
   ➤ *Task:* **Historical Trends**
➤ *Variable:* **8) GNPPC GHAN**
         9) GNPPC GUAT
         10) GNPPC KOR

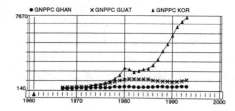

The graph shows that while South Korea started with the lowest GNP per capita of the three nation-states in 1967, its growth in GNP per capita was stunning compared to that of the other two countries.

The clear question is, Why was South Korea able to develop so rapidly when Guatemala and Ghana were not? Why has it succeeded in the progression compared with the other two? We may not be able to answer this question conclusively, but we can explore some of the data that will give us a picture of how and why development takes place.

While South Korea's development may seem miraculous, it was not done without help. In some ways, South Korea benefitted greatly in the 1960s and 70s from the strife that tore apart the Korean peninsula in the 1950s. Throughout the cold war, nation-states like South Korea were the focus of intense competition between the superpowers. The United States and its allies had a great stake in the success of the South Korean government and economy, so they were willing to pump large quantities of economic aid into a political and social setting that otherwise would have scared off donors and investors. Official development assistance (ODA) consists of grants and loans given directly to a government from another government or international organization. Our measure of ODA shows the net value received, which includes the amount paid back.

Data File: **DEVELOP**

Task: **Historical Trends**

➤ Variable: **17) ODAGHANA**

18) ODAGUAT

19) ODAKOR

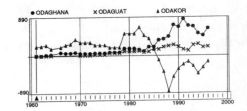

South Korea received more ODA from all sources than either of the other two nation-states. In 1986, South Korea began paying back more ODA than it received, thus its numbers on the graph become negative. South Korea also sought and received more loans from private and public sources than either Guatemala or Ghana.

Data File: **DEVELOP**

Task: **Historical Trends**

➤ Variable: **14) LOAN GHAN**

15) LOAN GUAT

16) LOAN KOR

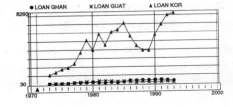

Typically, private lenders are unwilling to make loans where there is civil or political strife. Some authors use this as an argument for nation-states employing repression to maintain order (see Huntington, 1968). All three of the nation-states being discussed were led by autocratic, repressive rulers through much of the period being examined here, and each of them had at least one coup in which a popularly chosen political regime was overthrown by military leaders. Civil and political strife in South Korea drove some investors out, but loan guarantees through organizations such as the Overseas Private Investment Corporation (OPIC), an agency of the U.S. government, ensured that development funds were available in South Korea, in spite of the political and civil problems. The down side of private loans and some official direct assistance is that they increase a nation-state's debt.

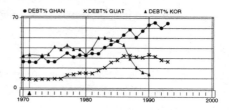

Data File: **DEVELOP**
Task: **Historical Trends**
➤ *Variable:* **5) DEB% GHAN**
6) DEBT% GUAT
7) DEBT% KOR

As we might expect since it had so many loans, South Korea had the highest external debt as a percentage of its GNP of the three nation-states throughout the 1970s and early 1980s. After 1982, Korean debt began to fall off as it began repaying the loans. Ghana's debt rose throughout the period of the data. By 1996, Ghana owed 65% of its gross national product.

While loans and ODA improve a nation-state's development chances, the debt they bring can slow economic development. Debt raises interest rates making it harder to get other loans and it can cause price inflation. The consumer price index (CPI) measures inflation by noting the proportional increase or decrease in prices relative to a particular year. For our data, the index year is 1987. In 1990, the CPI for Ghana was 226. This means that prices had increased by 126% (226 − 100 = 126) since 1987.

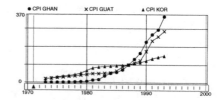

Data File: **DEVELOP**
Task: **Historical Trends**
➤ *Variable:* **2) CPI GHAN**
3) CPI GUAT
4) CPI KOR

Prices rose moderately in Korea throughout the period of the data. Both Guatemala and Ghana had substantial problems with consumer inflation, especially in the 1990s. Inflation slows development because it makes it difficult to buy necessary capital. Inflation is caused by many things including printing too much money and spending too much on the government.

Population growth can also slow economic development because it places strains on social services and depresses wages. We will explore the relationship between economic development and population growth rate in Exercise 12. For now, we will examine the population growth of the three nation-states in our case study.

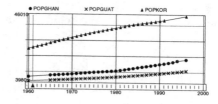

Data File: **DEVELOP**
Task: **Historical Trends**
➤ *Variable:* **20) POPGHAN**
21) POPGUAT
22) POPKOR

Korea had the largest population growth throughout the period of the data followed by Ghana and then Guatemala. The rate of South Korean population growth actually fell from 2.6% per year in 1966 to 0.9% in 1991. This contrasts with both Guatemala and Ghana. Guatemala's annual rate of population growth remained constant around 2.9% throughout the data while Ghana's rate of growth rose from 2.1% per year in 1966 to 3.0% in 1991.

Economic growth requires both economic and social infrastructure. Investment, loans, and aid must be coupled with education, health care, and income redistribution to create conditions that can sustain development. Education is both a cause and an effect of economic development. Sustained industrial production requires a technically educated workforce, but such technical education cannot occur without the economic conditions that support it. Education levels vary significantly among the three nation-states in our case study. Access to education can be measured by the proportion of children of secondary school age who are actually enrolled in school.

Data File: **DEVELOP**
Task: **Historical Trends**
➤ Variable: **23) SCH GHANA**
24) SCH GUAT
25) SCH KOR

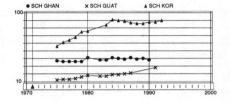

The historical trends graph shows that South Korea had the highest proportion of children enrolled in secondary education of the three nation-states. It also shows that for both South Korea and Guatemala, this proportion increased from 1975 through 1991. For Ghana, however, the proportion of eligible children enrolled in secondary school stayed relatively constant and actually fell in recent years.

There are many ways to measure economic development. We have been using GNP per capita as our primary indicator of the health of an economy. Other measures attempt to account for human and social conditions related to development. We will explore some of these measures in this exercise, but one very important social indicator is the life expectancy from birth. Life expectancy is measured as the average age that a population achieves. Since economic underdevelopment often increases infant mortality, life expectancy is usually lower in less developed countries.

Data File: **DEVELOP**
Task: **Historical Trends**
➤ Variable: **11) LIFE GHAN**
12) LIFE GUAT
13) LIFE KOR

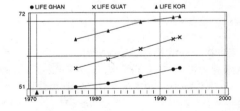

The bad news is that life expectancy from birth remains distressingly low in both Ghana (56.4 years in 1993) and Guatemala (65.3 years in 1993). The good news is that all three countries have had substantial improvement in life expectancy over the period of the data.

So, what has been South Korea's secret to economic development? We certainly do not have all the answers here, but we can shed some light on the question. South Korea's development was tied up with cold-war politics. Because of its history and strategic geography, South Korea received a large amount of aid and loans from the developed capitalist economies. South Korea was able to manage its inflation rate well and reduce its rate of population growth. South Korea was also able to capitalize on its long cultural tradition of valuing education. Did South Korea find the proper mix of policies that placed it at the head of the economic progression? To some extent, yes, but South Korea also benefited from its position in the cold war that broke down some of the structural barriers to development faced by other nation-states. Our data do not seem to resolve the development dilemma conclusively.

THE SOCIAL CONSEQUENCES OF ECONOMIC DEVELOPMENT

As we mentioned in the last section, there are many consequences and causes of development. During the late 1970s, U.S. strategies for promoting international development shifted from those related directly to supporting economic growth to what was called the "basic human needs" approach. Basic human needs focused on development strategies that improved the overall quality of life. This strategy did not ignore investment and economic infrastructure. Indeed, without economic growth, quality of life is unlikely to improve. Nevertheless, the strategy was based on a recognition that development meant more than growth in the GNP. Part of the reason for this strategy was that unequal distribution of income throughout the less developed countries meant that benefits from overall economic growth accrued only for those at the highest end of the income distribution. We can examine the level of income distribution with a variable in the NATIONS data file called $ RICH 10%. This variable shows the percentage of the GNP that is received by the richest 10% of the population. In a perfectly equal income distribution, the richest 10% of the population should receive 10% of the national income. Higher values of $ RICH 10% indicate unequal income distribution.

➤ *Data File:* **NATIONS**
➤ *Task:* **Mapping**
➤ *Variable 1:* **124) $ RICH 10%**
➤ *View:* **List: Rank**

RANK	CASE NAME	VALUE
1	Zimbabwe	55.5
2	Swaziland	54.5
3	Gabon	54.4
4	Ecuador	51.5
5	Nepal	50.7
6	Honduras	50.6
7	Brazil	48.3
8	Mauritius	46.7
9	Zambia	46.4
10	Kenya	45.4

Zimbabwe had the most unequal distribution of income in our data with the richest 10% of the population receiving over 55% of the national income. If you look further down the list, you will see that in six countries more than half the national income went to the richest 10%. In our data, the least amount that went to the top 10% was 20.5% of the national income—twice as much as you would see with a perfectly equal income distribution. In spite of several years of stunning growth rates in GNP, many countries were still suffering from the social impact of dire poverty. Health care, access to proper nutrition, education, and housing were not being improved.

The clearest measures we have of overall physical quality of life are life expectancy from birth and infant mortality per 1,000 live births. Since high infant mortality dramatically reduces average life expectancy, these two variables are highly correlated. We start by exploring the levels of these two variables across the world.

Data File: **NATIONS**

Task: **Mapping**

➤ Variable 1: **64) LIFE EXPCT**

➤ Variable 2: **63) INF. MORTL**

➤ Views: **Map**

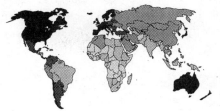

LIFE EXPCT -- AVERAGE LIFE EXPECTANCY (TWF 1994)

r = −0.955**

INF. MORTL -- NUMBER OF INFANT DEATHS PER 1,000 BIRTHS (TWF 1994)

The statistically significant correlation of −0.955** shows that the two variables are correlated such that high values of life expectancy are associated with low values of infant mortality. The maps clearly show that life expectancy is generally high in North America and Europe and low in the less developed regions of Latin America, Africa, and Asia. We can see what the values for these two variables are for various nation-states.

Data File: **NATIONS**

Task: **Mapping**

Variable 1: **64) LIFE EXPCT**

Variable 2: **63) INF. MORTL**

➤ Views: **List: Rank**

RANK	CASE NAME	VALUE
1	Japan	79.18
2	Iceland	78.86
3	Sweden	78.08
4	France	78.00
5	Switzerland	77.99

RANK	CASE NAME	VALUE
1	Somalia	162.70
2	Afghanistan	158.90
3	Western Sahara	155.50
4	Angola	148.60
5	Sierra Leone	145.00

Japan had the highest average life expectancy from birth (79.1 years). Scrolling down the list the United States ranked 24th with an average life expectancy of 75.8 years. Uganda and Somalia were at the bottom of the list with average life expectancies of 38.4 and 32.9 years respectively. Somalia also had the highest infant mortality rate at 162.7 per 1000 live births.

Exercise 11: The Development Dilemma

These data are very disturbing evidence of underlying structural violence in the world economy. That is, the distribution of wealth and economic productivity itself has a violent impact on people's lives in the same way that warfare does. Poverty kills people. An average life expectancy of 38 years means that many people die due to lack of access to basic human needs. We have alluded to the relationship between life expectancy and the GNP per capita. We should explore that relationship.

Data File: **NATIONS**
➤ Task: **Scatterplot**
➤ Dependent Variable: **64) LIFE EXPCT**
➤ Independent Variable: **53) GNPPC94**

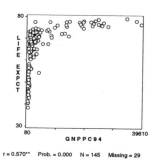

r = 0.570**   Prob. = 0.000   N = 145   Missing = 29

The graph shows a dramatic relationship between life expectancy and GNP per capita. Small changes in GNP per capita generate substantial improvements in life expectancy at the low end of the GNP per capita scale.[2] Increases in GNP per capita above about $10,000 produce little improvement in life expectancy. This relationship between GNP per capita and life expectancy has been called "the economic law of life, " which can be stated as "wealth cannot only buy a higher standard of living, it also buys life itself" (Kohler and Alcock, 1976:355). While basic human needs are still being addressed by development agencies, the focus of economic development strategies has shifted more to targeted economic growth and economic reform strategies.

ECONOMIC DEVELOPMENT ASSISTANCE

Throughout the cold war, the United States and its allies used economic aid as a carrot to attract the interests of nonaligned states in the struggles for the balance of power. Many programs, such as the Food for Peace program of the United States Agency for International Development, were intended to provide assistance to local populations with the hopes of winning hearts and minds to the Western Bloc. After the cold war ended with the fall of the Soviet Union in 1991, the United States no longer had the incentive to provide as much aid. We can use our data to explore the amount of economic assistance given by the major economic powers over time.

➤ Data File: **DEVELOP**
➤ Task: **Historical Trends**
➤ Variable: **26) FRANCE**
       27) JAPAN
       28) UK
       29) USA

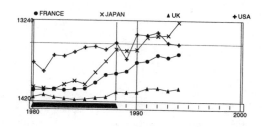

---

[2] Since the data in the graph are better represented by a curve than a straight line, the Pearson's correlation coefficient is not an appropriate measure of the relationship between the two variables. More advanced techniques for analyzing curvilinear relationships do confirm the correlation between GNP per capita and life expectancy.

The graph shows that the United States is no longer the largest donor state. U.S. foreign assistance leveled off and then fell during the 1990s. Japan is now the largest contributor to direct international assistance. France is also close to the United States in its donation of economic aid.

Our discussion of international economic development has, perhaps, left many questions unanswered. One of the questions we asked earlier is how development should be measured. One way to measure economic development is the GNP per capita. This gives us a good overall sense of the productivity of an economy, especially if it is observed over time. GNP per capita, however, tells us nothing about income distribution; that is, it does not tell us who benefits from economic change. GNP per capita also tells us nothing about the effect of economic change on meeting basic human needs, which can be a serious problem, especially if the income distribution is heavily skewed toward the richer members of the society. You can now explore some of these questions in the following worksheets.

WORKSHEET

NAME:

COURSE:

DATE:

EXERCISE

11

REVIEW QUESTIONS

Based on the first part of this exercise, answer True or False to the following items:

The GNP per capita of the non-industrialized Asian nation-states is higher, on average, than the average GNP per capita of the Latin American nation-states.　　T　F

According to the progression view of economic development, the less developed countries merely need to find the right mix of economic and political policies and resources to achieve economic development.　　T　F

According to the living pyramid view of economic development, the only way that a nation-state can sustain economic growth is to find a way to get around the structural barriers that are a natural part of the world economy.　　T　F

There is no apparent relationship between the level of cultural conflict in a society and its level of economic development.　　T　F

A primary good is one that can easily find a market in the international economy.　　T　F

According to our data, less developed countries tend to export primary goods and import secondary goods.　　T　F

South Korea has always had a higher GNP per capita than Ghana.　　T　F

South Korea's rate of population growth actually fell between 1966 and 1991 while Ghana's rate of population growth rose.　　T　F

The economic law of life implies that nation-states with high GNP per capita will also have high life expectancy.　　T　F

Japan is now the largest donor of official development assistance.　　T　F

EXPLORIT QUESTIONS

1.　In the preliminary section of Exercise 11, we discussed that there are other ways to measure development than the GNP or GNP per capita. Here, we will explore and compare these various methods for measuring development. Some of these methods, like GNP per capita, measure one aspect of development with the hope that other factors related to development are highly correlated with the one measure. Other methods develop an index that combines the scores of many variables to try to account for the multidimensional nature of development. Development is multidimensional because it must encompass both the ability of the economy to produce value and the effects of that value in meeting the basic human needs of the population.

a. Compare the ranking of each country in the table below on GNP per capita in 1994 (GNPPC94) with the ranking of the country on life expectancy from birth (LIFE EXPCT). We know that these two variables are highly related, but explore their values on a case-by-case basis.

➤ *Data File:* **NATIONS**
➤ *Task:* **Mapping**
➤ *Variable 1:* **53) GNPPC94**
➤ *Variable 1:* **64) LIFE EXPCT**
➤ *View:* **List: Alpha**

Country	Rank on GNPPC94	Rank on LIFE EXPCT
Gabon*	_____	_____
Namibia	_____	_____
Spain	_____	_____
Saudi Arabia*	_____	_____
United States*	_____	_____

* Denotes major oil reserves.

2. The United Nations Development Program (UNDP) developed an index to measure aspects of development beyond economic performance. The Human Development Index (HDI) uses a mathematical weighting procedure to combine measures of life expectancy, adult literacy, school enrollment, and gross domestic product per capita into one index. Another development index known as the Physical Quality of Life Index (PQLI) combines measures of literacy, infant mortality, and life expectancy into one index. Compare the three measures of development (GNPPC94, HDI, and PQLI) using scatterplots and fill out the table below.

Data File: **NATIONS**
➤ *Task:* **Scatterplot**
➤ *Dependent Variable:* _____
➤ *Independent Variable:* _____
➤ *View:* **Reg. Line**

	Dependent Variable	Independent Variable	r =	Significant?
PLOT 1	59) HDI	82) PQLI	_____	Yes No
PLOT 2	59) HDI	53) GNPPC94	_____	Yes No
PLOT 3	82) PQLI	53) GNPPC94	_____	Yes No

Which development index is more strongly correlated to GNP?   HDI   PQLI

3. The World Bank places nation-states in categories of economic development based primarily on GNP per capita. The United Nations Development Program also categorizes nation-states, but it uses the Human Development Index. Use a cross-tabulation to compare these two categorization schemes and fill in the table below.

> Data File: **NATIONS**
> ➤ Task: **Cross-tabulation**
> ➤ Row Variable: **38) DEV WLDBANK**
> ➤ Column Variable: **37) DEV UNDP**
> ➤ View: **Table**
> ➤ Display: **Column %**

		UNDP HUMAN DEVELOPMENT INDEX		
		Low HDI Countries	**Medium HDI Countries**	**High HDI Countries**
World Bank	**Low Income**	# Cases _____	# Cases _____	# Cases _____
		Column % _____	Column % _____	Column % _____
World Bank	**Med Income**	# Cases _____	# Cases _____	# Cases _____
		Column % _____	Column % _____	Column % _____
World Bank	**High Income**	# Cases _____	# Cases _____	# Cases _____
		Column % _____	Column % _____	Column % _____

a. The World Bank and the UNDP categorization schemes are significantly similar.   T   F

b. The World Bank and the UNDP have the greatest difference when comparing the Low categories.   T   F

c. It is impossible to infer from this comparison that the World Bank Index is better than the Human Development Index.   T   F

4. Below is a list of four factors that might affect a country's level of development. Choose two of the factors to further examine which measure of development is better.

Factors that may affect development (column variable)

42) ECON REG	Level of economic regulation
128) TARIFFS2	Level of import tariff
8) AGRIC	Percent of GDP accounted for by agriculture
39) DISTRIB	Percent of national income received by the richest 10%

First examine the relationship between the World Bank categories and your two selected factors.

Data File: **NATIONS**
Task: **Cross-tabulation**
Row Variable: **38) DEV WLDBANK**
➤ *Column Variable:* _____
➤ *View:* **Table**
➤ *Display:* **Column %**

Fill in the table below with the results of your first cross-tabulation. (Note: If the variable you selected does not have all the columns shown below, leave that column blank.)

a.   Factor 1 (Variable Name and Number): _____

	Low	**Medium**	**High**
Low Income	# Cases _____	# Cases _____	# Cases _____
	Column % _____	Column % _____	Column % _____
Med Income	# Cases _____	# Cases _____	# Cases _____
	Column % _____	Column % _____	Column % _____
High Income	# Cases _____	# Cases _____	# Cases _____
	Column % _____	Column % _____	Column % _____

b.   Factor 2 (Variable Name and Number): _____

	Low	**Medium**	**High**
Low Income	# Cases _____	# Cases _____	# Cases _____
	Column % _____	Column % _____	Column % _____
Med Income	# Cases _____	# Cases _____	# Cases _____
	Column % _____	Column % _____	Column % _____
High Income	# Cases _____	# Cases _____	# Cases _____
	Column % _____	Column % _____	Column % _____

Now examine the relationship between the World Bank categories and your two selected factors.

Data File:	**NATIONS**
Task:	**Cross-tabulation**
➤ *Row Variable:*	**37) DEV UNDP**
➤ *Column Variable:*	_____
➤ *View:*	**Table**
➤ *Display:*	**Column %**

Fill in the table below with the results of your first cross-tabulation. (Note: If the variable you selected does not have all the columns shown below, leave that column blank.)

c.   Factor 1 (Variable Name and Number): _____

	Low	Medium	High
Low Income	# Cases _____	# Cases _____	# Cases _____
	Column % _____	Column % _____	Column % _____
Med Income	# Cases _____	# Cases _____	# Cases _____
	Column % _____	Column % _____	Column % _____
High Income	# Cases _____	# Cases _____	# Cases _____
	Column % _____	Column % _____	Column % _____

d.   Factor 2 (Variable Name and Number): _____

	Low	Medium	High
Low Income	# Cases _____	# Cases _____	# Cases _____
	Column % _____	Column % _____	Column % _____
Med Income	# Cases _____	# Cases _____	# Cases _____
	Column % _____	Column % _____	Column % _____
High Income	# Cases _____	# Cases _____	# Cases _____
	Column % _____	Column % _____	Column % _____

5. Our discussion in Exercise 11 did not provide a conclusive answer to what causes economic development. Your work above may not provide a conclusive answer to which development measure is the best. Nevertheless, based on your work, what advice could you give the president of a less developed country? In your answer, be sure to reference your results in questions 2–4.

EXERCISE **12**

MANAGING THE GLOBAL COMMONS

Tasks: Cross-tabulation, Historical Trends, Mapping, Univariate, Scatterplot
Data Files: NATIONS, HISTORY, FPELITES

THE GLOBAL ENVIRONMENT—A LABORATORY FOR UNDERSTANDING INTERNATIONAL RELATIONS

International relations is a science of international events. We have been consistent throughout this book in using a three-level approach for explaining these events. The three levels of analysis—system, state, and individual—are not arbitrary. They are derived from the historical political organization of international life. Individuals make decisions, but they do so in the context of the nation-state system at this point in history. This allows us to identify the state as an aggregate actor that can, like an individual, have preferences and act upon them. The interaction of these individuals and states in the absence of a world government creates a system of rules and practices that define and constrain the types of actions the individuals and states can take. While the levels of analysis are theoretical constructs, we have not dealt with them abstractly. The different levels of analysis have provided us with concrete explanations of war and peace and economic prosperity. It would help us understand international relations even further if we could apply these ideas to a single issue as a case study. The global environment provides us with an excellent case study for this purpose.

Air and water pollution are not bounded by international borders. The acid rain created by nitrous oxide emissions in Ohio kills fish in lakes in Canada. When the nuclear reactor at Chernobyl in the Ukraine exploded in 1986, radiation spread across Eastern Europe and into Scandinavia. The global environment is affected by more than just wandering effluents. Problems like the declining ozone layer in the upper atmosphere and global warming are system problems that neither are created by one nation-state nor can be corrected by one nation-state. They demand a systemic response in a system without government.

The actions of each nation-state individually contribute to the problems and to the solutions. These actions have benefits and costs that affect the nation-states' choices about the environment. Nation-states must choose policies that protect their own interests, even when those interests may be at odds with systemic solutions. Thus, as in issues of national security or economics, nation-states attempt to identify their interests and make policies accordingly.

Whenever actions are taken in the name of a population, the interests of members of that population are important in determining the interests of the whole. National policies are aggregate responses to the interests of some set of individuals. In a democratic society, those policies should reflect a broad base of the public interests while in an autocratic society, the policies reflect the interests of a small

209

elite. In addition to the effect of individuals on policy, the environment is directly affected by individual actions. The choices we make to dispose of a can or recycle it collectively affect the problem of pollution.

Thus, the global environment gives us a laboratory for examining how international relations works. We can see how the organization of the system itself affects responses to systemic problems. We can see how nation-states define their interests in ways that either decrease or increase pollution. Finally, we can see how individuals support anti-pollution policies and how individuals make choices that help or hurt the environment. As we examine these issues, we will need to draw upon our knowledge about international law and organization, and our understanding of the sources of conflict in the system and the differential distribution of resources that determine the types of policies that are possible.

THE GLOBAL ENVIRONMENT AND THE INTERNATIONAL SYSTEM

At the turn of the 21st century, the world population has topped 6 billion people. This population is now doubling about every 36 years. That means that by 2036 there will be 12 billion people. Some analysts predict that population growth combined with limited resources and diminished productivity due to pollution will seriously overburden the earth's environment resulting in catastrophic collapse causing billions of deaths (see Meadows et al. 1992). We can explore the growth of the world population during the latter half of the 20th century with the data in the HISTORY file.

➤ *Data File:* **HISTORY**
➤ *Task:* **Historical Trends**
➤ *Variable:* **58) WORLD POP**

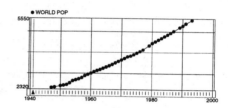

Estimated world population

Regardless of the validity of such dire predictions, it is clear from the graph that world population is increasing at a rapid rate. Rising population has many important effects on the global environment. More people put more demands on food supplies and natural resources. More people create more air and water pollution and solid waste that must somehow be disposed. More people also create greater strains on social and economic systems as they seek employment, health care, and other services.

When faced with ever-increasing population strains, the interactions of sovereign nation-states create a situation that Garrett Hardin (1968) referred to as "the tragedy of the commons." The tragedy of the commons occurs when autonomous actors share a common resource. It is best described by the narrative that Hardin used to define it. Imagine a village of shepherds who share a common pasture. At first, the grazing area is large enough to support all the shepherds with as many sheep as they want. As the village grows, the pasture land becomes stressed. Each shepherd must decide whether or not to add sheep to his or her flock. The benefits of adding a sheep accrue only to the individual shepherd, but the costs of the additional sheep are borne by all, making the incremental cost of one sheep to one shepherd much less than the potential return. With this cost calculation, each autonomous shepherd is inclined to add sheep until the pasture is ruined and all the sheep die. Hardin's point is that in a system of sovereigns, there is little incentive to sacrifice individual benefit to aid the commons when the costs of the commons depletion is shared by all. In international relations, this means that nation-states are bound in a world that does not by its character encourage environmental stewardship, yet is facing serious strain on its ecology.

Two examples of the tragedy of the commons at work in international relations are the so-called greenhouse effect and the depletion of the ozone layer. The greenhouse effect is caused by accumulation of certain gasses, most notably carbon dioxide (CO_2), in the upper atmosphere. These gases, like the windows of a greenhouse, allow sunlight in but do not let radiant heat out. Thus, if too much carbon dioxide accumulates, the temperature of the earth will gradually rise, which could alter world climates, cause extinctions of sensitive species, and melt the polar ice caps. We can explore the accumulation of carbon dioxide using data from the Mauna Loa observatory in Hawaii.

Data File: **HISTORY**
Task: **Historical Trends**
➤ Variable: **9) CO2**

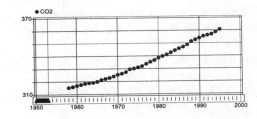

CO_2 concentration in the atmosphere in parts per million

The graph shows annual average concentrations of carbon dioxide in parts per million. It is clear that CO_2 is accumulating at a rather dramatic rate.

Two of the controversies over the greenhouse effect are whether or not this accumulation causes global warming and what the source of the CO_2 is. We do not have the space or the ability to explore either of these questions in depth, but we can examine some of the data that contribute to the argument. Has the earth been heating up? We can answer this question with surface temperature data throughout the 20th century gathered at a variety of sites and compiled by the U.S. National Aeronautics and Space Administration (NASA).

Data File: **HISTORY**
Task: **Historical Trends**
➤ Variable: **44) TEMPCHG**
45) AVG TEMPCH

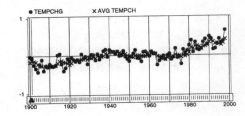

Changes in average global surface temperatures

The variable TEMPCHG measures the change in annual average temperature in degrees centigrade (C) from year to year. That is, if the average world temperature over all locations over 365 days in 1980 was 14.0°C and it rose to 14.39°C in 1981, then the data for 1981 would show an increase of +0.39. The extreme fluctuations from year to year can be dampened by looking at a 5-year running average using the variable AVG TEMPCH. This flattens out the hills and valleys to give a clearer picture of the trend in world temperature. Regardless of which variable we use, it is clear that average annual surface temperature has risen by an increasing rate during the 20th century. Opponents of the greenhouse theory point out that different measuring techniques generate different results. For example, NASA's own attempt at measuring atmospheric and surface temperature with space-based satellites since 1978 shows no significant rise in global temperature.

The second controversy about the greenhouse effect is the source of the greenhouse gases. Carbon dioxide is created by combustion of fossil fuels (like gasoline or coal). It is absorbed by green plants, the oceans, and rainfall. Proponents of the global warming theory point out that humanity is generating more and more CO_2 pollution with its cars and industry at the same time it is cutting down the forests. Opponents of the theory claim that humans are responsible for only a small portion of the CO_2 in the upper atmosphere and that natural processes, especially volcanic eruptions, generate many times the CO_2 that any human endeavor does.

In addition to affecting the carbon cycle, deforestation threatens important species of plants and animals and can have a detrimental effect on weather cycles. Deforestation is increasing due to the pressures of population expansion that demands more farmland and living space, increasing demand in the timber industry, and cutting trees to make way for mining and industrial use. The variable WOODS90–95 in the NATIONS file shows the difference in forested land between 1990 and 1995 in hectares.[1]

➤ *Data File:* **NATIONS**
➤ *Task:* **Mapping**
➤ *Variable 1:* **121) WOODS90–95**
➤ *View:* **Map**

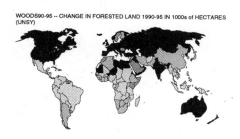

WOODS90-95 -- CHANGE IN FORESTED LAND 1990-95 IN 1000s of HECTARES (UNSY)

Dark shaded (red) parts of the map had no decrease or actually increased their wooded areas while light shaded (yellow) parts had decreases in the wooded areas. Forested land increased in the industrialized North from 1990 to 1995 but decreased dramatically in the less developed South. If we look at the ranking of WOODS90–95, we can see just how much forest each country gained or lost.

Data File: **NATIONS**
Task: **Mapping**
Variable 1: **121) WOODS90–95**
➤ *View:* **List: Rank**

RANK	CASE NAME	VALUE
1	United States	2943
2	Uzbekistan	1130
3	Kazakhstan	964
4	Canada	873
5	France	804
6	Greece	704
7	Belarus	344
8	New Zealand	217
9	Norway	135
10	Latvia	125

The ranking shows that the nation-state with the largest increase in forested land, the United States, expanded its forest by about 2.9 million hectares while the country that lost the most forest, Brazil, cut down over 12.7 million hectares of trees. Between 1990 and 1995, our data show that the world lost a

---

[1] A hectare is a metric measure of land area equivalent to 10,000 square meters, or 2.471 acres. An American-style football field is about 1.03 acres, or .42 hectare.

net total of 55,623,000 hectares of forest land. This is a good example of the tragedy of the commons. The cost of the loss of each hectare of trees is borne by all of us as it contributes to global warming and as it places pressure on potentially valuable threatened species, but the benefits accrue only to those who cut down the tree. Thus, countries like Brazil may not be swayed by arguments about the greenhouse effect because the costs are distributed to all but the benefits are gained only by Brazil.

Ozone (O_3) is an interesting chemical. In the lower atmosphere, ozone is one of the key elements of automobile pollution that causes health hazards. Hot, hazy summer days in urban areas are likely to result in ozone alerts with the accompanying warning that the young and old should avoid going outside. The upper atmosphere normally has a layer of ozone that is beneficial. Ozone absorbs ultraviolet radiation from the sun that can cause skin cancer. Chlorofluorocarbons (CFCs) are chemical gases that are used for a wide variety of consumer and industrial purposes. CFCs have been used as the propellant that causes hair spray to spray out of the can. They have also been widely used as coolants in refrigerators and air conditioners and as industrial fire suppressants. Unfortunately, when these useful chemicals reach the upper atmosphere, they react with ozone and deplete the ozone layer. Holes in the ozone layers have been discovered over the poles. The variable CFC in the HISTORY file shows chlorofluorocarbon concentrations in the atmosphere over time.

➤ Data File: **HISTORY**
➤ Task: **Historical Trends**
➤ Variable: **8) CFC**

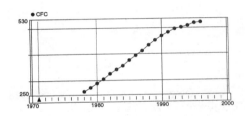

Atmospheric concentration of CFC-12 parts/trillion

Like CO_2 concentration, CFC concentration rose dramatically through the 1980s and early 1990s, but it started to level off after 1992. This was due, in part, to the response of nation-states at the system level to the problem of ozone depletion. The connection between CFCs and ozone depletion has been well established scientifically since the early 1970s. In 1981, the United Nations Environmental Program (UNEP) set up a working group to address the problem of ozone depletion. The group convened the Vienna Convention on the Protection of the Ozone Layer in 1985. The Vienna Convention produced only a general statement by 22 nation-states to take appropriate measures "to protect human health and the environment against adverse effects resulting or likely to result from human activities which modify or are likely to modify the ozone layer" (Vienna Protocol, Article 2, Section 1). There was little mention of specific policies and almost no discussion of CFCs.

After a long series of meetings on the ozone problem, the Montreal Protocol on the Substances that Deplete the Ozone Layer was signed by 29 individual nation-states and the European Economic Commission in 1987. The Montreal Protocol banned production of specific substances, including CFCs, that were known to deplete the ozone layer. There are now over 165 signatories of the protocol. Its effectiveness has been mixed. Chlorofluorocarbon production has been almost eliminated in most of the economically developed states, but it has increased in many less developed nation-states and the ozone holes are getting larger. As our data show, however, overall CFC production began to level off due to these international efforts. Thus, it is possible to avoid, or at least to reduce, the effect of the tragedy of the commons with systemic responses to environmental problems.

NATIONAL INTERESTS AND THE GLOBAL COMMONS

The tragedy of the commons begins with interests of the individual actors that are in conflict with what is best for the needs of the whole system. The developed countries have significantly reduced their production of CFCs because there are alternative chemicals. The alternatives, however, often require higher levels of technology and cost more to produce and use. Thus, less developed countries that are struggling to survive economically are less willing to adopt expensive environment-saving techniques. Less developed countries point out that the development in the North took place without any environmental controls. It is said that Pittsburgh in 1900 was in perpetual twilight, even at midday, because of the air pollution created by the steel mills. Less developed countries claim that they should not be saddled with the difficulties of trying to grow economically while protecting the environment. The industrialization of the North, however, has its costs.

> ➤ *Data File:* **NATIONS**
> ➤ *Task:* **Mapping**
> ➤ *Variable 1:* **57) GREENHOUSE**
> ➤ *View:* **Map**

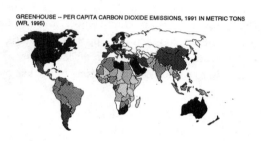

GREENHOUSE -- PER CAPITA CARBON DIOXIDE EMISSIONS, 1991 IN METRIC TONS (WR, 1995)

The map shows that, although much is made about the South's unwillingness to impose controls on its manufacturing, the largest contributors of greenhouse gases per capita are among the developed countries. It is not in the individual interests of these economically developed countries to take the steps needed to reduce carbon pollution. On the other hand, the less developed countries of the South are cutting down more trees as we saw earlier. If we add the WOODS90–95 variable to the GREENHOUSE map, we can see the correlation between these two variables.

> *Data File:* **NATIONS**
> *Task:* **Mapping**
> *Variable 1:* **57) GREENHOUSE**
> ➤ *Variable 2:* **121) WOODS90–95**
> ➤ *Views:* **Map**

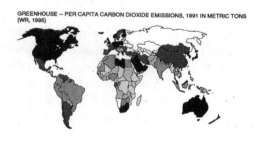

GREENHOUSE -- PER CAPITA CARBON DIOXIDE EMISSIONS, 1991 IN METRIC TONS (WR, 1995)

r = 0.225*

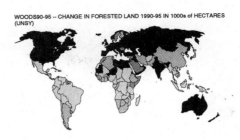

WOODS90-95 -- CHANGE IN FORESTED LAND 1990-95 IN 1000s of HECTARES (UNSY)

The correlation of 0.225* means that countries with high levels of greenhouse emissions were correlated with high levels of forest growth between 1990 and 1995, or alternatively, countries with low levels of carbon emissions had more deforestation. Thus, the developed countries are contributing to global warming through the emission of greenhouse gasses at the same time the less developed countries are contributing to global warming by cutting down their trees. Both sets of countries are acting in their individual interests, and these interests conflict with the needs of the global environment.

Earlier, we discussed the problems of world population growth, but what are individual state interests regarding population growth and how do policies of individual nation-states affect global population? Population growth rates vary widely from country to country.

> Data File: **NATIONS**
> Task: **Mapping**
> ➤ Variable 1: **79) POP GROWTH**
> ➤ View: **Map**

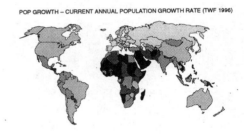

POP GROWTH -- CURRENT ANNUAL POPULATION GROWTH RATE (TWF 1996)

The map shows that population growth rates are highest in Central America, Africa, the Middle East, and parts of Southeast Asia. Another way to look at population growth is population doubling time. Doubling time is the number of years it will take for the population to double at the current rate of growth. The "rule of 70" is a way to convert growth rates into doubling time. Divide 70 by any growth rate to get the doubling time. We can see the population doubling times for nation-states in our data file with the variable POP DOUBLE.

RANK	CASE NAME	VALUE
1	Portugal	3500.0
1	Armenia	3500.0
3	Kyrgyzstan	1000.0
4	Trinidad & Tobago	875.0
5	Finland	700.0
6	Italy	538.5
7	Poland	500.0
8	Spain	437.5
9	Moldova	388.9
10	Belarus	350.0

Nation-states with the highest population growth rate have the shortest doubling time. We can see this by scrolling down to the bottom of the ranking. If the current rates of population growth continue, the population of most of the Sub-Saharan African countries will double in 20 to 30 years. By contrast, most of the European countries have doubling times over 100 years (France's doubling time is 206 years and the United Kingdom's population will double in 318 years). Why is it that many of the less developed countries in Africa and the Middle East have such high growth rates compared to the rest of the world? There are many causes of population growth including migration, high birth rates, and low death rates. One well-established phenomenon is the demographic transition that coincides with the process of economic development. Economic development quickly affects the growth rate by reducing the death rate of a population. If a medical clinic opens in a village, the death rates of the local population can immediately fall. The same is true when vaccination programs are introduced or new agriculture techniques increase yields. Decreases in birth rates, however, require sociological and cultural changes that take more time. Thus, for a while, the death rate falls quickly while the birth rate remains level. Population growth explodes during this interim period when death rates are low and birth rates are high. Eventually, economic development brings the cultural and sociological changes in a society that lower the birth rate. People who move to the city to get jobs in manufacturing find that large families are a liability. As agricultural development raises productivity, families realize that they no longer need large families for labor. They also realize that the lower death rates mean that more of their children will survive to become adults. All of these social and economic factors eventually reduce the birth rate and the growth rate of the population stabilizes. The process takes one to two generations (30 to 60 years). In the interim, population has soared.

It is well documented that most nation-states go through this demographic transition. The United States experienced its demographic transition in the middle of the 19th century. Latin America and Asia are just coming out of their transitions while many of the countries in Africa are in the middle of the transition. We can see the demographic transition with data from North Vietnam.[2] The French colonial administration did a census in Vietnam in 1936 that accurately recorded birth and death rates. The Communist North Vietnamese government also did accurate censuses throughout the 1960s and 70s and has continued to record these data after the country was reunited with the South in 1975. Since Vietnam is divided into provinces, it is possible to track demographic changes in the North over a significant period of time.

---

[2] The data and discussion about North Vietnam's demographic transition in this section are based on an article by Gavin W. Jones (1984).

➤ *Data File:* **HISTORY**
　➤ *Task:* **Historical Trends**
➤ *Variable:* **55) VN BIRTHS**
　　　　　 56) VN DEATHS
　　　　　 57) VN GROWTH

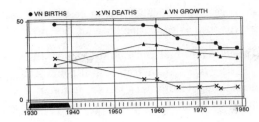

The graph shows that the death rate in North Vietnam began falling as early as the 1936 census but the birth rate did not begin to decrease until the late 1950s. The population growth rate increased throughout this period and did not decrease until the birth rate began to fall in the early 1960s. Thus, the contribution of an individual nation-state to global population growth is often due to its own economic development. While nation-states can institute policies such as birth control and education that will slow their own growth, it is nearly impossible to avoid the demographic transition in a developing economy. Population control programs are also expensive. It may not be in the interest of the independent nation-state to do that which will ease the global population problem.

THE INDIVIDUAL AND THE GLOBAL COMMONS

Each individual affects the global commons in at least two ways. First, each person affects the global environment by the lifestyle he or she chooses. We make decisions each day about whether to walk or drive, whether to recycle or not, or what to do with our waste products that collectively determine the health of the global environment. Should we use the old can of Freon in our basement to recharge our automobile air conditioner on a hot summer day or should we spend hundreds of dollars to have the system retrofit for a CFC-free refrigerant? Individuals also affect the global commons by their support for or opposition to governmental programs for cleaning the environment. Do we support taxes on our own consumption of gasoline as a way to reduce carbon emissions?

The demographic transition is a good example of how individual behavior affects both the state-level issues of national interest and the system-level issues of global population problems. As we mentioned earlier, birth rates decrease slowly in the face of economic development compared with death rates. Why is this? Birth rates are affected by social norms and beliefs about fertility and by the economic prospects of the family, while death rates are more likely to be affected by physical changes in medical care and nutrition. Norms and beliefs change slowly, but they can be affected by education. We can test the hypothesis that nation-states with higher education have lower birth rates with our data.

➤ *Data File:* **NATIONS**
　➤ *Task:* **Scatterplot**
➤ *Dependent Variable:* **79) POP GROWTH**
➤ *Independent Variable:* **44) EDUCATION**
　➤ *View:* **Reg. Line**

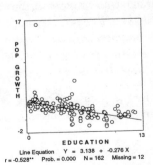

There is a strong statistically significant correlation (−0.528**) between education, measured as average years of school among people 25 years old or older, and the birth rate. The negative correlation means that as education goes up, the birth rate goes down.

The data on American Public Opinion and U.S. Foreign Policy permit us to explore individuals' support for international environmental policy. One question on the survey asked whether or not the respondent thought improving the environment was a very important foreign policy goal. We can explore this question using the combined general public and elite file.

➤ *Data File:* **FPELITES**
➤ *Task:* **Univariate**
➤ *Primary Variable :* **3) GOALENVI**
➤ *View:* **Pie**

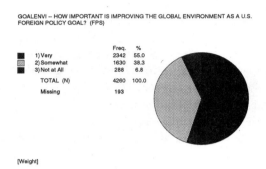

Clearly, a majority (55.0%) of the respondents, including both the general population and the foreign policy elite, think that protecting the environment was a very important U.S. foreign policy goal. Does this general support translate into support by members of the foreign policy decision-making elite?

Data File: **FPELITES**
➤ *Task:* **Cross-tabulation**
➤ *Row Variable:* **3) GOALENVI**
➤ *Column Variable:* **9) SAMPLE**
➤ *Views:* **Graph**
➤ *Display:* **Bar - Stack**

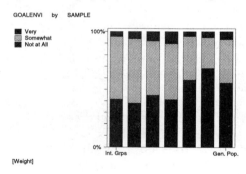

The bar graph shows that there are substantial differences in the support that various groups have for using foreign policy to protect the environment. Over 55% of the general population believe that protecting the environment is a very important foreign policy goal. It is no great surprise that this percentage is much higher than the percentage of the business elite who believe protecting the environment should be a very important foreign policy goal (only 38.1%). There is also more support among the general population for the environment than among the members of Congress.

Support for the environment as a foreign policy goal is affected by a number of individual characteristics. The environment is an issue of the young.

Data File: **FPELITES**

Task: **Cross-tabulation**

Row Variable: **3) GOALENVI**

➤ Column Variable: **1) AGE**

➤ Views: **Table**

➤ Display: **Column %**

GOALENVI   by   AGE
Weight Variable: WEIGHT
Cramer's V: 0.042 **

		AGE				
		Under 30	30-64	Over 65	Missing	TOTAL
GOALENVI	Very	522	1444	352	23	2319
		58.8%	54.8%	50.2%		54.8%
	Somewhat	323	1009	292	7	1623
		36.3%	38.2%	41.6%		38.4%
	Not at All	44	184	58	2	286
		4.9%	7.0%	8.3%		6.8%
	Missing	41	102	48	2	193
	TOTAL	889	2637	703	33	4229
		100.0%	100.0%	100.0%		

Nearly 59% of the people under age 30 believe that the environment is a very important foreign policy goal. Only 50.2% of those 65 and over think that the environment is a very important goal. Support for the environment in foreign policy is also affected by the individual's political ideology. The environment is a liberal issue.

Data File: **FPELITES**

Task: **Cross-tabulation**

Row Variable: **3) GOALENVI**

➤ Column Variable: **8) LIBCONS**

➤ Views: **Table**

➤ Display: **Column %**

GOALENVI   by   LIBCONS
Weight Variable: WEIGHT
Cramer's V: 0.119 **

		LIBCONS				
		Conserv.	Neutral	Liberal	Missing	TOTAL
GOALENVI	Very	728	1009	526	79	2263
		45.2%	60.1%	63.2%		54.9%
	Somewhat	735	598	249	48	1582
		45.6%	35.6%	29.9%		38.4%
	Not at All	148	71	57	12	276
		9.2%	4.2%	6.9%		6.7%
	Missing	49	88	18	39	193
	TOTAL	1611	1678	832	177	4121
		100.0%	100.0%	100.0%		

A large majority (63.2%) of the liberal respondents (both general population and elites) think that the environment is a very important goal in foreign policy. This compares to less than half (45.2%) of the conservative respondents.

Managing the global commons has provided us with an excellent laboratory for exploring international relations. Many environmental problems like overpopulation, global warming, and ozone depletion demand a systemic response, which is difficult to elicit in an anarchical nation-state system. The problem is embedded in sovereignty itself. As long as the costs of complacency are shared by all, individual nation-states have little incentive to sacrifice their interests to the interest of the whole. While individual people support protecting the environment as a goal of foreign policy, that view is not shared to the same extent by the government and business elites who often make policies affecting international relations. Nevertheless, there is some hope that cooperative international regimes supported by international organizations like the United Nations Environmental Program can slowly work to alleviate some of the strains on the global commons. The question that remains is, Can the anarchical system of sovereign states respond quickly enough?

NAME:

COURSE:

DATE:

REVIEW QUESTIONS

Based on the first part of this exercise, answer True or False to the following items:

The world population has now topped 6 billion people. If the population continues to grow at its current rate, it will double in about 36 years.   T   F

The tragedy of the commons occurs when the costs of using more resources are shared among many actors but the benefits accrue only to one actor.   T   F

Data on the surface temperature change of the earth during the 20th century do not support the theory of global warming.   T   F

Ozone is a major component of air pollution that serves no useful purpose for humankind.   T   F

Chlorofluorocarbon concentrations in the upper atmosphere have been increasing steadily with no sign of letting up since the 1980s.   T   F

The industrialized countries of the global North are the major contributors to greenhouse gas emissions among the nation-states.   T   F

The population explosion in less developed countries is due primarily to rising birth rates.   T   F

Nation-states with higher education levels tend to have lower birth rates.   T   F

From our data, the environment seems to be an issue of the young.   T   F

Because of the threat of environmental disasters, business elites, government elites, and the general population in the United States are all in agreement that the environment is a very important foreign policy issue.   T   F

EXPLORIT QUESTIONS

1. Throughout the preliminary section of Exercise 12, we observed differences in the environment between the global North and the global South and we attributed these differences to the level of economic development. We did not, however, test those observations. Differences in environmental status and policy based on economic development have become an important issue in international relations in recent years. Sometimes this issue is called sustainable development, because it deals with the possibility of economic development that does not disrupt the environment. We can use our data to explore some of the issues raised by sustainable development.

a.   We claimed in Exercise 12 that much of the rapid growth in population in the less developed world is due to the demographic transition. If that theory is valid, then birth and death rates should both be affected differently by the level of gross national product. Test these hypotheses by following the instructions and answering the questions below.

➤ *Data File:* **NATIONS**
➤ *Task:* **Scatterplot**
➤ *Dependent Variable :* **17) BIRTH RATE**
➤ *Independent Variable:* **53) GNPPC94**

Select the correct interpretation of this scatterplot from among the following choices:

1.   The birth rate rises as GNP rises.
2.   The birth rate decreases as GNP rises.
3.   The birth rate remains unchanged as GNP rises.

Data File: **NATIONS**
Task: **Scatterplot**
➤ *Dependent Variable :* **32) DEATH RATE**
➤ *Independent Variable:* **53) GNPPC94**

Select the correct interpretation of this scatterplot from among the following choices:

1.   The death rate rises as GNP rises.
2.   The death rate decreases as GNP rises.
3.   The death rate remains unchanged as GNP rises.

b.   Compare the two scatterplots. As GNP per capita rises, do deaths decline faster than births?

Yes   No

c.   Do these results support our hypothesis that the level of gross national product affects birth and death rates differently?

Yes   No

2.   If the theory of demographic transition is true, then we would expect that population growth rates will be much higher in less developed countries than in developed countries. We observed this with a map, but now we need to test this hypothesis.

Data File: **NATIONS**
Task: **Scatterplot**
➤ *Dependent Variable :* **79) POP GROWTH**
➤ *Independent Variable:* **53) GNPPC94**
➤ *View:* **Reg. Line**

a.   What is the correlation coefficient?

r = _____

b.   Is the correlation coefficient statistically significant?

Yes   No

c. There are two countries in the plot that are have exceptionally high birth rates. The correlation value is very sensitive to these outliers. Remove each outlier by clicking on OUTLIER and then REMOVE and answer the questions below.

	Country name	Correlation when removed
1. First Outlier	_____	_____
2. Second Outlier	_____	_____

3. An international convention on global warming was convened in Kyoto, Japan, in 1997. The protocol has stirred great controversy, especially in the industrialized nation-states because many less developed countries were exempted from the restrictions on greenhouse gas emissions. We observed in a map in Exercise 12 that the per capita emissions of greenhouse gases seem to be the greatest in the industrialized countries. We now need to test that observation.

> Data File: **NATIONS**
> Task: **Scatterplot**
> ➤ Dependent Variable : **57) GREENHOUSE**
> ➤ Independent Variable: **53) GNPPC94**
> ➤ View: **Reg. Line**

a. What is the correlation coefficient?

r = _____

b. Is it statistically significant?

Yes   No

c. Write a brief paragraph describing why you think less developed countries should or should not be exempted from the greenhouse emission restrictions. Use data to support your position.

APPENDIX: VARIABLE NAMES AND SOURCES

◆ DATA FILE: DEVELOP ◆

1) Date
2) CPI GHAN
3) CPI GUAT
4) CPI KOR
5) DEBT% GHAN
6) DEBT% GUAT
7) DEBT% KOR
8) GNPPC GHAN
9) GNPPC GUAT
10) GNPPC KOR

11) LIFE GHAN
12) LIFE GUAT
13) LIFE KOR
14) LOAN GHAN
15) LOAN GUAT
16) LOAN KOR
17) ODAGHANA
18) ODAGUAT
19) ODAKOR
20) POPGHAN

21) POPGUAT
22) POPKOR
23) SCH GHAN
24) SCH GUAT
25) SCH KOR
26) FRANCE
27) JAPAN
28) UK
29) USA

◆ DATA FILE: EUROPE ◆

1) COUNTRY
2) ALLY 1870
3) ALLY 1882

4) ALLY 1907
5) ECON ASST
6) OCCUPIED

7) VOTE

◆ DATA FILE: FPELITES ◆

1) AGE
2) DEFENSE
3) GOALENVI
4) GOALHUNG
5) GOALJOBS
6) GOALMKTS

7) GOALPOWR
8) LIBCONS
9) SAMPLE
10) SAMPLE2
11) THRIMMIG
12) WARCUBA

13) WARIRAQ
14) WARISR
15) WARPOL
16) WARSKOR
17) WEIGHT

◆ DATA FILE: FPSURVEY ◆

1) AGE
2) DEFENSE
3) ECONAID
4) EDUC
5) EMPLOYMT
6) GENDER
7) GOALALLY
8) GOALDEMO
9) GOALDRUG
10) GOALENVI
11) GOALHUNG
12) GOALJOBS
13) GOALNUC

14) GOALPOWR
15) GOALRHTS
16) GOALUN
17) GOALWEAK
18) IMPECON
19) IMPEMPL
20) IMPLIVNG
21) INCOME
22) LIBCONS
23) NEWSFP
24) NEWSINTL
25) PKEEP
26) RACE

27) RELIG
28) TARIFFS
29) THRCHN
30) THRJPN
31) THRRUSS
32) TRADEEU
33) TRADEJPN
34) USACTIVE
35) WARIRAQ
36) WARISR
37) WARPOL
38) WEIGHT

◆ DATA FILE: HISTORY ◆

1) Date
2) AGREEUS
3) AGREEUSSR
4) BAL TRADE
5) BAL TRADE2
6) BATTLESHIP
7) CARRIERS
8) CFC
9) CO2
10) DEF % FED
11) DEF % GDP
12) EVENT/ST
13) CONFL EVNT
14) COOP EVNT
15) ECON EVNTS
16) POL EVNTS
17) TOT EVNTS
18) EXPORTS
19) FDI DC
20) FDI LDC
21) GNPPC AFR

22) GNPPC ASIA
23) GNPPC IND
24) GNPPC LA
25) ICJ CASES
26) IGO
27) IMP CARS
28) IMP ELEC
29) IMP SHOES
30) IMPORTS
31) MIL EVNTS
32) NATION_MO
33) NGO
34) PEACE KEEP
35) PHONES
36) PRICE SEC
37) PRICE PRIM
38) RAIL TRAF
39) SAVE JAPAN
40) SAVE USA
41) SOVSTATES
42) SUBS USA

43) SUBS USSR
44) TEMPCHG
45) AVG TEMPCH
46) TRADE
47) FORTRAVEL$
48) USTRAVEL$
49) UNBUDGET
50) UNEMPLOYMT
51) UN MEMBERS
52) UN$PERCAP
53) VETO USA
54) VETO USSR
55) VN BIRTHS
56) VN DEATHS
57) VN GROWTH
58) WORLD POP
59) $/1000YEN
60) $/5PESOS
61) $/POUND

◆ DATA FILE: NATIONS ◆

1) COUNTRY
2) ACTOR EVTS
3) AFRICA1880
4) AFRICA1914
5) AGE15–64
6) AGREEUS85
7) AGREEUSA2
8) AGRIC
9) AID PCT
10) ALIGN CW
11) ARABLE
12) AREA
13) AREA2
14) ARMS EAST
15) ARMS WEST
16) BALTRADEUS
17) BIRTH RATE
18) BORDER
19) CIVIL LIBS
20) CIVIL WAR
21) CLINE80
22) COASTLINE

23) COLONY
24) COMPUTERS
25) CONF EVNTS
26) CONFLICT
27) CONFLICT %
28) COOP EVNTS
29) COOP %
30) CW TREATY
31) C.CONFLICT
32) DEATH RATE
33) DEBTPCT
34) DEFENSE PC
35) DEMOCRACY
36) DEMOCRACY2
37) DEV UNDP
38) DEV WLDBNK
39) DISTRIB
40) ECON DEVEL
41) ECON GROW
42) ECON REG
43) ECONORG
44) EDUCATION

45) FDI
46) FIGHT COPS
47) GNP 77
48) GNP 77B
49) GNP94
50) GNPPC65b
51) GNPPC77B
52) GNPPC85
53) GNPPC94
54) GNPPC94B
55) GOVTYPE70
56) GOVTYPE95
57) GREENHOUSE
58) GROUP77
59) HDI
60) ICJ CASES
61) ICJ JURIS
62) INDUSTRY
63) INF. MORTL
64) LIFE EXPCT
65) MIL FORCES
66) MNC HOST

DATA FILE: NATIONS cont'd

67) MNC HQ
68) MULTI-CULT
69) MULTICULT2
70) NATL PRIDE
71) NEIGHBORS
72) NONALIGNED
73) NUCLEAR
74) OIL
75) OIL2
76) OIL3
77) PKEEP
78) POP DOUBLE
79) POP GROWTH
80) POP77B
81) POP96
82) PQLI
83) PRIM EXP85
84) REGION
85) REGION IGO
86) RELIGION
87) RELIGION2

88) SANCTIONS
89) SAVINGS
90) SCIENTISTS
91) SINGER80
92) SOVDATE
93) STEEL
94) SURROGATE
95) TARIFFS
96) TERMTRADE
97) TRADE BAL
98) TRAV REST
99) TRMTRD85
100) TROOPS
101) UNCTAD1
102) UNDATE
103) UNEMPLYRT
104) UNHQ
105) URBAN GRWT
106) URBAN %
107) USAID65–75
108) USAID65B

109) USAID85
110) USARMS%
111) USTRADE97
112) WAR START
113) WAR45–91
114) WARPLANES
115) WARS
116) WARS 45–92
117) WARSHIPS
118) WARTANKS
119) WILL FIGHT
120) WINLOSE45
121) WOODS90–95
122) WTO
123) $ PER CAP
124) $ RICH 10%
125) % AGRIC $
126) % GDP ARMY
127) %FEM.HEADS
128) TARIFFS2

DATA FILE: WARACTOR

1) WARNUMB
2) COUNTRY
3) DEATHS
4) DEATHS2
5) FORCES

6) FORCES2
7) INITIATE
8) MAJPOWER
9) OUTCOME
10) POPULATION

11) POP2
12) WAR
13) WARTYPE

DATA FILE: WARHIST

1) DATE
2) COLONIAL
3) DEATHS
4) DEATHS 20C

5) IMPERIAL
6) INTERSTATE
7) MONTHS 20C
8) NATION MOS

9) WAR TOTAL
10) WARS
11) WARS5
12) DEATHS TOT

DATA FILE: WARS

1) WARNAME
2) WARNUMB
3) WARTYPE

4) ACTORS
5) DEATHTOT
6) FORCETOT

7) NATIONMO
8) REGION
9) YEAR

SOURCES
DEVELOP

The DEVELOP data file contains historical trend data related to economic development. The data cover the period 1960–1999, although not all variables contain data for all years. The data were collected from various sources. The source for each variable is noted in parentheses in the variable label. The key for the sources is shown below.

> IBRD/WT: International Bank for Reconstruction and Development (World Bank). World Tables (various years)
>
> UNSY: United Nations. *Statistical Yearbook of the United Nations* (various years). Print and CD ROM versions. New York: United Nations Publications.

EUROPE

The EUROPE file contains data on 38 European nation-states. The data were collected from many sources and coded by the authors, James Roberts and Alan Rosenblatt.

FPELITES

All the data in the FPELITES file were taken from the American Public Opinion and U.S. Foreign Policy Survey 1998 conducted by the Chicago Council on Foreign Relations. This file contains questions that were asked of both the general population sample and the foreign policy elite sample.

> CITATION: Chicago Council on Foreign Relations. 1998. American Public Opinion and Foreign Policy. (computer file) ICPSR Version. Princeton, NJ: Gallup Organization. Distributed by the Inter-University Consortium for Political and Social Research, Ann Arbor, MI.

FPSURVEY

All the data in the FPSURVEY file were taken from the American Public Opinion and U.S. Foreign Policy Survey 1998 conducted by the Chicago Council on Foreign Relations. This file contains questions that were asked only of the general population sample.

> CITATION: Chicago Council on Foreign Relations. 1998. American Public Opinion and Foreign Policy. (computer file) ICPSR Version. Princeton, NJ: Gallup Organization. Distributed by the Inter-University Consortium for Political and Social Research, Ann Arbor, MI.

HISTORY

The file HISTORY contains historical trends data covering the years 1900–1999. Not all variables have data for all years. The data were collected from many sources. The source for each variable is noted in parentheses in the variable label. The key for the sources is shown below.

> AAMA: American Automobile Manufacturer's Association
>
> BAILEY & DAVIS: Bailey, Sydney and Sam Davis. 1995. *The United Nations: A Concise Political Guide*. Lanham, MD: Barnes & Noble Books (page 22).

CALC: Calculated from other variables in the file.

COPDAB: Azar, Edward. 1978. Conflict and Peace Databank 1948–78 (computer file). Produced at the University of Maryland. Distributed by the Inter-University Consortium for Political and Social Research, Ann Arbor, MI.

COW: Singer, J. David and Melvin Small. 1993. Correlates of War Project: International and Civil War Data, 1816–1992 (computer file). Ann Arbor, MI: University of Michigan. Distributed by Inter-University Consortium for Political and Social Research, Ann Arbor, MI.

IBRD/WT: International Bank for Reconstruction and Development (World Bank). World Tables (various years)

IO: United States Department of Commerce. *Industrial Outlook*. Washington, DC: U.S. Government Printing Office.

JONES: Jones, Gavin W. 1984. *Demographic Transition in Asia*. Singapore: Maruzen Asia Press (page 209).

NASA: National Aeronautics and Space Administration web site: http://www.giss.nasa.gov/data/update/gistemp/

NASA: National Aeronautics and Space Administration web site: http://www.giss.nasa.gov/data/update/gistemp/

NOAA: National Oceanic and Atmospheric Agency, CO_2 monitoring project at Mauna Loa Observatory web site: (http://ingrid.ldgo.columbia.edu/SOURCES/.KEELING/.MAUNA_LOA.cdf/

OECD: Organization for Economic Cooperation and Development, Statistics Directorate. *Historical Statistics*, 1960–1994.

RIGGS: Riggs, Robert and Jack Plano. 1994. *The United Nations*. Second edition. Belmont, CA: Wadsworth Publishing.

RR: Coded from various sources by James Roberts and Alan Rosenblatt.

SAUS: U.S. Government Printing Office, *Statistical Abstract of the United States* (various years).

UN-ITSY: Department for Economic and Social Information and Policy Analysis, Statistics Division. 1994. *International Trade Statistics Yearbook*. Volume II. New York: United Nations Publications.

UNSY: United Nations. *Statistical Yearbook of the United Nations* (various years). Print and CD ROM versions. New York: United Nations Publications.

UNWIR: United Nations Conference on Trade and Development. 1995. *World Investment Report 1995*. New York: United Nations Publications.

UN-WWW: United Nations web site: http://www.un.org

WATSON: Watson, Bruce. 1991. *The Changing Face of the World's Navies*. Washington, DC: Brassey's Inc.

WR: World Resources Institute. 1998. *World Resources 1998–1999*. New York: Oxford University Press.

YIO: Union of International Associations. *Yearbook of International Organizations*. Website: http://www.uia.org/uiastats/stybv296.htm

NATIONS

The file NATIONS contains data on the 174 largest nation-states. The data were collected from many sources. The source for each variable is noted in parentheses in the variable label. The key for the sources is shown below.

CALC: Calculated from other variables in the file.

COPDAB: Azar, Edward. 1978. *Conflict and Peace Databank 1948–78*. Produced at the University of Maryland. Distributed by the Inter-University Consortium for Political and Social Research, Ann Arbor, MI.

COW: Singer, J. David and Melvin Small. 1993. Correlates of War Project: International and Civil War Data, 1816–1992 (computer file). Ann Arbor, MI: University of Michigan. Distributed by Inter-University Consortium for Political and Social Research, Ann Arbor, MI.

FITW: Gastil, Ramond D. 1995. *Freedom in the World,* New York: Freedom House.

HDR: United Nations Development Program, *Human Development Report* (various years). Print and computer versions. Oxford: Oxford University Press.

ICJ: International Court of Justice, Yearbook (various years)

IISS: International Institute for Strategic Studies 1997. *The Military Balance 1997/1998*. Oxford: Oxford University Press.

JULIUSSEN: International Institute for Strategic Studies, 1997. *The Military Balance 1997/1998*. Oxford: Oxford University Press.

NBWR: Kurian, George T. 1991. *The New Book of World Rankings*, Third edition. New York: Facts on File.

OGJ: *Oil and Gas Journal*. (Vol. 95, January, 1997)

PON: United Nations Children's Fund. 1996. *The Progress of Nations*. New York: UNICEF.

RR: Coded from various sources by James Roberts and Alan Rosenblatt.

SAUS: U.S. Government Printing Office, *Statistical Abstract of the United States* (various years).

STARK: Coded and calculated by Rodney Stark, MicroCase Corp.

TABER: Taber, Charles S. 1989. *Power Capability Indexes in the Third World*. Chapter in Richard Stoll and Michael Ward. Boulder, CO: Lynne Reinner Pp. 36–37.

TWF: United States Central Intelligence Agency *The World Factbook* (various year).

UN-WWW: United Nations web site: http://www.un.org

UNCTAD: United Nations Conference on Trade and Development. 1964. *Proceedings of the United Nations Conference on Trade and Development*. Volume I: *Final Act and Report*. New York: United Nations.

UNWIR: United Nations Conference on Trade and Development. 1995. *World Investment Report 1995*. New York: United Nations Publications.

USACDA: United States Arms Control and Disarmament Agency. *World Military Expenditures and Arms Transfers* (various years).

USDOS-UN: United States Department of State. *Voting Practices in the United Nations, 1985*. Report to Congress.

USDOS-WWW: United States Department of State web site: www.state.gov

USOFAC: United States Office of Foreign Assets Control. United States Department of the Treasury. web site: www.treas.gov/ofac/

WCE: Barrett, David B. Editor. 1982. *World Christian Encyclopedia* Oxford: Oxford University Press.

WDI: International Bank for Reconstruction and Development (World Bank) *World Development Indicators 1998*.

WDR: International Bank for Reconstruction and Development (World Bank) *World Development Report* (various years).

WR: World Resources Institute. *World Resources* (various years). New York: Oxford University Press.

WT: International Bank for Reconstruction and Development (World Bank) *World Tables* (various years).

WVS: World Values Study Group. *World Values Survey, 1981–1984 and 1990–1993.* Ann Arbor: Institute for Social Research, Inter-university Consortium for Political and Social Research.

WILLETS: Willets, Peter. 1978. *The Non-Aligned Movement: The Origins of a Third World Alliance.* New York: Nichols Publishing.

WRIGLEY: Wrigley, Charles. 1967. United Nations Roll-Call Voting in the General Assembly. Computer file distributed by the Inter-University Consortium for Political and Social Research, Ann Arbor, MI.

WARACTOR

The data in the WARACTOR file are all taken from the Correlates of War project (COW). Each record represents one actor's experiences in one international war that started between 1816 and 1992.

CITATION: Singer, J. David and Melvin Small. 1993. CORRELATES OF WAR PROJECT: INTERNATIONAL AND CIVIL WAR DATA, 1816–1992 (computer file). Ann Arbor, MI: Inter-University Consortium for Political and Social Research (distributor).

WARHIST

The data in the WARHIST file are all taken from the Correlates of War project (COW). Each record represents data on international wars during one year between 1816 and 1992.

CITATION: Singer, J. David and Melvin Small. 1993. CORRELATES OF WAR PROJECT: INTERNATIONAL AND CIVIL WAR DATA, 1816–1992 (computer file). Ann Arbor, MI: Inter-University Consortium for Political and Social Research (distributor).

WARS

The data in the WARS file are all taken from the Correlates of War project (COW). Each record represents one international war that started between 1816 and 1992.

CITATION: Singer, J. David and Melvin Small. 1993. CORRELATES OF WAR PROJECT: INTERNATIONAL AND CIVIL WAR DATA, 1816–1992 (computer file). Ann Arbor, MI: Inter-University Consortium for Political and Social Research (distributor).

REFERENCES

Baldwin, David. 1979. "Power Analysis and World Politics." *World Politics* 31:161–194.

Barnhart, C. L., ed. 1966. *The American College Dictionary*. New York: Random House.

Bull, Hedley. 1966. "Society and Anarchy in International Relations." Chapter in *Diplomatic Investigations*, edited by Herbert Butterworth and Martin Wight. Cambridge: Harvard University Press.

Carr, Edward H. 1939. *The Twenty Years' Crisis: 1919–1939*. London: Macmillan and Company.

Claude, Inis L., Jr. 1971. *Swords into Plowshares: The Problems and Progress of International Organization*. 4th ed. New York: Random House.

Clausewitz, Karl von. 1962. *On War*. Translated by J. J. Graham. New and revised edition. London: Routledge and Kegan Paul.

Cline, Ray. 1980. *World Power Trends and U.S. Foreign Policy in the 1980's*. Boulder, CO: Westview Press.

Dahl, Robert A. 1957. The Concept of Power. In *Behavioral Science* 2:201–215. Reprinted in *Political Power: A Reader in Theory and Research*, edited by R. Bell, D. V. Edwards, and R. H. Wagner, 346–359. New York: The Free Press.

Dougherty, James E., and Robert L. Pfaltzgraff, Jr. 1996. *Contending Theories of International Relations, A Comprehensive Survey*. New York: Longman.

Fukuyama, Francis. 1992. *The End of History and the Last Man*. New York: The Free Press.

Garraty, John A., and Peter Gay, eds. 1981. *The Columbia History of the World*. New York: Harper and Row.

Hastedt, Glenn P., and Kay M. Knickrehm. 1991. *Dimensions of World Politics*. New York: Harper-Collins.

Hardin, Garrett. 1968. "The Tragedy of the Commons." *Science* 162:1243–1248.

Hersh, Seymour M. 1991. *The Samson Option: Israel's Nuclear Arsenal and American Foreign Policy*. New York: Random House.

Huntington, Samuel P. 1968. *Political Order in Changing Societies*. New Haven: Yale University Press.

Kegley, Charles W., and Eugene R. Wittkopf. 1997. *World Politics: Trends and Transformation*. New York: St. Martin's Press.

Kindleberger, Charles. 1973. *The World in Depression, 1929–1939*. Berkeley: University of California Press.

Köhler, Gernot, and Norman Alcock. 1976. "An Empirical Table of Structural Violence." *Journal of Peace Research* 13, no. 4: 343–356.

Jones, Gavin W. 1984. "Population Trends and Policies in Vietnam." Chapter in *Demographic Transition in Asia*, edited by Gavin W. Jones. Singapore: Maruzen Asia.

Mackinder, Sir Halford. 1904. "The Geographical Pivot of History." *Geographical Journal* XXIII, pp. 421–444.

Meadows, Donella, Dennis Meadows, Jørgen Randers, and William Behrens III. 1974. *The Limits to Growth*. 2nd ed. New York: Universe Books.

Meadows, Donella, Dennis Meadows, and Jørgen Randers. 1992. *Beyond the Limits*. White River Junction, VT: Chelsea Green Publishing Company.

Morgenthau, Hans. 1952. "Another 'Great Debate': The National Interest of the United States." *American Political Science Review* 64 (December) pp. 961–988.

Morgenthau, Hans and Kenneth Thompson. 1985. *Politics among Nations, The Struggle for Power and Peace*. 6th ed. New York: Alfred A. Knopf.

Olson, William C., and Nicholas G. Onuf. 1985. "The Growth of a Discipline: Reviewed." Chapter in *International Relations: British and American Perspectives*, edited by Steve Smith. Oxford: Basil Blackwell.

Richardson, Lewis F. 1960. *Statistics of Deadly Quarrels*. Pittsburgh: Boxwood Press.

Rummel, Rudolph. 1972. *The Dimensions of Nations*. Beverly Hills, CA: Sage Publications.

Rourke, John T. 1999. *International Politics on the World Stage*. 7th ed. Guilford, CT: Dushkin/McGraw-Hill.

Singer, J. David, Stuart Bremer, and John Stuckey. 1972. "Capability, Distribution, Uncertainty, and Major-Power War." Pp. 19–48 in *Peace, War, and Numbers*, edited by Bruce M. Russett. Beverly Hills, CA: Sage Publications.

Singer, J. David, and Melvin Small. 1994. *Correlates of War Project: International and Civil War Data, 1816–1992*. Ann Arbor: Inter-university Consortium for Political and Social Research. (Codebook)

Singer, J. David, and Paul F. Diehl, eds. 1990. *Measuring the Correlates of War*. Ann Arbor: University of Michigan Press.

Small, Melvin, and J. David Singer. 1982. *Resort to Arms: International and Civil Wars, 1816–1980*. Beverly Hills, CA: Sage Publications.

Sprout, Harold, and Margaret Sprout. 1965. *The Ecological Perspective on Human Affairs with Special Reference to International Politics*. Princeton, NJ: Princeton University Press.

Tickner, Ann. 1988. "Hans Morgenthau's Principles of Political Realism: A Feminist Reformulation." *Millennium: Journal of International Studies* 17, no. 3 (Winter): 429–440.

UNCTAD. 1964. *United Nations Conference on Trade and Development I: Final Act and Review*. New York: United Nations.

UNCTAD. 1995. *World Investment Report 1995*. New York: United Nations.

Waltz, Kenneth. 1979. *The Theory of International Relations*. New York: Random House.

Wolfe, Marshall. 1974. "Development: Images, Conceptions, Criteria, Agents, Choices." *Economic Bulletin for Latin America* 18:1.

Wolfers, Arnold. 1959. "The Actors in International Politics." Chapter in *Theoretical Aspects of International Relations*, edited by William T. R. Fox. Notre Dame, IN: University of Notre Dame Press.

Wright, Quincy. 1942. *A Study of War*. Volume I. Chicago: Chicago University Press.

Young, Crawford. 1977. *The Politics of Cultural Pluralism*. Madison: University of Wisconsin Press.